SIX-GUN LAW
Volume 2

The Westerns of
Rory Calhoun,
Rod Cameron,
Sterling Hayden and
Richard Widmark

SIX-GUN LAW
Volume 2

The Westerns of Rory Calhoun, Rod Cameron, Sterling Hayden and Richard Widmark

by Barry Atkinson

Midnight Marquee Press, Inc.
Baltimore, Maryland, USA; London, UK

Copyright © 2018 Barry Atkinson
Cover design and interior layout: A. Susan Svehla
Copy Editor: Linda J. Walter

Midnight Marquee Press, Inc., Gary J. Svehla and A. Susan Svehla do not assume any responsibility for the accuracy, completeness, topicality or quality of the information in this book. All views expressed or material contained within are the sole responsibility of the author.

Without limiting the rights under copyright reserved above, no part of this publication may be reproduced, stored in or introduced into a retrieval system, or transmitted, in any form, or by any means (electronic, mechanical, photocopying, recording or otherwise), without the prior written permission of the copyright owner or the publishers of the book.

ISBN 13: 978-1-936168-84-2
Library of Congress Catalog Card Number 2018952708
Manufactured in the United States of America

First Printing by Midnight Marquee Press, Inc., October, 2018

Dedication

to Dad

CONTENTS

8	Foreword
11	Chapter 1: Richard Widmark: Blond and Unpredictable
16	Chapter 2: Rory Calhoun: Bad Boy Come Good
20	Chapter 3: Rod Cameron: The Unsmiling Ladykiller
22	Chapter 4: Sterling Hayden: The Reluctant Film Star
26	Chapter 5: Widmark: Seven Western Classics, 1948-1959
50	Chapter 6: Calhoun in the Saddle, 1949-1954
66	Chapter 7: Cameron at Universal, 1939-1948
86	Chapter 8: Hayden: Tall Man Riding, 1949-1955
110	Chapter 9: Calhoun: Good-Looker with a Gun— The Classic "Bs" 1954-1958
138	Chapter 10: Cameron: 1948-1957
178	Chapter 11: Hayden at The Alamo, 1955
184	Chapter 12: Widmark at The Alamo, 1960
195	Chapter 13: Cameron: 1963-1966
206	Chapter 14: Hayden: 1957-1975
220	Chapter 15: Calhoun: 1963-1990
236	Chapter 16: Widmark: 1961-1988
267	Chapter 17: Filmography
283	Bibliography and Acknowledgment

FOREWORD

"*Six-Gun Law* is getting the most buzz out of any of your books. I do not know if you had another Western book in you, but if you did…" So said my publisher, Gary Svehla, in an email to me dated January 22, 2016. OK, I emailed back, I'll give it some thought and come back to you. But if I did write a second volume along similar lines to the first, detailing the careers of Randolph Scott, Audie Murphy, Joel McCrea and George Montgomery, which cowboy stars would I concentrate on? Not John Wayne, James Stewart, Gregory Peck, Henry Fonda or any of the major stars—they've been written about many, many times before. No, it would have four among the not-so-major stars, those stalwarts who populated the low- to medium-budget Western year in, year out, their movies mostly going the rounds as second features, the unsung heroes of the Western sphere giving pleasure to packed audiences without ever hitting the Hollywood heights. However, I knocked that one out of the saddle, bucking my own trend by kicking off with Richard Widmark, a true Hollywood great, and an underrated one at that. Widmark wasn't a Western star to the exclusion of everything else he did; rather, he lent his highly watchable talents to the genre and in doing so came up with a fistful of absolute classics, especially the eight he made between 1948 (*Yellow Sky*) and 1960 (*The Alamo*). Widmark was darned good in practically everything he did, bringing an edgy vitality to the horse opera—and most of his oaters were big-budget productions with notable directors in the driving seat. His is a name not readily associated with the Western, so the aim here is to correct that particular issue; catch *Garden of Evil*, *Backlash* and *The Law and Jake Wade* and you'll see what I mean.

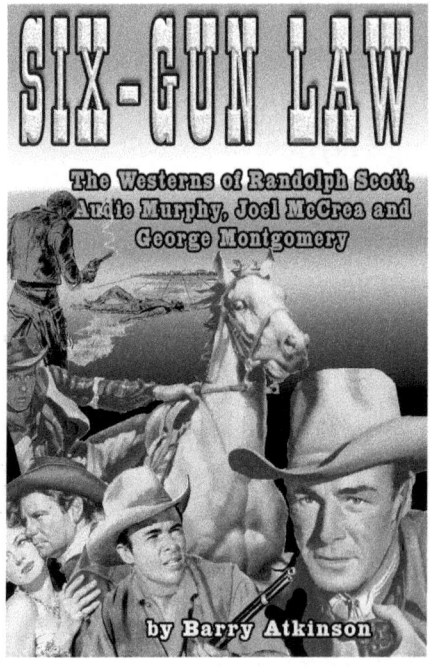

Rory Calhoun was next, an actor comparable in some respects to George Montgomery (the same could be said of Rod Cameron), a reasonable player in his own field blessed with personable features who looked great in the saddle. A lot of his '50s Westerns—*Powder River*, *Dawn at Socorro*, *Four Guns to the Border* and *Red Sundown* among the list—are vital additions to the genre, and some of his '60s output wasn't all that bad either. Calhoun's female devotees probably outnumbered his male fans, meaning that even today, both sexes can enjoy one of his sagebrush sagas, the men for his prowess on the gun (Calhoun nearly always played gunslingers), the women for the kind of Latin looks masculine Hollywood hunks were blessed with 50 to 60 years ago, long before the male of the species decided to get in touch with their feminine side!

Rod Cameron, like Calhoun, wasn't by any stretch of the imagination a great actor: Rugged looking, stern of expression, spitting out terse one-liners and very handy with both fists and guns, he played practically the same character in all 35 Westerns he appeared in. But again, Cameron came up with a list of essentials: *Panhandle*, *Stampede* and *Brimstone* are true '40s classics; *Short Grass*, *Ride the Man Down* and *Southwest Passage* are as good as any B-Western of the 1950s; and 1965's *The Bounty Killer*, although strictly a Dan Duryea oater, is marvelous stuff. Hack directors such as Lesley Selander, Joseph Kane, George Sherman, Fred F. Sears, Ray Nazarro, John Sherwood and Joseph H. Lewis brought out the best in actors of Cameron and Calhoun's limited abilities, constructing solid (if over-familiar at times) storylines and gun-filled action

to back up the leading man's efforts over 70-85 minutes. The countless Westerns these B-heroes starred in, firmly rooted in Old West folklore, owe their durability and expertise to directors like Selander who, over the years, have been criminally overlooked by mainstream movie writers in favor of John Ford, Anthony Mann and other big names responsible for making cowboy pictures with much larger budgets. Selander and company produced the goods quite often on peanuts; we must all remember that.

Sterling Hayden presents another side of the story altogether. Here was an actor who despised the Hollywood star system and was only in it for the dough;

his passion lay in another direction, the sea and boats. Hayden was tremendously effective in crime *noir* thrillers, a milieu which he reserved for his best performances; in Westerns, this was not always the case. This double-edged sword, a noticeable characteristic trait throughout Hayden's varied film career, will be expanded upon later, but anyone who writes him off for his occasional sloppy work in a Western does so at their own peril. *Hellgate*, *Kansas Pacific*, *Shotgun*, *Top Gun* and *Terror in a Texas Town* showcase the blond giant pulling his weight in the genre, while the outlandishly camp *Johnny Guitar* just has to be experienced to be believed. Hayden's oaters are so different and inconsistent that they beg to be watched, if only to work out what the hell the six-foot-five guy with the expressionless face was actually thinking about when he was making them!

Like Scott, Murphy, McCrea and Montgomery, the subjects of volume one, the four showcased in this second volume were all perfectly capable of playing their tough roles with ease because of their hard, uncompromising upbringing (especially true in Calhoun's case). They were also naturals in the saddle, born to ride, even Hayden, their combined output in the field an enduring reminder of how, many, many years ago, the Western movie reigned supreme over all others. So let's hit four divergent trails out West with four contrasting meaner-than-hell hombres and see how they coped, in true Western tradition, with bad guys (when they weren't being bad guys themselves), Indians on the warpath, sexy saloon dames, trigger-happy gunmen, cavalry detachments, double-crossing partners, devious land-grabbers, crooked logging-grabbers, corrupt lawmen, ladies (and tomboys) in peril, dishonest town officials, the construction of railroads on schedule across hostile terrain, the felling of timber and, in two instances, the legendary battle of the Alamo, all filmed in and around America's breathtaking untamed, rocky native scenery. You won't be bored for a single second!

CHAPTER 1

RICHARD WIDMARK: BLOND AND UNPREDICTABLE

In an era of predominantly tall, dark Hollywood leading men, Richard Widmark stood out. Five-foot-ten inches in height, of slight build, blue eyes and smooth, fair complexion (inherited from his father, who was of Swedish descent), Widmark was by no means the type of good-looking matinee idol that female members of the audience used to swoon over in the 1940s. Compare him to Victor Mature's heavyweight six-foot-two-inch, black-haired villain-turned-snitch in Fox's *Kiss of Death* and you'll spot the difference immediately. He wasn't a method actor, either. Like many of the Hollywood greats, Widmark the person was Widmark up on the big silver screen, never afraid to play unsympathetic (to audiences), deeply troubled, hard-boiled, not always honest, characters with an edgy, nervy dynamism, tapping into the psychological peculiarities of whoever he was portraying without ever over-emphasizing the fact, an ordinary kinda guy but *not* ordinary, a natural at using a sleight of hand performing ability that, in hindsight,

Widmark hit the big-time as Tommy Udo in *Kiss of Death*

many could not match. For example, he was a past master at switching from friendly to menacing in the blink of an eye by shutting up his enemies with a pronounced withering stare, a noticeable quality in his role playing. His mastery and intuitive touches in this field sneaked up on you without you ever being aware of it, the true sign of a great.

In many ways, Widmark was an acting enigma. True, if any seasoned movie buff is asked the question "Do you know who Richard Widmark is?" they will reply, "Yes, I do." But if asked "Name one of his films," the answer may not always be forthcoming. He was a reliable star player not really known for any one particular movie, except perhaps *Kiss of Death* and *The Alamo*, and maybe that was because he was so unlike his contemporaries who, in the main, were taller and darker. As stated, he stood out from the pack, a one-off, always eliciting a worthwhile performance, nearly always starring in grade A pictures and, to his credit, refusing to mingle with Hollywood's hedonistic, self-indulgent society; it's impossible to pinpoint any one actor who was remotely similar to him, in looks and in style. To this end, Richard Widmark, a well-known name in the echelons of Hollywood, was rather unique.

Although Widmark wasn't a Western leading player in the true sense of the word and was never really associated with the genre in the way that, say, James Stewart, John Wayne, Audie Murphy and Randolph Scott were, he made some darned fine Westerns, bringing a keyed-up intensity to the milieu which few others could equal—the seven he starred in between 1948 and 1959 are out-and-out classics. His overall 19-oater contribution obviously counted for something—Widmark was inducted into the Western Performers Hall of Fame at the National Cowboy & Heritage Museum in Oklahoma City in 2002. Widmark was a dependable actor, very rarely putting a foot wrong over 76 movies (including those made for television) spanning a period of 45 years. From psychotic punks (*Kiss of Death*, *Road House*), to neurotic villains (*The Street with No Name*), to *noir* two-bit chancers (*Night and the City*, *Pickup on South Street*), from professionals (*Panic in the Streets, *The Cobweb*) to battle-weary soldiers (*Halls of Montezuma, Destination Gobi*) and even Vikings (*The Long Ships*), an obsessive warmonger (*The Bedford Incident*), detectives (*Madigan*) and horror (*To the Devil a Daughter*), Widmark consistently delivered the goods in his trademark flat, Midwestern drawl, a massively underrated Hollywood star of the old school who deserves far more recognition than has been given his due—often overlooked by historians for actors with far less talent than Widmark possessed.

Richard Weedt Widmark came into the world on December 26, 1914 in Sunrise Township, Minnesota, the elder of two sons born to Ethel Mae Barr (of half English, half Scottish ancestry) and Carl Henry Widmark, a traveling salesman who later owned his own bakery. Before he was a year old, the family relocated to Sioux Falls, South Dakota, the first of many such family changes of address in Widmark's young life. A quiet, studious and highly intelligent boy, almost classical-looking from being blessed with fine-boned features, he moved around the Midwest a great deal because of his father's occupation, the family eventually settling in Henry, then Princetown, Illinois. Like so many of his generation, Widmark was hooked on the movies from a very early age, four in his case, his grandmother, a big film fan (especially of cowboy star Tom Mix), taking him and brother Donald to catch the likes of *Dracula* and *Frankenstein* in the 1930s; the young Widmark studied speech patterns as well as acting techniques (he was fascinated by the way Boris Karloff spoke in his deep, English tones), becoming a much-lauded public speaker and scholar at high school (he also wrote articles for the school newspaper and was a star football player), winning several oratory awards before attending Illinois' Lake Forest College, his ultimate plan to enter the legal profession. Studying stagecraft, the acting bug took over (Spencer Tracy was Widmark's favorite actor), banishing forever a possible vocation as a lawyer. After graduating with a Bachelor of Arts degree in 1936, he took on the role of Assistant Director of Speech and Drama on a salary of $150 a month, a role that led him to quit college in 1937, move to New York and enter the world of radio in 1938—his debut *Aunt Jenny's Real Life Stories*. During 1941 and 1942, he played newspaper reporter David Farrell in *Front Page Farrell*, a major radio drama hit of the time; his extensive (and just as successful) radio work also included *Gang Busters*, the *Molle Mystery Theater*, *The Inner Sanctum Mysteries*, *Ethel and Albert* and *Joyce Jordan, M.D.* In 1942, Widmark married college sweetheart/playwright Ora Jean Hazlewood, a union that

lasted 55 years up to her death in 1997; in 1999, he married Henry Fonda's third wife, Susan Blanchard. Financially secure because of his prolific radio programs, Widmark's first stage appearance was on Broadway in 1943 in the play *Kiss and Tell*. He was refused entry into the World War II combat arena because of a perforated left eardrum (he entertained the troops in plays during the war as a member of the American Theater Wing; brother Donald, a bomber pilot, was shot down over Nazi Germany and, as a result, suffered failing health during the 1950s). After the war he continued his stage career and caught the eyes of 20th Century Fox's scouts when appearing in Chicago in *Dream Girl* with June Havoc. Offered a seven-year contract in late 1946, he was given a script to read concerning a psychotic murderer on the trail of a police informer, a malevolent character light years away from those he had played on radio and in the theater ("The script struck me as funny and made me laugh, the guy was such a ridiculous beast."); his subsequent screen test landed him his first major film part in 1947 as giggling sociopath Tommy Udo in Henry Hathaway's seminal crime thriller *Kiss of Death*, a career choice that shot him to instant stardom, earning him the Golden Globe for New Star of the Year plus an Oscar nomination for Best Supporting Actor. Yet Widmark, hired on a salary of $1,000 a week, wasn't Hathaway's first choice for the iconic part—he thought the actor's fine, smooth features, fair looks, slight frame and high forehead made him look much too intellectual to play a killer psycho. Following a heated row with the cantankerous director, Widmark, disillusioned with the whole movie business, stormed off the set, only to be persuaded to return, Fox studio boss Darryl F. Zanuck overruling Hathaway by insisting that Widmark was the right man for the job—not unknown East Side nightclub pianist Harry the Hipster, whom the director had unaccountably favored. Zanuck, as it turned out, was proved right in his assessment of Widmark's latent talent—*Kiss of Death* was a huge critical and commercial success, creating an unforeseen impact; a new star was born, albeit a rather unusual one. Widmark's sniggering, heartless, cold-eyed hoodlum, almost antihero in concept (as would many of his future characters be—in many of his films you can detect that notorious chuckle), holding the attention over heavies Victor Mature and Brian Donlevy. He would go on to become one of *film noir*'s most memorable unhinged loonies. The scene of Widmark hurling wheelchair-bound Mildred Dunnock down a flight of stairs caused censorship problems in Britain ("It's better to be remembered for a laugh than not to be remembered at all," he said later in interviews).

Thereafter, Widmark, because of his offbeat, to some degree sinister, threatening attitude, allied to a distinctive slow tonal delivery (plus his brilliant portrayal of Tommy Udo), was cast in a series of Fox *film noirs* (*The Street with No Name*, 1948; *Road House*, 1948; *Night and the City*, 1950; *Panic in the Streets*, 1950) with big-name directors at the helm. His first Western, *Yellow Sky*, debuted in 1948; he became very popular very quickly, his hand and footprints were immortalized in concrete outside Grauman's Chinese Theater in 1949. The actor

Playing the Dauphin in *St. Joan*

eventually severed connections with Fox in May 1954, dissatisfied with the studio system's penchant of being shunted from one production to the next with little input of his own, feeling the need for more artistic control over future film work and steadfastly refusing to be typecast. So you could go and see *The Law and Jake Wade* in 1958 armed with the knowledge that the actor's previous two roles had been the Dauphin in United Artists' *Saint Joan* (one of his rare flops) and a military investigator in United Artists' *Time Limit*—his last sagebrush saga, *The Last Wagon*, was released two years previously. It was a sign of his singular virtuosity, a virtuosity that made him eminently watchable. Widmark never stayed within the Western sphere to the extent of anything else that was offered, the man content to take on varying roles as and when they appeared, but those he did make were, in the main, splendid examples of the genre, benefiting from his slightly dangerous, unpredictable persona and blond looks—all six of his '50s oaters are absolute essential additions to the Western arena, individualistic, classy and adult-oriented, among the best produced during this highly productive period for the cowboy movie, as we shall discover in chapter five of this book.

CHAPTER 2

RORY CALHOUN: BAD BOY COME GOOD

Born on August 8, 1922 in Los Angeles, Francis Timothy McCown, son of a professional gambler and of Irish ancestry, spent his early years in Santa Cruz, his father dying when he was only nine months old. His mother remarried, to Nathaniel Durgin, Francis sometimes going by the name of Frank Durgin. The family was poor and hit hard times, forcing young McCown, by sheer necessity, to drop out of high school into a life of teenage crime and juvenile delinquency. Aged only 13, he stole a revolver from a hardware store, was apprehended by the law and packed off to the California Youth Authority's Preston Reformatory School at Ione. Managing to escape from the adjustment center, he embarked on a robbery spree, targeting jewelry stores and drove a stolen car across state lines to avoid the police. Recaptured, McCown then spent several long-term spells in prison, including the U.S. Medical Center for Federal Prisoners in Springfield, Missouri, San Quentin prison and the Federal Reform School at El Reno, Oklahoma, where he met the Reverend Donald Kanally, a Catholic priest and the one man he credits for putting him on the straight and narrow. ("He took me in hand, teaching me to respect myself; he taught me values I hadn't learned as a youngster.")

Paroled from San Quentin just before his 21st birthday, six-foot-four McCown, nicknamed "Smoke" because of his cigarette addiction, took on a variety of labor-intensive jobs including lumberjack, miner, cowpuncher, boxer and truck driver. In 1943, while out riding in the Hollywood Hills, he accidentally bumped into Alan Ladd, whose wife, Sue Carol, was a movie agent. It only needed one glance at the young, tall and exceedingly dishy stranger on horseback, with piercing blue eyes and black wavy hair, for Carol to arrange a screen test for McCown through the offices of Hollywood mogul David O. Selznick. He passed on looks alone—this was a period in Tinseltown's history when male hunks like McCown were snapped up by producers and groomed for their possible box-office sex appeal, never mind what little acting capability they may or may not have possessed. Signed by 20th Century Fox, his first film role was an uncredited soldier in *Something for the Boys* (1944), followed in the same year by *Sunday Dinner for a Soldier*, again as an uncredited soldier, and Laurel and Hardy's *The Bullfighters* (1945), as an uncredited matador. *Where Do We Go From Here?* (1945, another soldier) was followed by his first "major" role, as pugilist James J. "Gentleman Jim" Corbett in United Artists' *A Man Called Sullivan*; listed 12th on the cast list

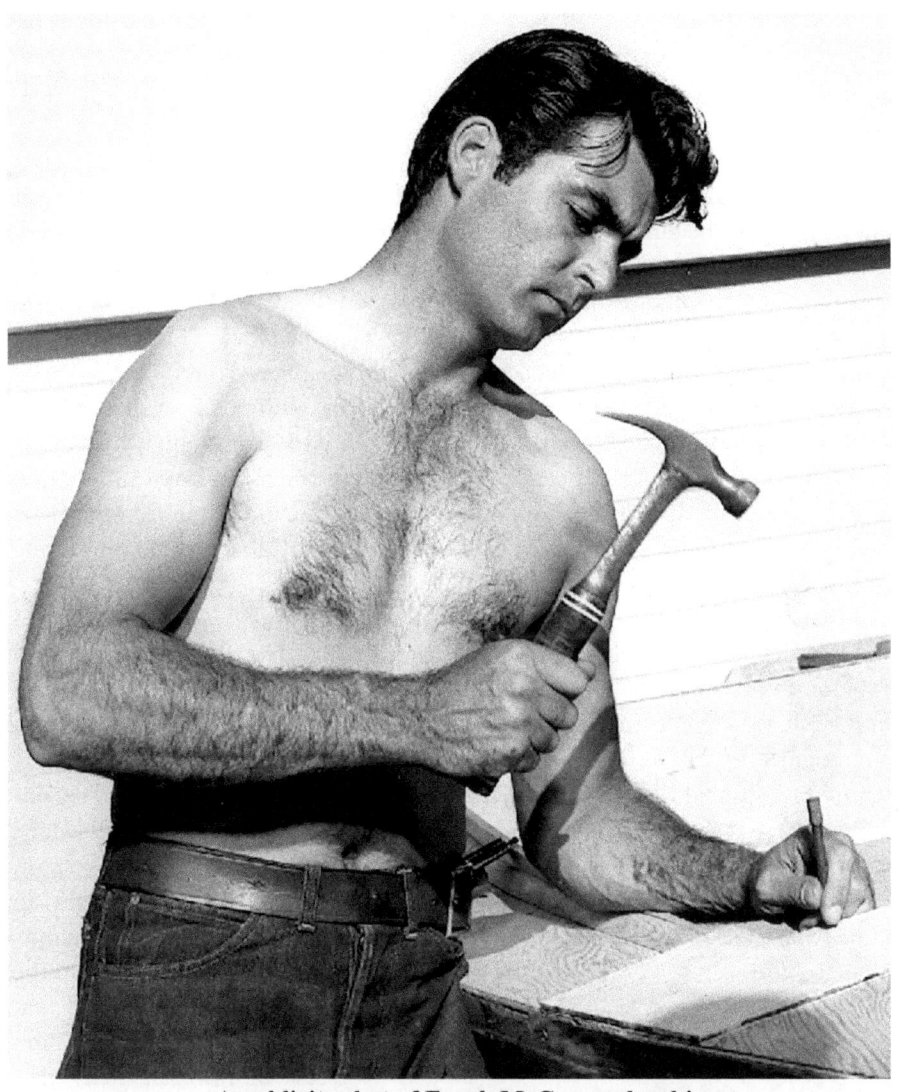

A publicity shot of Frank McCown—hunk!

he was billed as Frank McCown. It was Calhoun's career break, a chance to display his boxing prowess and impressive physique, not unnoticed by fellow star Linda Darnell (the pair had a fling during filming). After appearing (uncredited) as a boxer in *Nob Hill* (1945), Fox, disappointed at his lack of progress, dropped him from their roster: Henry Willson, Selznick's personal agent and chief talent scout, then changed McCown's name to the fancier Rory Calhoun (Troy Donahue was the first suggestion, later reused on actor Merle Johnson, Jr.). The dashing Calhoun caught the paparazzi's eye while escorting actress Lana Turner to the premier of Alfred Hitchcock's *Spellbound* in October 1945, an event stage-managed by publicity-hungry Selznick to push his faltering star into the public limelight.

In fact, Calhoun's love life would prove to be as stormy and colorful as his early years in crime. Although the volatile good-looker was married twice, to Mexican singer Lita Baron, 1948-1970 (three daughters), and Australian journalist Susan Rhodes, 1971-1999 (one daughter), he was an out-and-out womanizer, carrying on affairs with sex goddess Lana Turner, French actress Corinne Calvet (he proposed marriage in 1947, then changed his mind, wrecking her apartment and shooting at the girl when she demanded a reason for his unacceptable behavior), Yvonne De Carlo, Rhonda Fleming, Betty Grable, Julie Adams, Rita Hayworth, among scores of others, notoriously responding to Baron when she filed for divorce on the grounds of adultery with 79 named women, "Heck, she didn't even include half of them." He also had a fifth daughter, Athena, a result of a 12-month affair in 1958 with actress Vitina Marcus, who was later named "The World's Most Beautiful Showgirl." Calhoun was a dark-haired, highly fanciable rogue sporting a flashing smile, a real charmer, and the ladies loved him, a part he fully played to the hilt both on and off screen, but the untapped talent was there—it only needed the right moment, and the right director, to come along for it to flourish.

That "right moment" was United Artists' *noir* thriller *The Red House*, directed by Delmer Daves and released in 1947 after Selznick had decided to loan out Calhoun to other studios to promote his investment more widely. He was fourth on the bill, slowly but surely climbing the ladder—at last receiving top billing in Paramount's *Adventure Island* (1947), slipping to third starring opposite Shirley Temple and Ronald Reagan in Warner Bros.' *That Hagen Girl* (1947), and regaining the top spot in *Miraculous Journey* (Sigmund Neufeld Productions, 1948); he was now earning around $3,000 a week. He then starred in his first-ever Western, *Massacre River* (Allied Artists, 1949), a genre which served him well right up to *Bad Jim* (Delaware Pictures, 1990) and brought the best out of his admittedly marginal gifts in the acting profession. It was on the strength of his success in *Massacre River* that Fox offered Calhoun a new contract in 1949, deciding to utilize his good looks by teaming him with the studio's more glamorous actresses, a part which suited the six-footer down to the ground.

Rory on horseback, 1943

How does Rory Calhoun fare in the Western stakes against his many con-

temporaries? Could he act? His forte in the busy Western arena was playing professional gunslingers; ex-gunslingers, retired gunslingers, reformed gunslingers or gunslingers still on the job. Add to that his trademark abrupt, blunt delivery and indisputable handsome features and you had a cowboy hero almost up there with the best of them, one of the champions of the mid-range cowboy flick. So natural ability and an agreeable screen presence more than compensated for any aspirations Rory may have harbored in starring in a film based on the works of William Shakespeare. He fitted the bill nicely, looked the business on a horse, handled his opponents well by utilizing his old boxing skills (fistfights in Calhoun oaters were bruising affairs), and charmed the women off the trees. Perhaps there wasn't such a thing as a Rory Calhoun Western like there was a Randolph Scott or Audie Murphy Western, his name not having quite the same resonance and impact with audiences, but he nevertheless was capable of coming up trumps—*Four Guns to the Border*, *Dawn at Socorro* and *Red Sundown* are as good as anything Scott, Murphy, John Wayne or James Stewart ever appeared in, and produced on much lower budgets to boot. Given the right material, Rory Calhoun made some spiffy little Westerns that are as enjoyable today as they were all those years ago, a Hollywood jobbing actor, like so many minor star celebrities, operating on the sidelines, simply getting on with the job without all the ballyhoo sometimes connected with it. And Calhoun's horse operas were occasionally somewhat refreshingly different from the norm, as we shall find out in the coming chapters.

CHAPTER 3

ROD CAMERON: THE UNSMILING LADYKILLER

Six-foot-four Rod Cameron was born Nathan Roderick Cox on December 7, 1910 in Calgary, Alberta, Canada. As a youngster, he led a normal, uneventful childhood (in complete contrast to the three other stars featured in this book), aspiring to become a member of the Royal Canadian Mounted Police before getting hooked on Hollywood and the movies. He became involved in the welfare of juvenile delinquents at various schools and orphanages, including Calgary's St. Mary's School for Indian Children, before heading south and working on the Manhattan Holland Tunnel project in New York. Moving to Hollywood for coaching lessons, his strapping frame stood him in good stead for the role of stunt double and bit player, signing with Paramount in 1939 (although loaned out to other studios) and appearing uncredited in a number of productions between 1939 and 1940 (*The Old Maid* with Bette Davis, *Stagecoach War*, *If I Had My Way*

with Bing Crosby and *Rangers of Fortune*). Slowly, he began to get noticed, receiving credits and featuring in *The Quarterback* (1940), *Christmas in July* (1940) and, ironically, as a corporal in what would have been his chosen profession, *North West Mounted Police* (1940) with Gary Cooper. As his career staggered on (Cameron even starred in a horror movie, *The Monster and the Girl*, in 1941), he struck a chord with audiences playing square-jawed Agent Rex Bennett in the Republic serial *G-Men vs. the Black Dragon* and its follow-up, *Secret Service of Darkest Africa*, both 1943, Cameron's movie breakthrough year. He then signed up with Universal-International; their current cowboy star, Johnny Mack Brown, had left for Poverty Row outfit Monogram Pictures and they needed someone rugged, tall, dark and handsome to fill his boots. He was 13th on the cast list in United Artists' 1943 unremarkable oater *Wagon Wheels* (50-year-old silent star Richard Dix's last Western)—a year later, in *Boss of Boomtown*, he was top, and never looked back on a career path that not only took in Westerns, his main area of operation, but crime, adventure, comedy, war and even science fiction and horror.

Tough guy Rod Cameron lights up.

Not having the tough upbringing of Rory Calhoun or Sterling Hayden showed in Cameron's overall performances. He was what many might term an "ordinary jobbing actor," neither good nor bad, slightly one-dimensional in approach, not so great in the versatility bracket. The only bit of controversy surrounding his life was his marriage to Dorothy Eveleigh in 1960; she was the mother of his second wife, Angela Louisa Alves-Lico, who he had wed in 1950, producing a boy, Anthony; his first marriage was to Doris C. Stanford, lasting three years (1936-1939), a daughter, Catherine, the result of the union. Although a rumor spread around the film set that he had had another daughter from a secret liaison, this has never been substantiated.

Therefore, in reviewing his Westerns, you have to concentrate on the film itself rather than Cameron's display, which rarely altered from one production to the next. His acting style was a basic mix of brusque delivery, stern expression (Cameron smiling was a rare event) and an uncompromising directness in dealing with women, banking on his rough and ready charm and physique to bowl them over without the need for any kind of courtship; he was straight in there from reel one. Although an inch shorter than Sterling Hayden, he managed to look bigger on screen, his well-built frame filling a shirt nicely; like Hayden and Calhoun, his fistfights were almost examples of how to box, unflinching, punishing, brutal and vicious. Rod was perfectly at home in the familiar surroundings of the B-Western and seemed quite content with what he was doing, unpretentious to a fault. Fans couldn't ask for anything more.

CHAPTER 4

STERLING HAYDEN: THE RELUCTANT FILM STAR

Sterling Relyea Walter was born on March 26, 1916 in Montclair, New Jersey. Following the death of his father, he was adopted at the age of nine by James Hayden and his name was changed to Sterling Walter Hayden. As a child, he traveled around a great deal, living in coastal towns in New England, Massachusetts, Pennsylvania, Maine, Washington, D.C., and New Hampshire, attending Wassookeag High School in Dexter, Maine. Hayden, a lanky, restless youth, developed a love of the sea during his teenage years which mushroomed into a lifelong passion, dropping out of school when he was 16 and taking on the job of mate on a schooner. Other nautical trades included a seaman on the Grand Banks, a fireman, earning his master's license on a trading vessel in the Caribbean and, in 1937, serving as mate on the *Yankee*, embarking on a world cruise. Aged only 22, he took his first command on the rigger *Florence C. Robinson* in 1938, skippering the craft from Massachusetts to Tahiti.

Publicity shot of "The Most Beautiful Man in the Movies"

Hayden was now a virile, strapping six-foot-five-inch piece of male beefcake, blessed with rugged, blond good looks, plus a deeper than deep voice. After a stint as a male model, he came to the attention of producer/director Edward H. Griffith, who put him through acting lessons and signed him to a Paramount contract in 1940, promoting the unknown performer as "The Most Beautiful Man in the Movies" and "The Beautiful Blond Viking God." (Hayden later said he "winced. But the money was good."). He starred in two films in 1941, *Virginia* and *Bahama Passage*, meeting Madeleine Carroll on the set of *Virginia* and marrying her in February 1942. But the lure of the water, and importantly the war, was too much for Hayden to ignore: He loved to live life to the fullest and quit Hollywood, joining the U.S. Marine Corps as a commando under the pseudonym of John Hamilton and undergoing a series of adventures that would fill a book—but not this book! In a distinguished military service career, he was, at one point, an OSS agent ferrying supplies and gun running from Italy to Yugoslavia to aid the partisans in their fight against Nazi occupation, receiving the Silver Star for gallantry in action. Forever accused of dabbling in Communism by some of his critics, which he had briefly flirted with shortly after the war (and regretted doing so), he left active duty in 1945 to resume his career in the film industry, an industry that he openly admitted he hadn't much time for. The cash came in handy to help finance all things connected to the sea and boats (he owned his own ship, *The Wanderer*, often taking off in her without notification, even writing a book about the vessel in 1963), plus alimony payments, and that was about it. Acting wasn't his bag. His friends reinforced his bull-headed, couldn't-give-a-dime attitude: "Hayden's wild," they said. "He's kinda nuts, but you gotta hand it to him. He doesn't give a damn about the loot, or stardom or things like that. Seafaring is all what he wants." In 1976, writer Skiles Howard called Hayden "A force of nature … an element … but he can act." In his somewhat candid autobiography *Wanderer* (Knopf, 1963), the following lines sum up Hayden's cynical put-down of the acting profession: "Why did you never write? Why, instead, did you grovel along,

Hayden aboard his beloved *Wanderer*

through the endless months and years, as a motion-picture actor? What held you to it, to something you so vehemently profess to despise?" In writing this, it becomes evident that Hayden classed himself as a free spirit not to be tied down, never happier than when the waves were beneath his feet, unconcerned with Tinseltown's vagaries, temptations, politics and self-obsessive ways.

Hayden's personal and highly unconventional lifestyle, his resolve to buck the Hollywood vogue of near-hedonism and the cult of celebrity, was just as colorful as his fearless war exploits. He divorced Carroll in 1946 ("Wartime separations ended it," he admitted) and married/divorced Pasadena dress designer Betty Ann de Noon three times, from 1947 to 1958, eventually settling with Catherine Devine McConnell from 1960 to his death in 1986. Six children were produced as a result of these multiple marriages. Hayden was often involved in bitter custody battles over the four he had had with de Noon, leading to a near-permanent state of being broke.

He could also be cavalier with money, financing through Republic Pictures his own sea voyage to Tahiti in 1958 with his four children at a cost of $50,000, the aim being to shoot a documentary of the voyage *and* to leave the movie capital, with all its glossy, shallow (to his eyes) trappings, behind. The documentary was never made: He was forced to repay Republic the entire cost of footing the bill for the trip and infuriated bosses at Warner Bros. by reneging on a deal to co-star in the romantic drama *A Summer Place*, which he was reluctant to do anyway (his fee would have been $40,000); throughout his life, Hayden was constantly short of money because of his reckless spending. He unashamedly enjoyed the booze and smoked dope and made no attempt to disguise the fact, apprehended at Toronto airport in 1980 for going through customs with "a small quantity of weed in my case."

In 1947, Sterling Hayden starred in his third movie, Paramount's *Blaze of Noon* (that year, he was paid $70,000 by Paramount for doing, in his own words, "nothing"). His first Western, released in 1949, was *El Paso*. Due to his towering height (he was one of Hollywood's tallest actors) and mean, glowering features, producers often cast him in the role of a heavy, as witnessed in John Huston's classic *noir* heist thriller, *The Asphalt Jungle* (MGM, 1950), one of his most famous parts; he was also outstanding in Stanley Kubrick's *The Killing* (United Artists,

1956), another *noir* classic, and was offered the part of Tarzan after Lex Barker quit the role in 1953; he rejected it out of hand, going on to star in Westerns, crime, war, satire and gangster thrillers right up to 1981.

Hayden's performances throughout his career, but mainly in the '50s and anything other than crime *noir*, were governed by his contemptuous attitude toward filmmaking, Hollywood, the star system and everything connected to the movie industry. He disliked looking at himself on screen, 1973's *The Long Goodbye* being the one and only exception (he *did* admit to wanting to appear in *The Killing*). Actors were "pawns," he "couldn't stand the work," most of his character roles were "bastards spewn out onto screens across the world," he reckoned that if he had had the money he'd buy up and burn every negative to every film he had made, he only worked "when I got broke" and "you didn't need a special talent to star in a motion picture." "Incredible … parlaying nine years at sea into two decades of posturing" and to producers: "When you took me on, who did you *really* want for the picture?"—with comments like this, it's a miracle that the man ever turned in a decent acting display and continued to hang on in there for 40 years. True, a certain robotic stiffness comes across in some of his Western scenes (as in most of *Arrow in the Dust* and the first part of *The Iron Sheriff*), a remoteness that is a puzzle until one stops and remembers what the man was like away from the film set. But if Hayden chose to cruise on autopilot, so be it; at least, in his own words, he didn't "posture," content to turn up, run through his lines and collect his wages at the end of the shoot. He was in it for the money that provided much-needed capital for his seafaring adventures—pure and simple. Looking back on his career, he seemed to have reserved his prime acting displays for anything *other* than Westerns: His hoodlum, Dix Handley, in *The Asphalt Jungle*, is six-foot-five-inches of sneering intimidation, a once-in-a-lifetime role (director Huston, a Hayden fan, said to the actor: "They don't know what to make of a guy like you in the business.") It's a pity that, except on the odd occasion, this screen-burning intensity failed to translate over into his oaters, but why that was we shall never know.

So Sterling Hayden's 17 Westerns (he made four others that hovered on the Western fringe, not included in this volume) are a mixed bunch, but captivating insofar as most are not your traditional, standard cowboy fare. Perhaps *Flaming Feather*, *Arrow in the Dust*, *Shotgun* and *The Last Command* could be classed as such; certainly, *Hellgate*, *Johnny Guitar*, *Valerie* and *Terror in a Texas Town* could not. That's why I have included the man's Westerns in this book. He wasn't a Western star in the same sense that Randolph Scott, Audie Murphy, Joel McCrea and George Montgomery, the four dudes covered in *Six-Gun Law*, were, but what he starred in makes idiosyncratic Western viewing of a different kind, Hayden's sheer physical presence and charisma compensating for his "I couldn't give a damn about all this" inclinations. If anyone reckons that Sterling Hayden was a lousy cowboy actor, watch *Hellgate*, *The Last Command* or *Shotgun*, and think again!

CHAPTER 5

WIDMARK: SEVEN WESTERN CLASSICS, 1948-1959

Following his sensational screen debut as Tommy Udo in *Kiss of Death*, Richard Widmark was catapulted into the unusual and enviable position of being an A-lister from the word go; hardly any B-movies would come *his* way, he was that good. Fox, glad to have a novel, newly discovered bankable star on their hands, quickly cast him in two *noirs*, as a crime boss in *The Street with No Name* and playing an unhinged roadhouse owner in *Road House*, both released in 1948 and capitalizing on the actor's success at getting under the skin of Udo's damaged psyche. His first foray into the world of the Western was as Dude in William A. Wellman's $2,000,000 *Yellow Sky* (Fox, 1948), the first of two oaters he made that were set within the boundaries of a desert ghost town. Filming took place in California's Death Valley National Park and the Alabama Hills, Lone Pine, in July 1948, with temperatures soaring to 120°, home to scorpions and Gila monsters, a real-life ghost town constructed on the Lone Pine site. Widmark, unlike the other cast members new to the world of Hollywood horses, had a great deal of trouble mastering his steed in the sweaty conditions, suffering from uncomfortable saddle sores. Billed third behind Gregory Peck and Anne Baxter, his tight-lipped tinhorn gambler was coldness personified, contrasting with the blinding heat of the rugged Lone Pine mountainscapes, which were beautifully shot in stark black-and-white by Joseph MacDonald. *Yellow Sky* counts as one of a number of movies taking as their template Shakespeare's *The Tempest*: A group of strangers (in this case Peck and his gang) burst in upon two people living in isolation (Baxter and Grandpa James Barton), arousing all kinds of hidden emotions, particularly Baxter's deep-rooted lust for Peck, which is blatantly reciprocated in a couple of A [adult]-rated scenes, leading to jealousy within the ranks; burly John Russell has his own plans for Baxter, never mind what Peck thinks. Producer Lamar Trotti's concise script, taken from a W.R. Burnett story (he also co-wrote), cut down on verbal gymnastics, characters spitting out one-liners through gritted teeth in a rough, tough scenario; here, Peck did a sublime impersonation (intentional or otherwise) of Gary Cooper, *the* specialist in monosyllabic one-liners!

1867: Peck, Widmark, Russell, Robert Arthur, Harry Morgan and Charles Kemper, after holding up a bank and chased by a posse of cavalry, negotiate wa-

terless salt flats and wander half-crazed with thirst into the abandoned town of Yellow Sky. Tomboy Baxter, very handy with a gun, rifle and fists, sees that the outlaws are fed and watered and fends off Peck's clumsy advances ("You smell. Even Apaches are cleaner than you," she storms at him), while in the background, gold-hungry Widmark plots to take over as *de facto* leader and steal Baxter's hoard of riches worth $50,000, hidden inside a mine passage. Wellman frames his characters up close, *noir* fashion, Widmark's smooth, sun-baked blond features mirroring the harshness of the landscape, the delivery clipped ("Never mind the girl. Where's the gold?"), Peck involved in a series of standoffs with the compassionless gambler and his ambitions ("Dude's the leader, is that it?"), telling his compatriots to "shut up" if they show signs of stepping out of line and ordering Baxter to "stop swinging your hips all over the place." Peck, shaven, cleaned up and attired in fresh new duds, tries it on with Baxter for a second time. She responds, and in a moment of undisguised lust, claws at Peck's back in a savage embrace; he's the man for her, even though she refuses to admit it ("I thought you were enjoying it," he says as, perspiring, she pushes him off in a state of agitation). It all culminates in the inevitable showdown—Arthur succumbs from a fatal bullet wound while

Harry Morgan, Richard Widmark and Robert Arthur, a mean looking bunch in *Yellow Sky*

Peck, loyal to Baxter and old-timer Barton, guns down Widmark and Russell in a saloon (only shots are heard) and returns to town with survivors Morgan (the new Dude!) and Kemper, redeeming himself by handing back the stolen money to the bank manager ("It's all there. Every cent we took."). Outside of town, Peck presents Baxter with a hat purchased from a lady and, with Barton in tow, the five ride off with the gold into the wilderness.

If you've ever wondered what a major motion picture is like without a requisite score, watch *Yellow Sky*. Apart from Alfred Newman's opening and closing music (reprised from 1940's *Brigham Young: Frontiersman*) and Kemper singing "I'm Sad and I'm Lonely," this is one Western bereft of any incidental musical tonalities—only the sound of the wind whistling through those tumbled-down buildings is heard. The rest is a brooding silence. Does this add or detract from what's taking place? It must be said that in some sequences, music is urgently required to boost the tension and nuances, almost crying out for an accompaniment. However, it does lend the production a certain atmospheric air of desolation and realism and, in retrospect, is rather unique, not to mention a brave gamble by Fox at the time (52 years later, Robert Zemeckis dispensed with a soundtrack for the entire middle section of *Cast Away*, to telling effect). All in all, *Yellow Sky* still stands as one of the late '40s finest Western hours, a stylish, solid, great-to-look-at outdoors drama with the accent on a disparate group at odds within a confined setting rather than all-out gun-blazing action, with bad guy turned good guy Peck in outstanding form, as, in fact, are the entire cast. As for Widmark, although not the lead, his quiet, simmering threat is the perfect counterfoil to Peck's brusque, commanding boss, like a rattlesnake waiting for the right opportunity to strike. In his first-ever Western, Richard Widmark struck all the right notes; the *New York Times* labeled the movie "a scorcher."

From 1948 to 1954, Widmark cut his teeth on a series of meaty roles in some notable productions, directed by Hollywood star names: Jules Dassin's *Night and the City*, Elia Kazan's *Panic in the Streets*, Joseph L. Mankiewicz's *No Way Out* (1950), Lewis Milestone's *Halls of Montezuma* (again 1950, a stellar year for the actor), Robert Wise's *Destination Gobi* (1953) and Samuel Fuller's *Hell and High Water* (1954), among others. His next high-flying Western, 1954's $3,000,000 *Garden of Evil*, saw him billed third behind Gary Cooper and Susan Hayward. If *Yellow Sky* had suffered in places from a lack of music, then Henry Hathaway's stunning, little-remembered opus had it in abundance, courtesy of top Hollywood composer Bernard Herrmann, one of only two Westerns he scored (disregarding TV work), the other being United Artists' *The Kentuckian* in 1955. Herrmann, famed for his successful collaborations with Alfred Hitchcock and the fantasy works of effects ace Ray Harryhausen over at Columbia, orchestrated a stunning soundtrack to perfectly match the primordial landscape used for location filming—Mexico's volcanic Uruapan region. The omnipresent Paricutin volcano (last seen erupting during the final stages of Fox's 1947 swashbuckler *Captain from Castile*) and the buried church of Juan de las Colchas provided stunning set pieces; at any moment, you half expected to see a denizen from the Jurassic Age stride out of the banana jungles and cactus groves, so evocative was the maestro's magnificently noisy, brooding score. In fact, scenery plays a major part in *Garden of Evil*, the forbidding volcanic, ash-strewn hills shot

Widmark deals the cards in *Garden of Evil*.

in vivid colors by Jorge Stahl, Jr. and Milton R. Krasner, a point not going unnoticed by the critics who found the film's visual impact, and Herrmann's score, occasionally overpowering the plot. Thanks to Herrmann and the rugged locales, *Garden of Evil* drips in a highly unusual combination of Western and semi-fantasy ambience, almost unique in looks and mood. Why it remains shunted to the back of the '50s Western pile is a complete and utter mystery.

Stuck in a small one-horse Mexican village after their boat has broken down and faced with the depressing prospect of six weeks of idleness stretching ahead of them, three adventurers, holed up in a saloon, jump at the chance of $2,000 each, offered by gun-toting Susan Hayward. Her husband (Hugh Marlowe) is injured, trapped inside a gold mine situated in a remote part of the country inhabited by Apaches, and she needs help in getting him out. Widmark plays Fiske, another tinhorn gambler role (although more amenable than his gambler in *Yellow Sky*), Cooper is the silent man of action (which suited him down to the ground), Cameron Mitchell the hot-headed bounty hunter. Mexican Victor Manuel Mendoza joins the group, who first have to negotiate a perilous mountain ledge before heading off into the wilds, Hayward destroying the Mexican's markers—only she, and she alone, knows the way; nobody else will get to know about it. Hayward is one feisty, single-minded temptress, wrapping men around her little finger, as Mitchell finds out to his dismay; he unwisely makes a caveman pass at her, is violently rebuffed and ends up being punched senseless by Cooper, rolling around in a campfire and sobbing like a baby as Widmark looks on, highly amused (Coop and "Dick" hit it off, both on set and off.)

It's interesting to compare Widmark, in his second Western, to 53-year-old Cooper, in his 34th (including silents). In a movie where nobody smiles (well,

Coop does manage the odd flicker), Widmark's garrulous Fiske is up against Coop's reticent, stone-faced Hooker, summed up in an opening line of dialogue when Widmark remarks to Cooper "Say, you've heard of getting blood out of a stone, haven't you?" A second exchange is just as witty: Widmark (as Rita Moreno gyrates seductively toward them): "I've found that pretty women speak the same language all over the world." Cooper: "What about the ugly ones?" Widmark, drily: "Never listened." Coop's script (screenplay: Frank Fenton) was probably half the length of Widmark's and, at times, he looks in pain, probably due to recurrent shoulder problems and stomach ulcers that plagued him in later years. But Coop is Coop—

French poster for *Garden of Evil*

you know nothing at all about the man in this setup except that he used to be a peace maker, but that is sufficient enough for the audience. His economical underplaying of characters was as legendary as the man himself, so all can be forgiven! And everyone in the movie is on a short fuse, including Widmark.

After 42 minutes of the long arduous journey out, the mine is reached, Marlowe rescued, his broken leg patched up. The man turns out to be an ungrateful, embittered, self-pitying grouch, amazed that Hayward ever came back to someone as worthless (in his eyes) as him, but the Titian-haired lass has her eyes set on the gold, callously rejecting Widmark's caring overtures ("You're nothing at all. Nothing."). Riding off to escape the Apaches, first Cameron, then Marlowe and Mendoza are brutally killed, leaving Cooper, Hayward and Widmark to once more negotiate that vertigo-inducing mountain track, a pack of Indians hard on their heels. Widmark sacrifices himself on the ledge, succumbing to an arrow in the chest, allowing Cooper and Hayward to ride away from that "Garden of Evil," maybe to set up house and start a new life together. A fabulous adult, intelligent Western that pits a small group of misfits against each other in a wild, hostile terrain, a motion picture deserving reappraisal as the American genre classic it most certainly is; Cooper's box-office clout, Widmark's analytical but easygoing card sharp plus Hayward in full flow made for a deeply rewarding trip out West with a marked difference.

As Ben Devereaux in *Broken Lance*

Widmark's final appearance for Fox before severing connections with them to go freelance was as Ben Devereaux in 1954's *Broken Lance*, directed by Edward Dmytryk and budgeted at $2,000,000, a major critical and commercial hit practically guaranteed because of white-haired Spencer Tracy's monolithic presence. Widmark was fourth on the bill, his part an unsympathetic one, the venom-filled eldest of cattle baron Tracy's four sons siding with siblings Hugh O'Brian and Earl Holliman over Robert Wagner, a half-breed whose Indian mother, lovely Katy Jurado (nominated for an Oscar), is Tracy's second wife. Loosely based on Shakespeare's *King Lear* (sons substituted for daughters) and a remake of the company's *House of Strangers* (Joseph L. Mankiewicz, 1949), *Broken Lance*, shot in Arizona and looking splendid in the new CinemaScope format (Joseph MacDonald's superb pristine color brought the sweeping vistas to vivid life) was another adult-oriented Western (A-rated in Britain) containing solid performances all round. It

Spencer Tracy confronts his sons in *Broken Lance*.

gave Widmark the rare opportunity to star alongside Tracy, his acting hero, and, like many oaters of this period, highlighted the antagonism felt toward the downtrodden native Indian, in this case Jurado, Tracy's doe-eyed, almost subservient, wife an outcast virtually shunned by the local community. Wagner got most of the screen time and made a good fist of it, playing the son taking a three-year rap on account of Tracy ransacking a copper mine that is polluting the local water supply and thereby poisoning his herds. Delectable Jean Peters supplied the love interest, unconcerned that Wagner was half-Indian despite warnings from her father, Governor E.G. Marshall, to stay away from the boy. With Wagner in prison, argumentative Widmark, bitter over his upbringing and feeling that Tracy always took him for granted, gains control as head of the Devereaux Ranch after his father dies from a heart attack, with plans to pay Wagner off on his release with a "take it or leave it" business proposition, his two brothers content to go along for the ride and keep Widmark happy.

Richard Murphy and Philip Yordan's screenplay worked on many levels (racial prejudice; sibling rivalry), *Broken Lance* becoming a tad talkative in the middle section, but with bull-headed screen legend Tracy on full throttle, who cared (his courtroom scene, where he refuses to give a straight answer to a straight question and ends up cross-examining the prosecutor, is a blueprint in acting bravura, showcasing Tracy at his irascible best, as is his standoff with mine owner Robert Burton). The film ends with the expected showdown between eldest and youngest brother ("You're his little pet. You always were," sneers Widmark to Wagner), Widmark shot dead by Indian Eduard Franz following a ferocious fistfight between the two among rocks, Widmark about to finish Wagner off with a rifle bullet. The final scene is deeply moving in its sheer unspoken simplicity, Wagner (he breaks a lance near his father's grave as a sign of peace) and Peters riding off in a buggy, Jurado, back with her tribe, looking on, pleased that her son has found the woman of his dreams, one who will accept him for what he is, a lone wolf howling high on a rock, perhaps the spirit of Tracy saying a fond farewell to the young couple and the son he thought most of. "Refreshingly serious," wrote the *New York Times*, *The Hollywood Reporter* adding "a hard-hitting Western."

Up until now, Widmark wasn't classed a Western lead in the traditional sense of the word, not by the studios or the fans. All that was about to change, albeit not on a permanent basis. Parting company with Fox in May 1954, he took on his own projects, hired by Universal-International in 1956 to headline *Backlash*, a superb, relatively obscure (for a 1950 cowboy flick) oater directed by John Sturges, budgeted at just over a million dollars. Universal's Westerns of this period were a cut above the rest—noisy, brash, violent and fast-moving. *Backlash* didn't buck the trend. Filmed around the arid Arizona localities of Sonoita, Cortaro and Patagonia and dressed in Irving Glassberg's sparkling Technicolor hues, Sturges' streamlined sagebrush saga-cum-detective story took in fractured kinship, double-dealing, standoffs a-plenty, a fragile romance built on mutual mistrust and warring Apaches. Herman Stein's bulldozing score drives the action to extreme limits. Similar to what happened to Randolph Scott in United Artists' *Abilene Town* in 1946, *Backlash* is probably the defining moment when Widmark stamped his authority on a Western and made it his own; he had found his spurs and could now carry such a production on his slim shoulders, his name pulling in the audiences. OK, he continued to branch out into other areas of cinema, never content to become simply a cowboy folk hero like so many of his contemporaries, but he undoubtedly matured into a formidable Western leading star, as *Backlash* conclusively proved.

Widmark's psychologically damaged Jim Slater is a man on a mission, seeking to kill the lowlife who left his father and four others to die at the hands of the marauding Apaches in Gila Valley, the party searching for $60,000 in buried gold.

Donna Reed cozies up to Dick Widmark in *Backlash*.

Frisky Donna Reed is a *girl* on a mission; her missing husband could have been one of those massacred and she wants to ferret out the real truth behind his disappearance. Reed meets up with Widmark and sparks fly. Her dubious sexual past (hinted at in Borden Chase's tight screenplay) means that Widmark never knows where he stands with her, smothered in passionate kisses one minute, being set up to be dispatched the next; for some reason best known to herself, she sees Widmark as the root of all her troubles. "You know, if I was smart, I'd see you out of here," he tells her as she tends to his shoulder wound. "Why don't you?" she answers. "I'm not smart. And you're good looking." *Backlash* is pretty complex for what many might perceive as a standard Universal '50s Western, top-heavy on Freudian symbolism and demanding 100% concentration, veering from an opening tense cat-and-mouse shoot-out taking place among craggy heights to the fraught Widmark/Reed on/off relationship, including a range war between rancher Roy Roberts and John McIntire's bunch of hired gunslingers, trigger-happy cowpoke William Campbell (dressed in black as Johnny Cool, out to carve a reputation for himself) plus two vengeful brothers in the form of screen toughs Harry Morgan and Robert J. Wilke thrown into the mix. You are never quite sure how the convoluted plot, riddled in all kinds of dark secrets and unrelated mini-dramas, secondary characters introduced then leaving, is going to resolve itself. Few if any

French poster for *Backlash*

explanations are offered, Sturges allowing the events to unfold with no tangible threads visible until the final denouement. Reed knows that McIntire is the rat that left his comrades to die, including her husband, and that the rogue rancher happens to be Widmark's father, the mysterious sixth man Widmark has been looking to kill! In a series of climactic showdowns set in the desert town of Sierra Blanca, Widmark, lightning fast on the draw, guns down both Morgan and cocky Campbell (he's already shot Wilke) and goes on the run in a corral from the uncaring father who left him as an infant. As he's about to shoot his own son, McIntire is fatally wounded by one of Roberts' posse, who have stormed the town to oust McIntire's gunmen; Widmark dispassionately stares at the bloodied corpse lying in the dust without any regrets or feelings of remorse and walks off with Reed.

Backlash, a fine example of the new kind of adult Western emerging during this decade that eschewed the family-type adventures of Roy Rogers, Gene Autry et al., played to all of Widmark's strengths ("Tough and mean," said *Variety*): Highly strung, tight as a bowstring, charismatic, intimidating, emotionally vulnerable at times, tough and quick-witted; and the actor's "Tommy Udo" chuckle is in evidence throughout, as is his trademark easy grin. It's down to his star quality that it made money, Widmark taking a basic wage of $50,000 plus a 50% share of the profits, netting him a tidy sum. Sure enough, the movie *is* unconventional and sparky, by no means your average oater, inconsistent in some areas perhaps but a disciplined little Western all the same, directed with a firm hand by Sturges in no-holds-barred style and containing blistering performances from the entire cast. On this showing, the main man could have forged out a successful career starring in nothing but Westerns, having now participated in four expensive horse operas, all of which had rung box-office tills. He now looked the part and at last appeared comfortable in the saddle (he even leaps onto his horse's back in *Backlash*) but chose not to stick to this career route.

Following United Artists' adventure thriller *Run for the Sun* (1956), Widmark returned to 20th Century Fox the same year to star as Comanche Todd in another high, wide and handsome Western yarn, *The Last Wagon*, directed with bite and an expert eye for landscape shooting by Delmer Daves. Set in 1873 and filmed against an awe-inspiring backdrop of gulches, creeks, canyons and bluffs around Arizona's remarkable mountainous Sedona region (Wilfred [Wilfrid] M. Cline's dazzling photography was a sight to behold), the movie saw Widmark, a white man who had lived with the Indians, playing a fugitive on the run, hunted down for the murder of three brothers (he slays the fourth, brutal sheriff George Mathews, who has treated him like an animal, tied to a wagon wheel, 20 minutes in: "I wanted to kill them and I did," he states at his trial near the end), redeeming himself by assisting six young survivors of an Apache massacre to negotiate their way to safety through the forbidding Canyon of Death. Racial prejudice rears its ugly head, as it so often did in the 1950s Western scenario: Hothead Nick Adams (the actor tragically died from a drug overdose in 1968 at the age of 36) doesn't trust Widmark an inch, while Stephanie Griffin loathes her half-sister, Susan Kohner, for having Indian blood coursing through her veins (Widmark later saves Griffin's life by sucking poison from her arm left by a rattlesnake, making the girl repent her spiteful feelings toward Indians and Kohner). To add sauce to a very tasty dessert, Felicia Farr, en route to get wed, falls head over boot heels in love with the renegade's dangerously sexy, rugged blond persona, while youngster Tommy Rettig hero-worships the man, a feeling that is reciprocated: Widmark's two sons and wife were savagely murdered by the gang of coyotes he has slaughtered; he sees in Rettig the boy that should have grown up beside him, a poignant motif in a Western bristling with exciting incident and crisp one-liners, courtesy of writers James Edward Grant, Gwen Bagni and director Daves.

Widmark, fleshing out the somewhat dubious antihero that was Comanche Todd into a person you could relate to, looked on top form in *The Last Wagon*, blond and slim, his light tan setting off his blue eyes and faded buckskins to perfection, his performance classed by *Variety* as "forceful." The action, from the knife-edge opening scene of Widmark being chased by the brothers through a series of bone-dry gulches, was violent (Widmark fells Mathews with an axe and knifes two Apaches to death), the dialogue racy for 1956 (jealous Griffin wondering whether Farr will offer herself to the tied-up killer during the night), hence the British "A" certificate [children must be accompanied by an adult]; okay, the closing section was ever-so-slightly schmaltzy, Widmark, on trial, being saved from the rope when Farr, Kohner, Griffin, Rettig, Adams and Ray Stricklyn all speak up for him, the judge letting the renegade off (justifiable homicide?) on condition that Farr takes him on as a husband. But the final scene of Widmark, Farr and Rettig galloping off into that spectacular Arizona wilderness to set up house is uplifting to the senses, a fitting conclusion to another shunted-to-the-sidelines Western classic in urgent need of critical reassessment. And never has Arizona's Sedona region been better presented than in Daves' stunner of a Western, embellished by a beautiful score from Lionel Newman, younger brother of noted composer Alfred Newman.

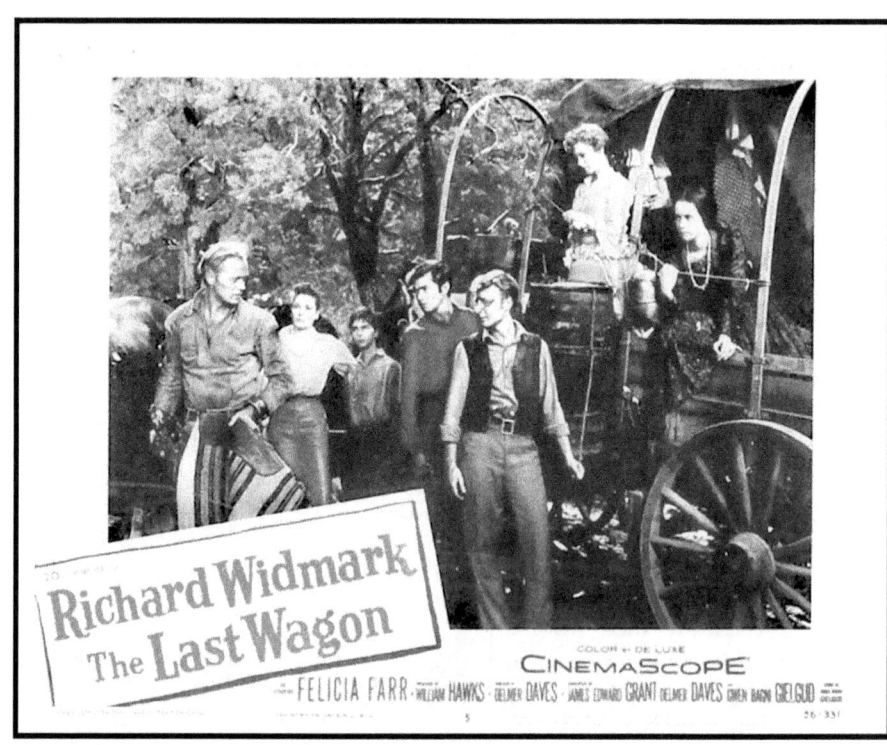

Western-wise, Widmark was on one heck of a roll: Five big-scale oaters were tucked under his gun belt, all produced on expensive budgets and all bringing in healthy profits; could things get any better? They certainly could—*The Law and Jake Wade* (MGM, 1958) is an absolute cracker, filmed around Lone Pine's Alabama Hills and Death Valley National Park on a budget of $1,540,000, Widmarks's second horse opera set in the locale of a desolate desert ghost town. Widmark shared top billing with Robert Taylor, John Sturges' thundering good Western mirroring the Randolph Scott/Budd Boetticher productions made between 1956-1960: A not-so-honest good guy pitted against an engaging bad guy, a magnetic villain who grabs all the attention, the scenario played out in a harsh, remote environment ("A must for a Western is isolation," stated Sturges in a 1960 interview). New trends in cinematic violence, spilling over into the Western format, guaranteed *The Law and Jake Wade* receiving an "A" classification in the United Kingdom when it was released in late 1958, the attack by Comanche Indians on the ghost town fairly graphic for its day and deemed unsuitable for minors. Although Widmark liked William Bowers' screenplay, taken from a story by Marvin H. Albert, and agreed to take on the role of yet another bad 'un, he later stated that he was never overly fond of the end results and disliked working in Sturges' favored "isolated" locale, strange when you consider his brilliant performance as outlaw Clint Hollister and the rapport he had with Taylor, the two bouncing off one another like the consummate professionals they were.

Marshal Taylor (Jake Wade) busts ex-partner Widmark (Clint Hollister) out of Morganville's jail, a debt repaid; Widmark busted *him* out of jail some years back following a bank holdup. Before going clean, Taylor had abruptly parted company with Widmark, hiding $20,000 of loot in a distant desert ghost town, having decided to give up robbing banks. Widmark, now freed, wants that money badly, planning to kill Taylor once he's got his hands on it. On home territory,

Widmark and Taylor on the trail in *The Law and Jake Wade*

the reformed outlaw and his fiancée, Patricia Owens, are abducted by Widmark and his gang, tied up and forced to head off into the mountains where, after three grueling days (Taylor's one escape attempt proves abortive), the ruined town is located. The place is soon under attack from Comanche Indians; all but Taylor, Widmark, Owens and Robert Middleton ultimately perish. The cash found in a grave, and with it a shooter inside the saddlebag ("I forgot about that one," admits Widmark, ruefully), Middleton and Owens gallop off, leaving the two war buddies to play cat-and-mouse among the wrecked buildings. Taylor brings down his old friend/foe with a single bullet; dropping his gun into the dust in regret at killing Widmark, he joins Owens and Middleton, riding away with the stolen takings.

"Don't try to follow me Clint. You remember, I'm pretty good with one of these," reminds Taylor to Widmark after breaking him out from behind bars in the opening sequence. "Yeah, yeah, I remember," drawls the blond one, flashing that easy grin. "But you're not as good as me. Just, uh, just prettier." As Taylor rides off, there's an unsettling shot of Widmark astride his horse, a look of cold malice on his face, allowing us a glimpse of his character's ruthless, amoral side. Yes, the teaming of black-clad, dark-haired Taylor with blue-jacketed, fair-haired Widmark is pure dynamite, thanks to Bowers' terse script. Widmark's Clint Hollister joins a long line of Western villains who are just so damn likeable—no wonder Taylor wears a look of resignation at the end after shooting him. Was it all worth it, just to see his one-time friend sprawled in the dust? The relationship between the two is edgy, based on a former trust now turned sour, each homing in on the other's foibles; Taylor feels guilt over the death of a boy during a raid (in fact, he's not responsible) while Widmark, in his mind, reckons he's been betrayed, whether he secretly admires Taylor or not. In yet another oater where nobody manages to raise so much as a flicker of a smile, cowboy hoodlum Henry Silva's slack-jawed, dead-eyed outlaw stands out, the support cast of DeForest Kelley, Middleton, Eddie Firestone and Owens perfectly willing and able to watch Widmark and Taylor snipe, snap and glare, the spectacular Lone Pine scenery captured in Robert Surtees' diamond-hard photography. As stated, the Comanche raid is graphic and gruesome, Silva succumbing to two arrows, Owens pushing an arrow into the face of a rampaging brave, a few touches of mock 3-D filming adding to the tension (arrows and war axes flung direct at camera). "There's your gun," says Taylor to Widmark in the climactic shoot-out, tossing the weapon into the deserted street. "I was gonna hand you yours," is the curt reply. "Well, you like me a lot better than I like you," a final comment from Taylor that sums up the parting of the ways and how the men viewed each other.

"I'm in charge." Widmark spells it out in *The Law and Jake Wade*.

Of particular interest to soundtrack buffs is Fred Steiner's stock score. Snatches of his sinister-sounding music cropped up in numerous TV Westerns of the period, including *Boots and Saddles* (1957-1958), *Rawhide* (1961-1964) and *Gunsmoke* (1960-1965). Sturges directed with an eye for dark interiors highlighted by harshly lit exteriors, framing his small group of protagonists against a panoramic backdrop of blue skies, rugged mountains, canyons and desert, an absorbing mix—yet, unaccountably, *The Law and Jake Wade* remains, to this day, vastly underrated, the critics unusually sniffy in their reviews, although agreeing that "the scenery is awesome and authentic." It's not by any means a kiddies' cowboys and Indians opus, being the sixth Widmark Western to receive a British "A" classification, more a study of a diverse bunch of characters on a mission that will sort out who's the winner, and who's the loser, and in this respect, there's a classic standoff between Widmark and Silva when the riders chance upon a couple of smoking, burned-out wagons, clear signs of an Indian attack. Coyotes are scrabbling over freshly dug graves and, unwisely, Silva fires his gun to scare them off.

"What's the matter with you?" snaps Widmark, aware of Comanches lurking in the vicinity.

"I'm sorry Clint, it's just that I can't stand them filthy coyotes. I didn't stop to think," replies Silva.

"We'll chisel that on your tombstone," is the snappish rejoinder.

Silva doesn't like that response. "I said I was sorry."

"Right about now I guess Jake's sorry, too, but that ain't keeping him from getting killed."

"Whadd'ya mean by that?"

"Ah, what do you care?"

Silva persists, pushing his luck. "I don't like people who talk to me like that."

One of Widmark's ice-cold stares results, a full six seconds long. Then "You don't, huh?" He slowly dismounts and approaches Silva who's suffering from a severe case of itchy trigger finger.

"So whadd'ya gonna do about it? Some more of that doin' without thinkin'?"

"I'll do plenty," snarls Silva, challenging Widmark's position as top dog.

Widmark smiles that lazy smile. "You gonna draw on me, Rennie?"

Silva goes for his gun but his holster's empty, the pistol lying on the ground. Widmark utters that throaty chuckle, hands Silva his weapon, spits, "I ought to shoot your ears off," and mounts up, threatening his bunch with a bullet in the back if they so much as think about running out on him. A riveting sequence displaying Widmark at his very best—and the same goes for the rest of the cast. Five golden minutes that admirably demonstrate what acting in a '50s Western was all about.

Hardcore Western fans will revel in Sturges' first-class horse opera and the chance to see two top-notch film stars on fire—the interaction between the two is priceless. Taylor, who wanted to steer his career path in the direction of the Western, is stern-faced but solid, while Widmark, a veritable coiled spring, is compulsively watchable, a lot looser and less rigid. The man is so utterly charming in a rough 'n' ready kind of way, a blend of menace and charm yet containing a vicious streak, that you are once again left wondering why he didn't lend his name to more movies of this caliber. In *The Law and Jake Wade*, you'll find, embodied in the form of outlaw Clint Hollister, the quintessential Richard Widmark Western performance.

Studio publicity shot featuring Taylor and Widmark

If *The Law and Jake Wade* is a Western masterpiece still waiting to be discovered, then "Dick" Widmark's next feature, *Warlock* (Fox, 1959), coming in on a budget of $2,400,000, lays claim to being *the* heavyweight psychological Super Western *par excellence* of the 1950s, easily one of the genre's top 10 in a decade overflowing with sagebrush saga must-sees and without doubt director Edward Dmytryk's finest hour behind a lens. The storyline, on the surface, is straightforward enough: The Utah mining town of Warlock, tired of being terrorized by power-mad Abe McQuown and his rowdy cowpokes from the San Pablo Ranch and losing one inept sheriff after another, decides to hire professional gunslinger Clay Blaisdell to put a stop to the rioting and clean the place up, following the callous shooting of the local barber. But Blaisdell brings with him enough emotional baggage to override anything those boys from the ranch can come up with; very soon, Warlock's citizens are regretting the day they employed the quick-draw marshal and his volatile sidekick, Tom Morgan. It's up to sensitive Johnny Gannon, the one decent cowboy from San Pablo, to be deputized and come up with a solution, not to mention the guts, to end the violence with McQuown's "regulators" and also run Blaisdell out of town, a forbidding set of tasks in any rookie lawman's book.

Simple, yes. But Dmytryk's multi-plotted soap opera-style Western for adults is anything *but* simple, once you strip away the layers and dig deep. *Warlock* is all about fractured relationships: Widmark (Gannon) wants to break away from bully-boy Tom Drake (McQuown) and his roughhouse tactics, sick of the whole charade, his loose cannon brother, Frank Gorshin, failing to understand Widmark's stance; Judge Wallace Ford rails against a "vigilante gambler gunman" being appointed at $400 a month, the citizens disagreeing with his protests—at first; attractive Dolores Michaels, brought up in a staid church atmosphere, unleashes her pent-up desires on rugged Henry Fonda (Blaisdell); Dorothy Malone's Lily Dollar nurses an almighty grudge against Fonda for gunning down her fiancé

Six-Gun Law

Widmark faces up to Henry Fonda in *Warlock*.

years back, even though he was a no-good loser ("You killed the only decent man I knew."); Widmark begins a prickly romance with Malone; and even gun hand DeForest Kelley suffers from a conscience of sorts, torn between Drake's mob and Widmark's newfound law-abiding beliefs.

But it's in the complex, and rather dark, association between Fonda and fellow gunman/ex-killer/gambler Anthony Quinn (as Tom Morgan) that raises *Warlock* onto a fascinatingly different level to your normal run-of-the-mill Western. The hint of homosexuality in Quinn's behavior toward Fonda didn't escape the

Anthony Quinn gazes at his hero in *Warlock*.

notice of the strict British Board of Film Censors when the film was released in the United Kingdom in May 1959, becoming Widmark's seventh "A" classified cowboy picture in a row. Fonda takes on the mantle of Quinn's hero figure, the club-footed "Black Rattlesnake of Fort James" hobbling after him like a lovesick puppy dog, caring for his every need and fussing around him in mother hen mode (note the nude female painting on Fonda's bedroom wall, a gift from Quinn, but not for *his* benefit!). He shoots dead the brother of Malone's fiancé, sent to kill Fonda, in order to protect him and lays into anyone who he views as a risk to the pair's partnership. "You come here again and talk to Clay behind my back and I'll kill ya. I'll kill anyone who's dangerous to Clay. Even you, Lily," he savagely spits at Malone. "Tom. Why do you do this?" she queries. "Because he's the only person, man or woman, who looked at me and didn't see a cripple" (The Blaisdell/Morgan/Dollar entanglement, based on unconscious sexual desire, matches the Wyatt Earp/Doc Holliday/Kate Fisher scenario in *Gunfight at the O.K. Corral*). The bald truth is that Quinn, deep down, is a weak and pathetic specimen of humanity, using Fonda as an emotional crutch, unable to form a close bond with anyone except his laconic friend. When Fonda tells Quinn he's marrying Michaels ("Even killers and gunmen have mothers, Miss Marlow," he says before she flings her arms around him passionately), the all-male relationship deteriorates; Quinn is crestfallen to the point of bursting into tears, insisting they move on to the next town after they've finished their business in Warlock. But Fonda has other ideas; the man has had enough of drifting from one assignment to the next, realizing he's the last of a dying breed, and wants to quit ("Maybe it's time. Maybe we run out of towns."). But can he? Killing is his chosen trade and has been his way of life for as long as he can remember; he wishes he could call time but can't, unable to accept a future, even with Michaels, by doing anything different other than using his fancy six-guns to keep the peace ("It's the way I live. It's the way I'll always live."). In Quinn's eyes, if Fonda moves on and allows deputy Widmark to enforce the law, he'd be nothing, no longer a hero. In a tense climax, the two have a standoff after Quinn gets inebriated, devastated by Fonda's intention of resigning ("We're finished here, Morg."), and goes berserk with two Colts. "I'm gonna have to run you out of town," says Fonda. "I'll go like a lamb. You'll be a hero again. That's all I want, Clay," whines Quinn, then states, "I'm better than you. I can beat you Clay." He does, shooting Fonda's hat off, but his partner aims for the belly and Quinn lies dead in the street. Full of anger and remorse, Fonda acts like an avenging angel from hell, burning the saloon to the ground during a thunderstorm and answering Widmark's call to shoot it out the next morning: "You can't stay here. Trouble and death follow you. Warlock's had enough of both." The showdown, which sees Fonda wearing his two gold-handled Colts, results in the gunman getting the drop on the deputy sheriff but throwing both weapons into

Tom Drake and Widmark exchange words in *Warlock*.

A knife wound won't stop Widmark's upcoming gunfight in *Warlock*.

the dust; smiling at Widmark and admiring his undoubted courage, he mounts his horse and rides off alone, his job finished, his future unclear. Widmark, having taken the entire San Pablo outfit minus unexpected ally Kelley into custody, is the new face of law and order in the mining town.

Other highlights in a powerful, well-structured Western: Fonda's first commanding appearance in the packed French Palace saloon, the temperature dropping by several degrees as he walks down the stairs in that trademark slow gait, hushing the noise in an instant, a gripping, expertly edited sequence dripping in frosty tension—Kelley bravely faces up to him but quickly backs down against that lightning draw, staring at the barrel of Fonda's gleaming pistol even before his gun has cleared leather ("Marshal. What if someone painted them handles black for you," suggests Kelley, referring to Fonda's infamous gold-plated shooting irons. "That might do," is the short reply. A long pause. Then, "But who's to do it?"), the *de facto* lawman laying down no-nonsense terms to Drake and his men; Fonda blasting down Gorshin in the street; Widmark's gunfight with Drake and one of his thugs, winning despite a knife wound in his right hand; the spectacular rocky scenery of Utah's Moab region, wonderfully captured by cameraman Joseph MacDonald; Leigh Harline's evocative music; and Robert Alan Aurthur's insightful script. Interestingly, Widmark was first considered for the role of Blaisdell but he advised against it, putting forward 54-year-old Fonda's name, which paid dividends. Although Widmark's name appeared top on the billboards, *Warlock* was Fonda's show all the way, a fact that Widmark later acknowledged. His steely-eyed, enigmatic gunman, speaking in that famous flat Nebraskan tone, mirrors the part he played nine years later in Sergio Leone's *Once Upon a Time in the West*; in *Warlock*, the actor turns in one of his most memorable movie performances, a deftness of touch evident for all to see in his quiet, understated study of Blaisdell's ice-cold personality that few actors could match today, a master class in authoritative technique, of how to pull it off without visible effort.

In a picture overflowing with class deliveries, Widmark and the galvanizing double-act of Fonda and Quinn stole the honors, making the film a huge commercial success for Fox, agreeing to those fans who required just that little bit more depth in their Western fare—and *Warlock* possessed depth in spades. The critics lapped it up as well, almost unanimous in their praise. "Pretty exciting … good, solid, gripping … colorful and noisy," enthused the *New York Times*. The *Motion Picture Herald* said "Big, well-produced … unusual plot complication … spirit and suspense," while *The Hollywood Reporter* commented "complicated storyline … devious cross-currents." *Variety* chipped in with "an adult Western in depth … class product," *Time* joking that it all boiled down to two things in the end: "Who is faster on the draw, and who is slower on the draw?"

Warlock was Richard Widmark's final Western (and movie) of the 1950s, a tremendous way to finish, a real man's picture, one that rewards repeated visits. True, out of 32 features made between 1947 and 1959, he had starred in only seven since 1948's *Yellow Sky*, but what a seven! Most stars would have been proud to include any one of them in their curriculum vitae, and it's a testament to Widmark's unobtrusive skills that all seven are supreme illustra-

Warlock was Widmark's final Western of the 1950s.

tions of just how great the genre could be, despite the fact that he was not looked upon by the public as another James Stewart or John Wayne figure; he dipped his toes into the Western pool, liked what he saw in the script, decided he'd take it on, came up with a humdinger and went on to other things. Very few he made after would measure up to this "Magnificent Seven," although his first of the new decade, John Wayne's troubled, $12,000,000 production of *The Alamo*, continued the 5-star trend. The involving, antagonistic circumstances surrounding the making of this epic classic Western will be fully discussed in chapter 12.

CHAPTER 6

CALHOUN IN THE SADDLE, 1949-1954

Rory Calhoun's first foray out West saw him playing Lieutenant Phil Acton in Allied Artists' *Massacre River*, released in 1949 (some initial prints were in Sepiatone), and he couldn't have chosen a more unusual oater to kick off his 41-year tenure as a Westerner if he had tried. Financed at $200,000, John Rawlins' trim little B-Western has *noir* written all over it (a sassy dame; unrequited love; broken friendships) and belies its modest budget on all fronts: Stunning black-and-white photography centered around Arizona's spectacular Canyon de Chelly National Monument at Chinle; forceful, dramatic music from composers John Leipold and Lucien Moraweck; and fine acting from a couple of good-looking hunks, Calhoun and Guy Madison (the pair were firm friends away from the cameras). Writer Louis Stevens' screenplay took us in a completely different direction after the initial *She Wore a Yellow Ribbon*-type start: Panoramic shots of Indians and cavalry galloping across the plains and through rugged canyons; Colonel Art Baker, commander of a frontier outpost (RKO's *Fort Apache* set from 1948 was used), promising Chief Iron Eyes Cody that Indian land beyond the so-called Massacre River will not be violated by the whites; tomfoolery in the shape of burly Emory Parnell, doing a fairimpersonation of Victor McLaglen's Sgt. Festus Mulcahy in John Ford's cavalry classic *Fort Apache*; and beefcakes Calhoun and Madison playfully fighting over the winsome charms of Baker's daughter, Cathy Downs. The gal once loved Calhoun but now favors Madison, the two promising to marry as soon as she returns from a trip to St. Louis.

So a standard opening to what many will consider a standard low-budget oater. But matters take a darker tone with the arrival of blonde Carole Mathews, a lady not to be messed with. She's turned up in nearby Jackson, the last town bordering the river, to reclaim her legitimate half of the Blue Star saloon, crooked Steve Brodie her unwilling partner. During a tussle with renegade Apaches, young Johnny Sands, Downs' brother, is badly wounded and brought into the saloon for emergency treatment by Madison. Mathews acts as doctor and operates, retrieving the bullet and falling head-over-heels in love with Madison who reciprocates her lust and is left in a quandary over his feelings toward Downs and his buddy-buddy relationship with Calhoun. Both suffer; the two lieutenants come to blows, Calhoun tries it on with Mathews to prove she's a no-good tart and Brodie is shot dead by Madison after the thug brutally assaults Mathews. Downs returns on the stage, crestfallen at the sight of Mathews canoodling with her gorgeous-looking beau, and matters reach crisis point when Sands, tooled up and gunning for Madison because of his sister's perceived betrayal, is shot in the back by Mathews. Madison, shouldering the blame, resigns his post, even though a promotion was in the offing, and we now have the classic *noir* scenario of a pair of doomed, scorned lovers heading off for a new life together in Colorado, vengeful Calhoun, in buckskins and double holster (everyone in this film wears a double holster) in hot pursuit, even if it means crossing the out-of-bounds Massacre River to confront the two people who have caused him so much grief.

Calhoun cleans up nice in *Massacre River*

Rawlins' riveting Western winds up in splendid tragic fashion, the director making full use of those towering cliff faces, rocky pinnacles and wide-open horizons to highlight the drama taking place beneath the craggy heights, Leipold and Moraweck's pulsating score adding to the tension. Calhoun and Madison engage in a ferocious fistfight and in a blazing skirmish with Apaches, Mathews is fatally wounded, dying in Madison's arms; the Indian chief acknowledges Madison's loss and retreats with his braves, the final few seconds showing Madison, now a civilian scout, accompanying a wagon train as Calhoun and Downs, together once more, look down from a ridge.

Massacre River is a little-remembered beauty, arriving just before the golden era of the Western, the 1950s, and a rarity worth tracking down. Calhoun acquits

Italian poster for *Massacre River*

himself with honors, easygoing one minute, hard-as-nails the next, a likeable performance that boded well for future projects out West. And there's no getting away from the fact that he had the matinee-idol looks to wow female members of the audience. The *New York Times* was less than complimentary: "A snarled romance … stilted, amorous bickering … is murder in more ways but one." Ignore those unfounded barbs—Calhoun's introductory Western is an undiscovered treasure from the genre's flourishing period and he does darned well in it.

20th Century Fox, impressed by Calhoun's success in *Massacre River*, offered their former star a new five-year contract (although he continued to be loaned out to other studios), putting him straight into *Sand*, released in 1949 and commercially unavailable as I write, faded prints taken from old tapes obtainable from gray market dealers only. The first of six Westerns he would make for the company, *Sand* was a modern-day horse opera (in more ways than one) based on cowboy writer Will James' 1932 novel and, as the opening line of dialogue states, relates the story of a horse, in this case Jubilee, a magnificent brown stallion worth $25,000, who goes on the run in the wilds after snatching a mare from a corral. Jubilee turns into a killer horse, is hunted first by Indians and then by the cowpokes at Coleen Gray's ranch before finally reunited with his owner, entrepreneur Mark Stevens. Why *Sand*? James writes in his book that "the little grain of sand within him starts to grow," a reference to either Calhoun's shady ranch hand (Chick Palmer) who eventually comes good, or the relationship between Stevens and Jubilee. Filmed around Colorado's picturesque Durango and San Juan National Forest areas, plus the Alabama Hills at Lone Pine, Charles G. Clarke's once vivid photography, nominated for an Oscar, has now been reduced to a muddy blur, the nightfall sequences almost impenetrable, making watching the movie a chore to sit through, even for horse lovers.

And those horse lovers will not be amused at the sight of Calhoun laying into the frisky steed with a stick, Jubilee trampling a rival stallion to death and the shooting of a horse, three scenes which would never be allowed to be screened in today's more conservative cinematic climate. The main problem with *Sand* is in the casting of the lead: B-actor Stevens, wooden throughout, should have made way for the more charismatic Calhoun, the two coming to blows over sex-hungry ranch boss Gray; what the girl sees in boring Stevens is a complete mystery, particularly as Calhoun has made *his* intentions perfectly clear. But Calhoun enjoyed playing characters with an immoral edge to them (like Richard Widmark, in fact), and may have turned down the chance to take on Stevens' role in favor of his more devious foreman—in many of his future Westerns, he would be the bad guy with a smidgen of decency lurking beneath the unprincipled, agitated surface, a not-so-saintly figure even when wearing a badge. In the end, after a protracted chase across country (wildlife footage of beavers and mountain cats is inserted at intervals), Jubilee recognizes his owner and calms down, Rory, who pockets $2,500 for roping him, departing for Texas, leaving Gray and her lover to get on with it under the approving stare of Charles Grapewin, her garrulous old grandpa. One of Rory Calhoun's rarest pictures, *Sand* benefits from his macho presence in a film full of underachievers, more a sign of his brooding dark persona than anything else—but he was slowly getting there and beginning to make his mark on paying audiences, though not quite the big box-office draw that Fox executives had once envisaged. "Competent," said the *New York Times*, adding that "the horse is more fascinating than the humans," true in regard to everyone except Calhoun.

"A non-stop Tune-Trip loaded with Laughs" screamed the posters to 20th Century Fox's *A Ticket to Tomahawk*, released in 1950, an *Annie Get Your Gun/Calamity Jane*-type frolic set in the Colorado mountain heights in December 1876. Richard Sale's comedy-cum-serious Western was a weird blend of knockabout farce, song and dance, silly sketches, crowds acting the fool, humorous dialogue (Sale

Calhoun in *A Ticket to Tomahawk*

wrote the script with wife Mary Loos) and conventional Western violence, notable for the second screen appearance of Marilyn Monroe, playing a dancing girl dressed from top to toe in yellow. Ex-vaudeville star Dan Dailey was Johnny Behind-the-Deuces, a footloose and fancy-free salesman purchasing a ticket from Epitaph to Tomahawk on the pioneering Tomahawk and Western railway. Trouble is, the locomotive, run by Walter Brennan, has to be hauled by a team of horses for the first 40 miles to Dead Horse Point due to lack of tracks, and then reach town, a further 20 miles, on time for the franchise to be officially rubber-stamped. Stage boss Mauritz Hugo sees the railroad as a threat to his business, instructing gunslinger Rory Calhoun (Dakota) to join the trek and ensure that the train doesn't complete the trip, whatever it takes. Monroe is one of four dancing gals also on the voyage and there to keep the peace is hot-tempered tomboy Anne Baxter (Kit Dodge, Jr.), deputized by her crusty grandpa, Sheriff Will Wright, and pinning a tin star to her pretty shirt; she's marshal on Wright's strict understanding that she steers clear of any predatory males, difficult when Dailey and Calhoun ("He's kinda pretty," Baxter says, eyeing up the dude astride his horse) are sniffing around her skirts. However, stern-faced, recalcitrant Chief Yowlachie (Pawnee) hovers like a menacing stone statue in the background, ready to plunge his tomahawk into the back of any man stupid enough to try it on with his sharpshooting mistress, a lass perfectly capable of fending for herself: Boot Hill Cemetery contains the bodies of six of her victims.

Does this scatty scenario work? Yes, thanks to the entire cast playing it alternatively for laughs, then straight, plus some wonderful scenic views of Colorado's rocky terrain, dressed in Harry Jackson's bright colors. The interlude where Dailey teaches lovely Baxter to "buss" (kiss) is a charming example of light comedic acting, performed exquisitely by the two attractive leads, *and* you get to see Monroe's shapely pins in a dance routine, Dailey joining the troupe and demonstrating his own superlative song and dance skills. Offset against this light-hearted mood are the more serious moments: Two of Hugo's men, poised to dynamite a bridge, are skewered with arrows; Calhoun is struck by a knife thrown by Baxter (you don't see the blade enter flesh), falling to his death into a ravine; Hugo dies after Yowlachie's tomahawk gets him in the back (again, it's left to the imagination); and the Arapaho attack on the train and wagons would do justice to an A-rated Western, not one specifically aimed at a family audience. A firework display on Funeral Peak ("Happy New Year" is spelled out); Dailey's old Indian pal, Chief Thundercloud, teaching his braves how to cheat at cards; the mayor of Tomahawk moving the town sign up to the decorative locomotive to fulfil its charter (the rails terminate on the outskirts of town); and some choice lines: Baxter to Wright: "I'm not a he. I'm a she. There's a difference, y'know!" Wright, as suspiciously protective as ever: "How d'ya find *that* out?" And Brennan, watching Baxter and Dailey canoodle: "They make a fine lookin' couple, don't they?" forcing ever-silent Yowlachie to utter his three-only words in the picture: "I couldn't say"—these all go to make *A Ticket to Tomahawk*, an amusing throwback to a distant era of good old colorful Hollywood entertainment, something of a guilty pleasure to enjoy, thanks to its sheer professionalism in all departments (Baxter and Dailey end up married with five kids, all girls) and Calhoun, like the movie, switching from charming to someone a little more sinister with ease. As the *New York Times* correctly stated, "It's a pretty good show."

"A pretty good show" didn't sum up Rory Calhoun's second film of 1950, Warner Bros.' unsatisfying and oddly tired-looking *Return of the Frontiersman*. Director Richard L. Bare specialized in comedy films, knocking out 63 10-minute shorts in the long-forgotten *So You Want/So You Think* series from 1942 to 1956. He was also the man responsible for Western star Randolph Scott's most bizarre, if not worst, oater, *Shoot-Out at Medicine Bend*, released by Warners in 1957. So the combination of Bare's erratic directorial style (if you can call it that), an anemic script (Edna Anhalt), singers Gordon MacRae (his only Western) and Julie London all at sea out West, Calhoun (Larrabee) as wooden as a sidewalk plank and a predominantly aged cast meant cowboy disaster all round, a "limp adventure" and "the sorriest of sagebrush sagas" as one critic mentioned (it resembles a 1920s penny dreadful-type good guys versus bad guys outing in color). Warner Bros.' resident composer, David Buttolph, threw everything into his score, a deafening barrage of orchestral noise designed to get the momentum going but failing; it worked a treat in *The Beast from 20,000 Fathoms* and *House of Wax* (two classic Buttolph scores), but not here. Occasionally, extremely loud soundtracks, however professional they may be, do not a good Western make!

It's 1872 in the town of Laramie and returning frontiersmen have replaced the murdering, robbing desperadoes in the West's "mad festival of shooting," or so the overly dramatic opening lines announce. We are then into a case of the "mistaken identity" scenario: Sheriff's son MacRae roughs up Edwin Rand in a saloon, Dad Jack Holt arresting him and Rand. On their release from jail, Rand is murdered and MacRae framed for the killing. Captured in a box canyon, MacRae is back behind bars but given a six-gun by smartly dressed friend Calhoun, a newspaper boss. Breaking out during a bank robbery, MacRae is wounded and somehow accused of being in with the bandits. Doe-eyed London leaps to his rescue and eventually, it comes to light that smarmy Calhoun is the villain behind the scam, arranging for Rand to be shot, the posse leaving the town unguarded to chase after innocent MacRae, thus enabling the bank to be bushwhacked in relative ease, a cowpoke dressed identically to the sheriff's son fooling everyone into thinking MacRae was in on the robbery. A climactic gun battle at the gang's mountain bolt-hole is followed by MacRae and Calhoun slugging it out under a waterfall; Calhoun loses the fight and is flung into prison, MacRae taking London for a buggy ride, no doubt to investigate what lies under her well-upholstered bodice.

A mundane B-movie by any other name, even from a giant studio like Warner Bros., *Return of the Frontiersman* did no favors to anybody, least of all Rory Calhoun, who looked bored to tears throughout, his Western stint in the saddle somewhat directionless at this stage of his career. MacRae seemed distinctly uncomfortable in cowboy garb [although he would be back in the saddle in 1955's *Oklahoma*] while all London managed to do was to flutter her huge eyelashes and avoid being groped by her hefty musical leading man. The only impression left after sitting through one of Rory Calhoun's lamest Westerns will be Buttolph's racket of a score ringing in your ears.

County Fair (Monogram, 1950) and *Rogue River* (Ventura Pictures, 1951) were followed by three Fox movies: The period drama *I'd Climb the Highest Moun-*

tain (1951) and two musicals, *Meet Me After the Show* (1951) and *With a Song in My Heart* (1952). Then, finally, Calhoun struck a chord with the movie-mad public in Jacques Tourneur's wonderfully evocative *Way of a Gaucho* in 1952, a part originally offered to Tyrone Power who turned it down. Budgeted by Fox at $2,240,000, Philip Dunne's screenplay, from Herbert Childs' novel, was similar in content to Victor Hugo's *Les Miserables*, focusing on the relentless pursuit of gaucho outlaw Martin Penalosa/Val Verde (Calhoun) by Major Richard Boone, aggrieved at having his right arm put out of action by Calhoun's flashing knife. Filmed in Argentina, with shots of California's Vasquez Rocks included for good measure, this was the Old West in South America circa 1875, the pampas replacing the plains, estancias standing in for ranches: Calhoun, arrested for the death of a man in a brawl during a festival, is released after childhood friend and patron Hugh Marlowe intervenes on his behalf and enrolled into the army, but his naturally rebellious nature sees him deserting, heading into the wilds and rescuing the lovely Gene Tierney from savage Indians. He's recaptured in a canyon ambush, spread-eagled in the military compound but set free by fellow inmates, roaming the desert wastes and eventually transforming himself into fierce bandit leader Val Verde, the scourge of the pampas, his gang of criminals and deserters raiding supply caravans, the emptied wagons hurled into mountain rivers. An embittered Boone is determined to hunt down his quarry, even when Calhoun and Tierney go on the run, heading toward Chile and the towering, snow-capped Andes where they are forced to turn back as Tierney is suffering pains through pregnancy.

There's a strong religious motif running through *Way of a Gaucho*, Calhoun painted as a free spirit that no man can shackle, not even Boone: Kindly Father Enrique Chaico takes on the mantle of his church protector when Calhoun and Tierney return to civilization, the fugitives becoming engaged in a game of cat-and-mouse with Boone's federal troops (much of it in the vicinity of an imposing

Richard Boone, Gene Tierney and Rory Calhoun in *Way of a Goucho*

cathedral), Marlowe, the country's National Deputy, doing his darndest to appease Boone's murderous instincts and paying with his life, trampled to death by a herd of stampeding cattle. The finale is rather abrupt yet uplifting, the lovers getting wed and then surrendering to Boone, Calhoun now, in his eyes at least, an honest man.

Beautifully photographed in rugged Argentine locations by Harry Jackson (there's a sublime image of Calhoun outlined against the setting sun, the screen blood-red, emphasizing the man's personal odyssey) and embellished by Sol Kaplan's melodic score, *Way of a Gaucho* possesses a strange timeless quality that renders it quite unique, even when viewed today. Parts of the film are extremely moving, such as the burial of one of Calhoun's gaucho comrades (Everett Sloane), murdered by Boone's men, his battered guitar placed on his lonely mountain grave, a nice touch; and Dunne's script [at the time] was amusing in places [but today seems shockingly offensive]: "As for me, give me one of these Indian women. They ask nothing more than to be beaten three times a day," says Sloane laughing, seeing Calhoun and Tierney kissing. Despite the *New York Times* calling Calhoun "sturdy but sullen," and commenting that the terrain was more impressive than the pursuit, the picture proved a big success when first released and promoted Calhoun's name to a wider public, now something of an on/off leading man; he carries the action on his broad shoulders with aplomb, his charm and ease in the role radiating from the screen, an assured performance all round, probably one of his best. In fact, it is at this precise point in time that Rory Calhoun's Western career took off; albeit it had taken a cowboy film set in Argentina to provide the lighted match to the fuse!

In *The Silver Whip*, rookie stagecoach driver Jess Harker (Robert Wagner) dreams of running the Silver City stage out of Red Rock with a team of six horses instead of shunting backwards and forwards to Wheat Creek with freight in a two-mule-driven cart. Despite reservations as to the youngster's competence, boss Luke Bowen (James Millican) gives the kid the chance he's been waiting for, a stage carrying a shipment of $27,000 in gold to Silver City as well as glamorous passenger Waco (Lola Albright), an old flame of Race Crim (Dale Robertson), a stagecoach guard of proven experience who joins the trip, riding shotgun. Jess is also given a silver whip for his promotion. Disaster strikes at the Buffalo Gap relay station: Outlaw Slater (John Kellogg) and his gang open fire on the stage and pinch the gold; Jess joins in the gunfight, hot lead flies, he gets wounded and rides off with the stage, returning to find his uncle dead and Waco fatally wounded—she dies in Crim's arms. Blamed for both deaths and the robbery, Jess is dismissed from his post but unexpectedly given the chance of redemption by peace maker Tom Davisson (Rory Calhoun) who deputizes the lad, the pair setting off to bring Slater to justice before Crim, thirsting for revenge, can pump him full of slugs. In a series of shoot-outs, the bandits are whittled down to two, their leader, Slater, caught after a tense game of hide and seek among rocks, the gold retrieved. Back in town, Crim, smarting after losing his prize, joins a lynch-hungry mob to grab the two outlaws from jail and hang them from the nearest tree; Jess confronts Crim and puts a bullet in his stomach, Davisson, who has been trussed up in a stable, freed and ordering the crowd at gunpoint to disperse. In the closing minutes, Jess marries sweetheart Kathy (Kathleen

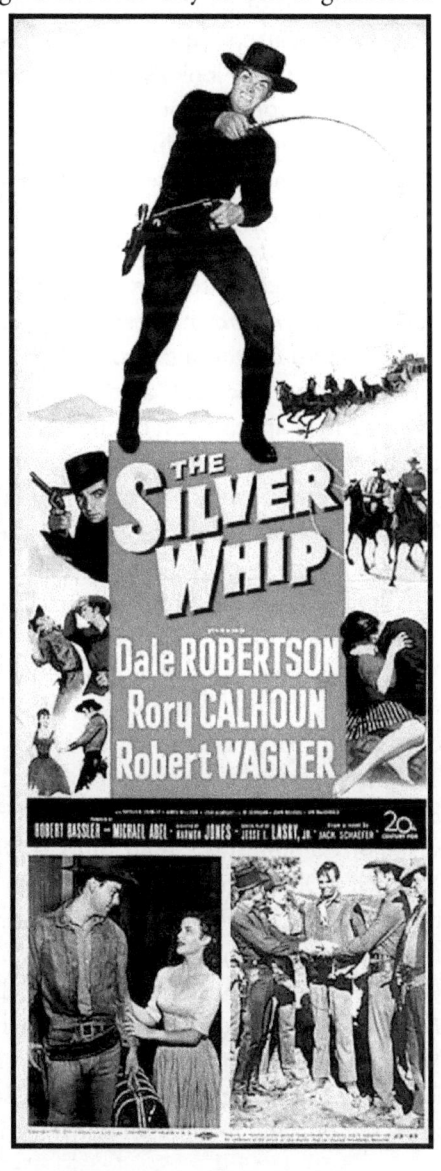

Crowley), tosses his whip away and departs on honeymoon, Crim, recovered, and Davisson waving him goodbye. The boy has now become a man.

Alfred Newman's title theme from *Yellow Sky* announced the start to Fox's 1953 oater *The Silver Whip*, directed by hack filmmaker Harmon Jones in rigorous fashion, the rugged hills and pine forests of California's San Bernardino National Park used to marvelous effect (black-and-white photography: Lloyd Ahern, Sr.). This pared-to-the-bone B-Western showcased a solid turn from Robertson as the dangerously edgy trigger-happy Crim, stealing the acting honors from Calhoun's good-guy sheriff, the two playing off each other's strengths and weaknesses like seasoned professionals, not the minor-league material they were perceived to be in some quarters. At times, fresh-faced 23-year-old Wagner seemed out of his depth beside mean-looking hombres Robertson and Calhoun but, to his credit, soldiered on, coming good by the final reel; like his somewhat naïve character, surviving a baptism of fire. The movie's highlight is Calhoun, Robertson and Wagner's six-minute chase over rocks and boulders to nab Kellogg, conducted without incidental music, a tautly edited sequence put across with real dash by Jones; the jail interlude contained echoes of Howard Hawks' *Rio Bravo* which was to appear six years later. If you can ignore Wagner's gravity-defying rock 'n' roll quiff, *The Silver Whip*, modestly budgeted even by 20th Century Fox's usual lavish standards and containing a concise script by Jesse Lasky, Jr. from a Jack Schaefer story (he wrote *Shane*), is a great little Western scoring highly on the excitement monitor that appears forgotten these days, admirably demonstrating just what can be achieved over 70-odd minutes on limited funds; it also underlined the dependable, if not overly expressive, masculine talents of Dale Robertson and Rory Calhoun, both now looking swell on the back of a horse.

The Silver Whip was swiftly followed by Fox's *Powder River* (1953), a loose rehash of a Randolph Scott vintage classic, *Frontier Marshal*, produced by Fox in 1939 and said to be the inspiration behind John Ford's *My Darling Clementine*. Writers Sam Hellman and Stuart N. Lake provided the script for *Frontier Marshal*, working with Daniel Mainwaring (aka Geoffrey Homes) on Calhoun's smart little dust-buster, based on the Wyatt Earp/Doc Holliday legend. Filmed in glorious Technicolor tones by veteran Edward Cronjager at Montana's Glacier National Park on a budget of $985,000, Louis King's oater took in the Earp persona in the shape of Calhoun (as Chino Bull), a Doc Holliday figure courtesy of Cameron Mitchell's Doc Mitch Hardin and two hot dames vying for both men's attention, Corinne Calvet (Frenchie Dumont) and Penny Edwards (Debbie). Even rival saloons were involved, *Frontier Marshal*'s The Bella Union and The Palace of Pleasure saloons reprised as, yes, The Bella Union and The Palace saloons! *Powder River* showed just how much could be crammed into a 78-minute second-feature Western without appearing rushed; from this early stage in his cowboy career, it lays claims to being one of Rory's finest, the actor carrying the action with his usual self-effacing manner, displaying oodles of charm.

Calhoun, an ex-marshal saddled with a reputation, has hung up his guns, prospecting for gold in the mountains with sidekick Frank Ferguson. When one of the Western's vilest of villains, Robert J. Wilke, turns up at Calhoun's camp with Carl Betz, intent on stealing the pair's horses, the two coyotes are sent packing. Calhoun rides into Powder River, picks up supplies and confronts saloon owner John Dehner, the brother of Betz, over the threat posed by his wayward sibling, also apprehending a local hothead (without the use of pistols) who has just plugged the sheriff. Calhoun is made temporary marshal; on his return to camp, he finds Ferguson shot dead, the gold pouches missing. Back in town, Rory is sworn in, taking on the marshal's job full-time, much to the delight of French saloon hostess Corinne Calvet who eyes up the lawman in his fancy new duds and likes what she sees (bearing in mind their real-life tempestuous on/off affair in 1947, the couple just about managed to get along without fighting during the shoot). "A lotta work around here. You won't get much sleep," she says, Calhoun tersely replying, "I don't need much." Soon there are two saloons in town, Calhoun arresting Calvet for dealing with loaded dice at the crap table while waiting for the opportunity to strap on his gun belt and eliminate Betz and his confederates.

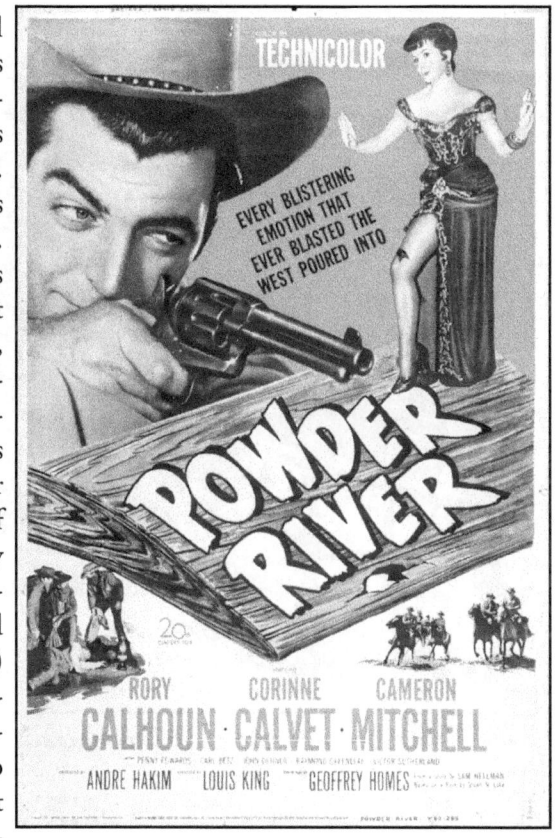

Into the proceedings steps aggressive Cameron Mitchell, wearing his Colt low down at knee height, lightning fast on the draw and, like Calhoun, an infamous gunman. The two form an uneasy alliance, egging each other on as to who has the quickest trigger figure. The man suffers from blackouts caused by a brain tumor and knows he's on borrowed time; Calvet unwisely falls for the tortured doctor and wants to care for him, a relationship strained by the appearance of Mitchell's sweetheart from out East, Penny Edwards. She wishes to rekindle her romance with Mitchell but he doesn't want to know ("I'm not a doctor anymore. You'll be marrying a dead man."); Calhoun takes a shine to the lovely lass, galloping off with her on a trip to the mountains (and Ferguson's remote grave) on his buckboard—Mitchell catching them together and seething with jealousy. Calhoun then arranges for a $300,000 gold shipment to be collected from the Homestead Mine, letting the town barfly spill the information to Dehner and his brother in an attempt to force Betz out of hiding for a showdown. After a shootout on a ferry, the gold is safely brought to town where a further revelation comes to light, adding more spice to an already highly convoluted (and overloaded) plot: Molten-tempered Mitchell confesses that *he* shot Ferguson in self-defense, claiming that he rode into Calhoun's camp and was fired at—but he still stole those nuggets, planning to ride off with the gold for a new, if somewhat short, life. In another gun battle at the stables, Edwards is badly wounded, Mitchell summoning his former skills and digging out the bullet, only inches away from her heart. The blazing finale sees Wilkes, Dehner and Betz biting the dust and Mitchell facing Calhoun in the expected standoff. The doctor shoots Calhoun's gun out of his hand but collapses in agony, dying from a brain stroke. As Calvet takes the stage for pastures new, Edwards elects to stay on in Powder River; no doubt, dashing Calhoun is the reason for her staying!

"A mess," and "bad ... baffling," wrote the *New York Times* unfairly. *Powder River* is neither; it's almost a testament to how darned good a Western could be knocked out on less than a million bucks. Performances across the board are fine, the edgy interplay between Calhoun and Mitchell is a delight, the film moves and the overall look reminds one of a distant time in Hollywood's history when shades of color glowed from the screen, unlike the dingy, digitally composed schemes prevalent in today's cinema. A note for film music buffs: A stock soundtrack was incorporated but keen-eared fans will detect refrains in the title music that were later used in Fox's 1958 X-rated [in the UK] psycho-Western, *The Fiend Who Walked the West*, the composer Leon Klatzkin.

Following a support role in Fox's 1953 box-office Marilyn Monroe winner, *How to Marry a Millionaire*, Rory Calhoun's final Fox Western saw him starring with the blonde bombshell for a third time in Otto Preminger's ill-fated $2,200,000 *River of No Return*, released in 1954 to promote two important cinematic events: The wonders of the new CinemaScope process, and sex-kitten Monroe's attempts at becoming a serious Hollywood actress. Calhoun was billed third behind Robert Mitchum and Monroe, appearing on screen for about 16 minutes, a card sharp by the name of Harry Weston, song and dance gal Monroe's husband-to-be. *River of No Return* falls into the category of "It's so bad, it's almost good—but not quite," thanks mainly to a notoriously difficult shoot: Preminger wasn't by any means first choice as director (William A. Wellman, Henry King and Raoul Walsh were in the frame), only hired on Fox chief Darryl F. Zanuck's insistence, a wrong choice as it turned out; Mitchum had little time for the end product; Monroe stated it was her worst-ever picture; both stars disliked Frank Fenton's clichéd script; and Preminger, never interested in the material in the first place, was forced into the project by contractual issues, departing for Europe immediately after the main 12-week shooting schedule, not getting involved in post-production work which was left to Jean Negulesco to tidy up and buying himself out of his contract with the studio. Monroe damaged her ankle during filming in the white water rapids on Idaho's Salmon River (principle location work was around Alberta's Banff National Park), Mitchum hit the bottle with a vengeance and the pair had to be rescued twice from a capsizing raft, Preminger determined that all involved performed their own stunts to save on overheads (Mitchum later disputed this, stating that stunt doubles were used in the more dangerous river sequences). The director also fell out with Monroe, fuming and arguing with her over her choice of voice/acting coach Natasha Lytess, who remained on set most of the time, giving her client instructions on how to perform a particular scene that were contrary to those of Preminger's.

The movie, renowned more for its troubles rather than what was shown on the silver screen, made a profit, thanks to Monroe's high voltage sex appeal and the novel CinemaScope format, but looked at today, *River of No Return* has many, many faults, not least of all the hackneyed plot which could have been sketched out in a few minutes: Mitchum, released from prison after shooting a man in the back, locates 10-year-old son Tommy Rettig in a mining camp and attempts to bond with the lad; the two head off up into the mountains to Mitchum's farm; Calhoun and Monroe arrive on a raft, bound for Council City where the gambler intends to file a stolen gold claim and marry Monroe; Calhoun steals Mitchum's

Calhoun and Monroe get close in *River of No Return*.

horse at gunpoint, galloping off *without* his fiancée; Mitchum, Monroe and Rettig take the raft to Council City over a series of rapids, encountering hostile Indians and prospectors; Monroe begins to admire Mitchum's homespun philosophy and masculine toughness; arriving at the city, Rettig, like his Pa before him, puts a bullet in Calhoun's back; and Mitchum, dragging Monroe out of a saloon on his broad shoulders, returns to the wilds with the golden-haired lass and his son to set up house. Most critics agreed with the audience—never mind the film itself, the mountain scenery was as spectacular as the Monroe scenery, her bodice straps continually falling below her shoulders, her cleavage and shapely legs on full widescreen display, as was the infamous Monroe glossy red pout. She acts the part well enough, singing four tuneful ditties, "One Silver Dollar," "I'm Gonna File My Claim," "Down in the Meadow," and "River of No Return," but there's little screen chemistry between her and big hitter Mitchum, even when animalistic lust gets the better of his senses and he assaults her on the ground. There's a desultory Indian attack, a pretty meaningless confrontation with a couple of murderous gold diggers, also on Calhoun's trail, umpteen (and embarrassing) shots of hard-faced miners turning all soppy into their beers when Monroe breaks into song (perched on a piano, strumming a guitar) and a lot of clumsy back-projection work when the trio are caught up in one raging torrent after another. As for Calhoun, he should have been allowed more screen time, his disreputable, almost feral, trigger-happy gambler a darned sight more animated than Mitchum's sleepy-eyed farmer—even 12-year-old Rettig livens up what many considered to be an overlong (even at 91 minutes) exercise in popularizing glamour goddess Monroe's provocative talents, Preminger's pacing of events found to be "lagging." Joseph LaShelle's color photography shone and the landscapes were magnificent, but this couldn't compensate for an outdoors adventure that failed to engage the emotions, almost a pseudo-Western in feel; it required an out-and-out action director like Raoul Walsh to give it some urgently needed grit and put fire in its belly.

Six-Gun Law (Midnight Marquee Press, 2015) dealt with the Western careers of Randolph Scott, Audie Murphy, Joel McCrea and George Montgomery, champions of the medium-budget oater during the 1950s. How, then, does Rory Calhoun's work up to 1954 compare to those four, and where does he figure in the Western hierarchy? He wasn't in the same league as Scott, Murphy or McCrea. You could easily place him on the same level as Montgomery from 1954 onwards when he really made his mark, even though he tended to gravitate toward non-Westerns like Richard Widmark; both were selective when it came to mounting a horse in front of the cameras, although Widmark was by far the better actor and a major Hollywood "name." Although not blessed with a wide acting range, Calhoun was competent enough in the performing stakes but *not* a name guaranteed to pull in the masses, unlike cowboy heavyweights Scott, Murphy and McCrea; he's one of a large number of borderline Hollywood stars who featured in some damn good B-Westerns without really making a huge impact, such as Rod Cameron, Stephen McNally, John Payne, Dale Robertson, Tim Holt and Sterling Hayden. Yet he had his audience: His dark good looks more than screen charisma carried the day; he could be truly excellent in his flashy, no-nonsense fashion on occasions, rather ordinary on others. But his output, however low- to medium-budget it may have been, greatly contributed to the 600-plus Westerns that appeared during this heady period of the genre's history and still make good viewing today; his 12 Westerns that would appear between mid-1954 to 1958 (13 when you include also-ran *The Spoilers*) typify the lean, mean guns 'n' bullets-style oater of that decade, exemplifying the best of Rory Calhoun as a cowboy star, and to Western aficionados, the best is good enough.

CHAPTER 7

CAMERON AT UNIVERSAL, 1939-1948

Rod Cameron's acting mettle was first tested in six Universal "B" trail busters churned out in 1944/45, Fuzzy Knight the main co-star, all coming in at just on the hour and all having virtually the same production team. They've dated badly and are primitive-looking in places, particularly when placed side by side with Westerns of the 1950s (and even most of the output from the 1940s), the genre's productive period. In a way, Cameron's early career at this juncture mirrored Randolph Scott's formative years in his 10 Zane Grey oaters produced by Paramount from 1932 to 1935; both periods allowed the actor in question to show his strengths, to develop from an uncredited stand-in to a name capable of topping a bill. In this respect, Universal's rough and ready potboilers served their purpose, pushing Cameron further up the fame ladder into the realm of the more superior "Bs" and even a few "As." Subtlety wasn't the name of their game, long-forgotten period pieces, everything filmed at helter-skelter pace, music blaring out to push the quick bursts of action along with very few breaks to give your ears a rest, plus a comedic element ever-present courtesy of Knight's clownish antics and mugging, ruining, in some instances, what might have been a more serious narrative, or as serious as it could get in this brief framework. *Boss of Boomtown* (1944), directed by Ray Taylor, was the kind of stuff kids used to see at the Saturday Morning Picture shows in England during the mid-'50s, more lengthy serial in design than short motion picture. Cameron played cavalry sergeant Steve

Hazard, continually brawling with fellow sergeant Tom Tyler, the pair provoking each other and raising their fists from the opening reel to the last. Ore shipments from the Golden Eagle Mine and army payrolls are being snatched in a series of stage bushwhackings, so Rod (based at Fort Rocky), partner Fuzzy Knight (as Chatter-box!) and treasury agent Sam Flint infiltrate the gang by becoming members of it, unmasking Jack Ingram and Robert Barron as the brains behind the heists. Two dames figure in the plot: Owner of the Bullion City Emporium Vivian Austin, "Miss Hollywood 1943" (she fancies Cameron and Tyler fancies her) and 4-foot-9-inch motor-mouth Marie Austin (she's Knight's bride-to-be) who hollers her way through one song without any appreciation from the saloon crowd (and who could blame them!). On hand to provide relief are Ray Whitley's Bar-6 Cowboys, dressed as a singing cavalry group who perform a couple of numbers while Cameron and company take a breather from all that dashing around (they featured in 14 movies, from 1937 to 1945).

Big, beefy, square-jawed, granite-faced Cameron fitted the bill nicely, his witty banter with Tyler crackling with friendly animosity, while Universal-International favored comic sidekick Knight (he starred in nearly 200 pictures, mostly in the same role) blundered his way across set as though he was auditioning for a part in a Marx Brothers' movie (the company well may have reckoned he was hilarious and indispensable; many Western fans thought otherwise). A stock score composed of music by Paul Sawtell and Hans J. Salter blasted away in the background, everyone accused everyone else of being in on the robberies and the whole lightning-quick shebang was done and dusted in 58 minutes after a smoke-filled shoot-out. Old-fashioned in looks (compare it to any of, say, Randolph Scott's '40s Westerns and you'll see what I mean), *Boss of Boomtown* was, as far as Cameron was concerned, a means to an end; five more were to follow before he entered the big time in *Salome, Where She Danced*, a classic guilty pleasure of sheer awfulness; more on that one later. Note: Vivian Austin retired from the film industry in 1947 through blindness brought on by severe health problems; her sight was later restored by her second husband, Doctor Ken Grow. She stated once that she found Cameron to be "very serious and very quiet on set. I liked him a lot."

Hot on the trail of *Boss of Boomtown*'s hoof prints came *Trigger Trail* (1944), another land-grabbing confection (a much-favored '40s theme in Westerns), George Eldredge the baddie in charge of a bunch of crooked investors, terrorizing and evicting settlers off their land in the Comanche Strip by claiming that they have no legal rights to their properties. In gallops Rod (as Clint Farrell), fresh from law school and packing a gun, coming to the rescue of the homesteaders and his father's own spread, the Flying F Ranch, before Eldredge's jackals, led by crooked lawman Lane Chandler, burn their ranches to the ground. Once we've gotten over the humorous sight of Fuzzy Knight (Echo) using his pet skunk Petunia as a ventriloquist's dummy, the movie springs into life courtesy of Lewis D. Collins' forceful direction, interrupted at intervals by Ray Whitley's Bar-6 Cowboys singing three numbers. Eldredge covets the settlers' land for the new Great Southern Railroad, which he runs; Cameron reckons that those who have lived there 21 years are entitled to stay put—and there's five weeks to go before those claims are legal. Following the death by shooting of young Robert "Buzz" Henry (pretty serious stuff in this kind of scenario), furious Cameron telegraphs Washington for guidance, an investigating government official is shot by Chandler using a high-caliber rifle, Knight bashes gunman Michael Vallon over the head with a guitar, thus escaping a .45 slug, Sheriff Eddie Dew isn't quite sure whose side he's on and Rod is wrongly arrested (not for the first time in this series!) for the murder of Chandler in a jail cell—heavyweight bruiser Dick Alexander is the culprit. Sentenced to three years hard labor on the road construction gang (but still wearing his fancy shirt), news comes through from Washington to Cameron via sprightly filly Vivian Austin that the squatters' rights are legal, and he's released, pronto. Following a shoot-out at the Flying F Ranch, Eldredge is placed into custody, his gang wiped out in a hail of hot lead. Cameron cuddles up to Austin to the sound of the Bar-6 Cowboys while, in the closing seconds, "plum crazy" Knight falls headfirst into a barrel of water after trying to grab his pet skunk for a much-needed perfumed bath. An enjoyably entertaining, fast-moving second entry in the series, even though Dew was a poor substitute for Tom Tyler from *Boss of Boomtown*—and goofy Knight, for once, is moderately amusing.

Third in the Cameron/Knight 1944 outings was *Riders of the Santa Fe* (aka *Mile a Minute*), 60 chaotic minutes directed by Wallace W. Fox in which Cameron (Matt Conway) doesn't strap on a gun belt until the last 10 minutes after Knight (Bullseye Johnson), in the 40th minute, appears in drag as George Douglas' fictitious Aunt Agatha, attempting to nab a map of Red Mountain's land rights secreted in baddie Douglas' office. He hopes to prove the crook has falsified records to enable him to control a vital waterhole, charging wranglers $1 a head to water their cattle, or buying up the herds at $9 a head, half the market price. After a Vaudevillian first reel in which Knight screeches a song horribly off-key and acts like a fairground attraction, getting punters [customers] to throw balls at his head, Douglas has the God-fearing mayor-elect shot and replaces him with Knight, a bumbling fool he reckons is so scatterbrained he'll do whatever is demanded of him. Wrong! Straightaway, Knight hires Cameron, a peace officer who doesn't wear a gun, using his fists and persuasive talk to enforce law and order, a cut-price Destry in all but name only (turns out he's nifty with a pistol anyway). When cattleman Eddie Dew comes up against Douglas and his henchmen over waterhole rights, Cameron sides with Dew while casting his eyes over Dew's sister, Jennifer Holt (actor Tim Holt's sister); he arranges for the steers to stampede into town, thus upsetting Douglas' plans to take over the place. Cameron then imposes a "No Firearms" policy, looking and sounding suspiciously like a young Randolph Scott in some scenes, and muscles his way through Douglas' boys without firing a shot, Ray Whitley's Bar-6 Cowboys singing and yodeling a couple of numbers (Whitley also plays Cameron's deputy). Douglas and his phoney land survey scam is found out, resulting in a furious shootout (all smoke, no bullets) after Dew's steers have been stampeded once again by brushfire. Cameron, at last armed, slugs Douglas senseless and is hailed as the town's hero by the grateful citizens. Average knockabout fun, with acting honors actually going to Knight who at least puts some energy into his performance, whether it's silly or not; Cameron appears stilted, Dew is blank-eyed and

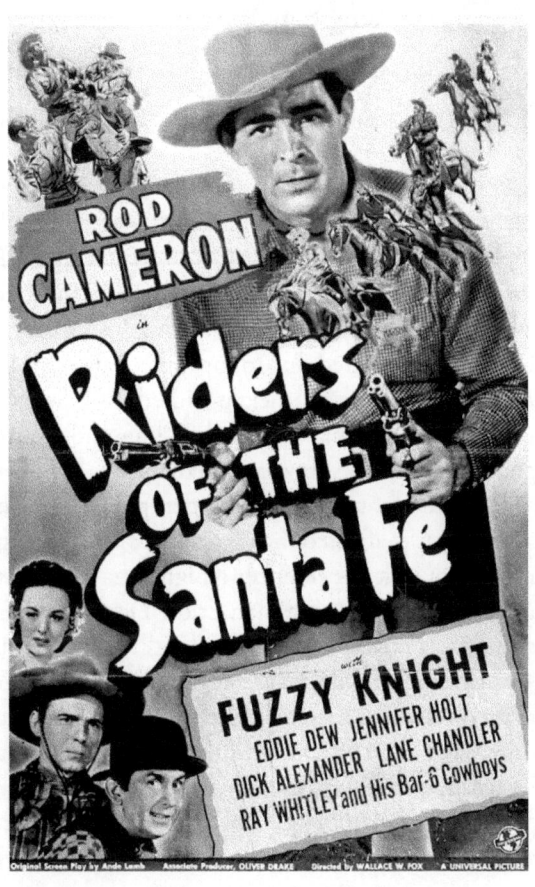

expressionless, Douglas looks like a 1920s screen villain and Holt flits around in the background doing very little. And is that shades of *The Mummy's Curse*'s score I can detect in Paul Sawtell's noisy, over-orchestrated stock soundtrack?

Lewis D. Collins' *The Old Texas Trail* (aka *Stagecoach Line*, 1944) was a tad too ambitious in plot design for a cheapo trail buster coming in just on the hour: Troubleshooter Cameron (as Jim Wiley) rides to the assistance of a stage ambush, is creased by a bullet and has his identity papers stolen by George Eldredge's henchman, Edmund Cobb; the gun tough then infiltrates Marjorie Clements' workforce (the Sandstone Stage Line) impersonating Cameron, the lass busy constructing a stage route from Texas to Arizona; Cobb is thus in a position to pass on information to Eldredge, who has ambitions to take on the line franchise himself, allying his cause to rotund crook Joseph J. Greene. Cameron, recovered due to insurance salesman Fuzzy Knight's administrations, is then mistaken for another of Eldredge's killers, Rawhide Carney, a wanted man, saloon boss Virginia Christine aiding and abetting the corrupt businessman by getting Clements' crew all fired up on liquor and feeling unhappy with their lot. Confusion reigns on the open prairie as Cameron, viewed by all as a deadly gunslinger, is arrested, held for trial on a first degree murder charge, the case dismissed on lack of evidence (Knight acts as defense lawyer, or tries to!). Clements' payroll is snatched, foreman Eddie Dew scratches his head in bewilderment, Rod dresses as a black-clad masked bandit and Knight lives up to his reputation as the worst insurance salesman ever to hit the Wild West, unable to sell a single policy to anybody (to his credit, Fuzzy actually turns in a decent bit of acting). Cobb is unmasked as an imposter while corrupt Greene joins an investigator at the end to hopefully prove that Clements' route isn't viable, aware that cohort Eldredge has planned to dynamite the Rock Creek Bridge that crosses the trail; the ruse doesn't work, the stagecoach, driven by Rod who has revealed his true identity, bouncing over an alternative rough track to complete its mission on time. In a climactic gunfight in which Eldredge's mob are cut to pieces, Cameron lassos the crook and the Sandstone Line is awarded the contract to build an East-West highway from Texas to Arizona. When Knight learns that Greene could face the noose, he wails, "Hang him? No! I just sold him a life insurance policy. And you were the one who put me up to it," he adds, pointing an accusing finger at grinning Cameron, who's more interested in the delights that Clements might have on offer under her decorative cowboy outfit than Knight's whining tones.

Ray Whitley's Bar-6 Cowboys are on hand to lend vocal (and yodeling) support to a convoluted exercise in B-movie thrills, William Lively's script a positive jumble of mistaken identities played out against a background of Paul Sawtell's musically arranged, and very loud, stock score. The cast go through the motions efficiently enough, Knight's scatty insurance salesman, H. Pinkerton "Pinky" Pinkley, the liveliest character on set—for a change!

Veteran director Lambert Hillyer, whose career dated back to 1917 and included a plethora of hour-long grade-Z Western quickies, was at the helm for 1945's *Beyond the Pecos* (aka *Beyond the Seven Seas*), featuring Fuzzy Knight as ex-seafarer Barnacle Pete Finnegan, his mobile boat, the *Sagebrush Susie*, hauled along the dusty trails by two horses to the sound of that quirky Knight leitmotif conjured up by composer Paul Sawtell, a talking parrot on board, an anchor tossed into the street when "disembarking" in Mesa City. What's more, Knight talks in nautical vernacular, wears a striped vest and looks, from a distance, like Popeye the Sailor. Before any self-respecting Western fan reaches for the "off" button, let it be said that *Beyond the Pecos*, combining Knight's tomfoolery (he sells hair restoring elixir concocted from local spring water) with two-fisted, pistol-packing action, is one of the best in the series, thanks to a more-or-less straightforward, although by now familiar, plot. Heavyweight, piano-playing swindler Gene Roth (he employs mute

Cameron and the Bar-6 Cowboys in *Beyond the Pecos*

Henry Wills to whip anyone interrupting him while tinkling the ivories) knows oil is on land owned by Robert Homans, so precipitates a range war between rancher Eddie Dew and Homans in the hope that he'll gain control of the Wagon Wheel spread. In troops Rod (Lew Remington), Homans' son, the tall stern-faced hombre bent on uncovering Roth's double-dealing practices. Jennifer Holt's uncle, crooked lawyer Frank Jaquet, owed debts by Homans and signing the Wagon Wheel's deeds over to Roth's grubby hands, is poisoned by Roth's gunman, Jack Ingram, just as he is on the point of spilling the beans. The murder is pinned on Cameron who, at the inquest, proves his innocence by hoodwinking Ingram into drinking from the same pitcher used on Jaquet; panicking, the killer begins to confess all before Roth shoots him and flees with his jackals—Cameron, Dew and the townsfolk in hot pursuit. The whole kit and caboodle winds up in a mass shoot-out, Roth's men defeated when Captain Knight fires three cannon balls into their ranks. Roth arrested and carted off to prison, Ray Whitley's Bar-6 Cowboys sing a melody, Cameron clasps Holt's hand, Dew treats us to a rare smile, even though he's lost out to Rod in the love stakes, and Knight feels the wrath of another dissatisfied customer whose hair hasn't grown after taking the Old West (*not* Old Eastern) magic tonic—it's fallen out!

The sixth and final Cameron/Knight adventure, 1945's *Renegades of the Rio Grande* (aka *Bank Robbery*) rattled through its paces over 57 minutes with clumsily handled gusto from director Howard Bretherton, Ande Lamb's script centered on the whereabouts of a map pointing the way to $50,000 stolen from the Vista

Cameron on his trusty steed in *Renegades of the Rio Grande*

Grande Bank; John James, in on the robbery with Glenn Strange's gang, passes the map to his brother Cameron (Buck Emerson) and dies from gunshot wounds. Cameron is then pursued by Strange's buckaroos and two Texas Rangers, Knight (as Trigger Bidwell) and Eddie Dew—he hides out in Jennifer Holt's hacienda, the Rancho Rio Lindo—the stolen money belonged to the Salezar family (Holt is the mistress) and Cameron wishes to return it. Unbeknown to all except stuttering, rubber-faced Knight, the map winds up tucked inside Strange's holster, uncovered after numerous saloon fistfights and shoot-outs, plus three tuneful ditties from Ray Whitley's Bar-6 Cowboys, a deafening soundtrack composed of score-snippets from nine composers (Dimitri Tiomkin is somewhere in the mix) assaulting the eardrums. To the melodic refrains of the serenading Bar-6 Cowboys (Whitley also takes on the role of Holt's foreman, a stilted performance), the camera fades out on Holt grabbing Cameron's hand (prelude to a romance?), thus ending a series of six Westerns high on energy, low on finesse and finances but still interesting, from a film history point of view, to take in, even 70 years after they were first conceived. Dew is as wooden as a buckboard, Knight is less stupid than usual (although unfortunately, he gets to sing a song and calls money "smackers," a term coined around 1915), the action roars along and Cameron, on autopilot for this entry, looks swell in a pressed white shirt. To his eternal credit, he had survived his low-budget baptism of fire with a straight face, not easy when paired with the manic Fuzzy Knight—the gateway now opened and it was time to move on to bigger and much better things.

Those "bigger and better things" commenced in fairly disastrous fashion with Universal's *Salome, Where She Danced* (1945), produced on a budget of $1,200,000, loosely based on the exploits of Irish actress/singer Lola Montez and going on to make twice that much at the box-office. A masterpiece of poor taste? A screwy guilty pleasure? A clunker of the first degree? A camp classic? You takes your choice as 23-year-old Yvonne De Carlo (Anna Maria Salome), in her first major motion picture (23 bit parts had preceded it), vamps her way from Berlin to San Francisco's Gold Coast in a series of utterly preposterous situations

The Westerns of Calhoun, Cameron, Hayden and Widmark

Cameron surveys the horrors of the Civil War in *Salome, Where She Danced.*

concocted mainly to push her up the scale into the higher echelons of Hollywood's top-ranking glamourpusses. Producer Walter Wanger also had plans to promote co-star David Bruce as a new swashbuckling Errol Flynn-type action hero (the two actors were close friends), but on this showing, his intentions ran dry. Bruce, forever famous for playing the parchment-skinned, grave-robbing zombie in 1943's *The Mad Ghoul*, remained impassive throughout, as in the scene in Drinkman Wells' saloon where, in a three-minute dance sequence, De Carlo turns on her seductive, sinewy charms to no avail—Bruce stands stock-still like a statue, staring, his features blank, and then walks out. As for Cameron, playing war correspondent Jim Steed, he's simply along for the ride; during the movie's final third, he's a bystander, superfluous to requirements, watching one man after another make a fool of themselves over De Carlo's flashing eyes and pouting red lips. It's a one-dimensional performance but, give the big guy his due, he must have been as mixed-up over the risible narrative as the rest of the cast and the audiences watching it put together.

In April 1865, the Civil War has ceased, leaving journalist Cameron at a loose end, scratching around for new assignments (he bumps into Graycoat Bruce, who wants to carry on fighting). A year later, he's in Germany, attending the Berlin Opera with Colonel Albert Dekker and Kurt Katch (Bismark), captivated by sexy Viennese singer/dancer De Carlo, first seen emerging from a giant shell and pirouetting her way through Swan Lake. Cameron worms himself into her affections, instructing the manipulative diva to find out from Dekker when hostilities between Austria and Prussia are due to commence and unmask troublemaker Katch; it would make good copy for his paper, *Leslie's Weekly*. Caught spying, De Carlo, her music teacher J. Edward Bromberg and Cameron flee to the Old West where, in the lawless Arizona town of Drinkman Wells, she puts on "Salome's Big Show" in tandem with Madame Marjorie Rambeau and wows Bruce, now an outlaw boss; he promptly rides back into town after fleecing the saloon of its takings and abducts her, totally smitten. Sitting beside the campfire, De Carlo, eyes shimmering with lust, forces him to see the error of his ways (by smooching and singing "O Tannenbaum"); a changed man, Bruce returns her to town and hands over the stolen loot (the place is subsequently renamed Salome, Where She Danced).

Next stop on De Carlo/Cameron's kitsch-laden, whistle-stop tour of America is San Francisco's Gold Coast, the gal now attracting the attention of wealthy Russian Walter Slezak; he buys her a $50,000 Rembrandt, she's after seducing the nobleman in order for him to finance her own opera house. Bruce turns up again, still a reformed character (but seeming dazed and forlorn), Cameron yearns for her caresses and Dekker arrives on the scene from Berlin to settle old scores. In an attempt to remove Bruce from the picture (De Carlo loves him, but god knows why), Slezak arranges for the outlaw's old gang to pretend to rob a Chinese junk full of jade and silk. Bruce goes along with the scheme, is bamboozled by Chinaman Abner Biberman (talking in a jarring Scottish/Chinese accent) and his crossbow-toting followers and treated to an oriental dance routine by De Carlo in sequins. "You're part of it, too?" he mumbles. "Are you angry?" she replies. "No," is the short answer and they kiss, De Carlo handing him a locket with her portrait inside. By this stage of the proceedings, paying customers at the time must have been thinking "You couldn't have made this stuff up if you tried," but, yes, more is to follow: Bruce and Dekker go head-to-head with swords on De Carlo's deserted stage; Dekker is run through and Bruce decides to return to Virginia as a shotgun guard on the Butterfield Stage Line. In a farcical climax, Bruce's stage is chased by Dekker's stage, the Russian out to arrest him for murder. The stage carrying Bruce crashes over a sea cliff; he's hauled up and handcuffed just as Cameron and De Carlo walk up. Biberman mouths a few words of Eastern wisdom, Bruce clambers into the coach next to De Carlo and Dekker, having second thoughts, tosses in the keys to the handcuffs, allowing the lovers to get on with their lives. Cameron, watching them kiss, looks as sorrowful as Bruce has done for the past 90 minutes. Well, at least he's left with De Carlo's locket containing her portrait, compensation for his loss.

Noted film critic James Agee's response was "The funniest deadpan parody I have ever seen." "Ridiculous," said *Variety*, mirroring the rest of the put-downs, Bosley Crowther of the *New York Times* adding, "The most fantastic horse opera of the year … squalid and splendorous." Charles Lamont's direction is okay, the Technicolor photography (W. Howard Greene and Hal Mohr) is sumptuous and Edward Ward's music thunders along without pause for breath. But why was it ever made? Why have an exotic damsel in distress placed in various unrelated locations, the lass pestered by a bevy of unsuitable suitors, when there's no dramatic thrust? "Love conquers all" appears to be the theme, the lovely De Carlo (shot in soft focus half the time) finally forcing a flicker of a smile to crease Bruce's immobile countenance; boy, was *he* hard work! Apart from De Carlo and Slezak, the acting overall is poor (De Carlo's dance choreography is bizarrely unpolished and all over the place, yet strangely erotic), the dialogue hitting new heights of absurdity, the narrative fraying at the seams. But it's oddly addictive; you want to go back and check that what you have sat through actually did exist as a motion picture, a bona fide turkey from Hollywood's golden age that has very few equals in its sphere (and certainly not in a Western), which, on hindsight, is just as well.

Charles Lamont, Cameron and De Carlo were reunited for 1945's *Frontier Gal* (aka *The Bride Wasn't Willing*) after Maria Montez and Jon Hall (on/off lovers at the time) had turned the script down; Montez was suspended by Universal for rejecting the project. Actually, Michael Fessier and Ernest Pagano's terse screenplay (they also produced) crackles with witty one-liners in an atypical Western that, over 92 minutes, veers from straightforward action to light comedy, a few musical interludes tossed in to keep audiences happy, which worked—the movie was a hit and, more than *Salome, Where She Danced* managed, made De Carlo a hot property in Hollywood. Shot in beautiful muted Technicolor tones by Charles P. Boyle around California's mountainous, wooded Kernville region and containing a lovely score from Frank Skinner, aided by Hans J. Salter, *Frontier Gal* is an engaging oddball mix that excites and brings a smile to the face—and any Western featuring Fuzzy Knight as a character that *doesn't* grate on the nerves must have a lot going for it.

First off, the picture is as politically incorrect as they come, but in 1945, who cared about such trifles? In his best role to date, Cameron (Johnny Hart) is seen galloping through the landscape pursued by a posse, falsely held accountable for the killing his partner. Evading capture, he rides into Red Gulch, looking the business in black shirt and white neckerchief. In the saloon, he brushes aside two toughs while Fuzzy Knight strums a guitar and whistles, homing in on singing De Carlo, the joint's "boss turkey." Cameron, true to type, ignores the usual romantic preliminaries and makes his play, grabbing De Carlo (much to knife-throwing boyfriend Sheldon Leonard's disapproval), calling her "beautiful" and marching the gal upstairs to her room in a sequence of events that goes something like this: Kiss. Slap. Another kiss. Another slap. A third kiss. A third slap. A fourth kiss. A fourth (but much weaker) slap. A fifth kiss. Then total capitulation, the hushed saloon crowd itching to rush home and practice Cameron's basic macho foreplay technique on their own partners. In the morning, after a night of lust, Cameron

Publicity shot of Rod Cameron

hints at rings, jewelry and a permanent relationship. "Now who's the boss turkey?" he teases De Carlo. "You are!" she exclaims with a big smile, taken aback by this tall stranger who has literally swept her off her feet. But at the end of the day, Cameron is concerned to learn that the saloon lass is anticipating the sound of wedding bells; he's in town to marry schoolmistress Jan Wiley, not to get hitched to De Carlo, and she's shocked by plans that don't include her. "What happened last night?" she enquires. "I like to tame colts," he replies. But they do get wed—at the point of De Carlo's pistol! Cameron, a $1,000 reward on his head, is then arrested for the manslaughter of his partner, receives two slaps from De Carlo ("I do not kiss convicts!"), escapes, rides into town, hauls his new bride off to his ranch and engages in more roughhouse honeymoon shenanigans; slaps, kisses, De Carlo throwing crockery before they end up in bed (whatever happened to his feelings for Wiley?). The sheriff, a deputy and shifty gunman Leonard arrive, take Cameron into custody and he serves six years behind bars. End of Act One.

Act Two: Cameron canters into Red Gulch six years later in the middle of a De Carlo musical number. "You gonna divorce me?" he grins before dragging her (not against her will) upstairs for more bedroom romping. She then drops a bombshell; they have a five-year-old daughter (delightfully played by seven-year-old Beverly Simmons), and Leonard, the real killer of Cameron's buddy, wants to marry De Carlo if she gets a divorce. The big man's having none of it; he wants to care for Simmons and whisks her off to his ranch where, after a spot of bottom-spanking to control the child's temper, she announces "Oh gosh! You love me!" In the background, Cameron's deadpan Cherokee manservant (Frank Lackteen) answers everything said to him with a "Ho" and Sheriff Andy Devine and two pals drop by, as does Wiley and her aunt,

Clara Blandick, summoned to add "a feminine touch here and there." The sight of three grown men peeling Simmons' clothes off prior to the tot going to bed would raise censorial eyebrows these days, as would the repeated scenes of spanking and slapping. Meanwhile, De Carlo closes her saloon in the hope that she can play happy families with Cameron ("Hate him?" she remarks to jealous Leonard. "I'll do anything he wants."), that is until she meets prim and proper Wiley and her stuffy aunt at the ranch, where the claws come out, the schoolmarm viewing her rival as nothing more than a saloon tart without a future. In a thrilling climax guaranteed to set the pulses racing, Leonard abducts Simmons, given chase by Cameron, Wiley, Blandick and Devine's posse, culminating in the tense rescue of Simmons, perched precariously on a wobbly, splitting log over a raging waterfall, by her father. Leonard falls to his death onto rocks after slugging it out with Cameron, Wiley and her aunt depart in a huff and Rod puts De Carlo across his knees, smacking her delicious backside.

"Daddy! You spanked Mummy!" cries Simmons, delightful to the end.
"You're darned tootin' I did," grins Cameron.
"That means you love her."
"That's what I've been tryin' to tell her."

The warring husband and wife kiss for the umpteenth time (no more slapping!) and are now free to set up house together with their handful of a daughter. *Frontier Gal* is, in modern-day vernacular, a feel-good 1940s Western, tough though heartwarming without resorting to sugary sentimentalism, an underrated picture that looks fine and dandy, containing sparkling love/hate interplay between the two leads; Cameron, assured and self-composed, had proved himself to be capable of carrying a production on his broad back and was now on a roll of sorts, content, for the time being, to stay within the Western sphere, a sphere which best suited his modest talents.

Frontier Gal possessed oodles of charm; Alfred L. Werker's *Pirates of Monterey* (Universal, 1947) had oodles of quasi-romantic baloney courtesy of skirt-chasing Mexican soldier Mikhail Rasumny, a member of gun runner Rod Cameron's troop who are on a secret mission, carrying fresh rifles to Monterey, to be used against Spanish Royalists attempting a coup in Old California circa 1840. For the first wearisome 26 minutes, Cameron (Captain Phillip Kent) and Rasumny get involved with two ladies, Maria Montez and Tamara Shayne; the pair may or may not be spies, and to complicate matters, Montez is betrothed to Spanish officer Phillip Reed, a friend of Cameron's. A sojourn at a harvest festival in Santa Barbara, more flirting and clowning (from Rasumny), a dance and a great deal of chat—where is all the action when it's needed? There's a brief spell (shot in Bronson Canyon) where Cameron's team is ambushed in a ravine but, until the climax, that's all there is. At the fort in Monterey, Major Gilbert Roland emerges as a traitor in the camp, arranging for his own brother to steal some of the rifles; the man is captured, then shot escaping, Reed wounded in the confrontation. The bedridden officer soon learns about Cameron romancing his gal right under his nose and heads for Roland's hacienda by the coast to shoot him, just as the pirates of the title disembark and charge up the beach to engage the Spanish militia. In a scene straight out of an Italian peplum movie, Cameron runs Roland through with his blade, the pirates are defeated, Cameron weds Montez (Reed is best man) and grizzled Rasumny succeeds in having his wicked way with Shayne.

"Tired …mechanical … desolate and drab," said the *New York Times* and they hit the nail on the head: *Pirates of Monterey* is one of those ultimately turgid pictures that is all dressed up with nowhere to go. Flashy cinematography (W. Howard Greene, Hal Mohr and Harry Hallenberger), an over-exuberant score (Milton Rosen) and attractive leads in Cameron and Montez do little to make amends for an adventure patently lacking *in* adventure, excitement, thrills and incident. Rod combines rugged good looks with a let's-get-down-to-business macho charm toward redhead Montez (this facet of his character would manifest itself in most of his future movies) but cannot save this disappointing Western-cum-pirate exercise from sinking, like its protagonists at the end, beneath the ocean waves.

Just before he broke from Universal, Cameron was loaned out to Allied Artists at the start of 1948, starring in Lesley Selander's marvelous *Panhandle*, photographed at Lone Pine by Harry Neumann in Sepiatone which lent the production a pronounced evocative air, akin to glancing at a scrapbook of the Old West and watching the pages spring to vivid life (the ever-productive Selander went on to make a further six movies with Cameron). A rough, gritty tale of revenge containing an elaborate score from Rex Dunn, *Panhandle* is Cameron's pivotal Western of the 1940s; it's his *Abilene Town* moment, the United Artists' 1946 actioner that put Randolph Scott on the map. Here, Selander's thunderingly good oater placed

Cameron on a similar footing, promoting him as a cowboy star to be reckoned with. Playing John Sands, he strides through the narrative full of purpose, 6-feet-4-inches of mean attitude, twin guns blazing as he comes up against saloon boss/town magnate Reed Hadley (dressed in flashy boots and sporting a studded double holster) and his varmints in the town of Sentinel; Hadley, who has designs on ruling the entire Panhandle region, was the reptile responsible for the murder of Cameron's brother Billy, a crusading newspaperman uncovering town corruption. Cameron himself has a reputation the size of Texas; legend states that he once caused Billy the Kid to back down in a standoff, and he's an ex-marshal/outlaw in the bargain, not that that matters one bit to trigger-happy young dude Blake Edwards (he co-wrote the script with John C. Champion, the pair producing). He's itching to beat Cameron to the draw, incensed at the lofty, double-holstered hombre sneeringly calling him Little Boy Blue in a crowded saloon *and* in front of his boss, Hadley.

Owner of a south-of-the-border trading post, Rod's secret past as a gunman is kept firmly under wraps until he's informed of his brother's death in Sentinel, shot in the back while going about his business. After a tense game of stud poker, Cameron pointing his gun at a card cheat (this scene is introduced to reinforce our hero as a man not to be messed with), he gallops off toward Sentinel and waylaid by three lawmen, bent on apprehending him from his time spent as an outlaw; he disarms all three in a corral. In Sentinel, Cameron books into the Blue Belle Hotel, thus setting up a series of confrontations with Hadley and his boys in the Last Frontier saloon. Hadley's the Big Wheel in these parts and knows why Cameron has arrived in Sentinel pushing his weight around, seething with jealousy when his secretary, Anne Gwynne, falls head over heels in lust with Rod. "He's beautiful!" she coos to Hadley after meeting the tall, dark stranger. However, Cameron has a second attractive female vying for his attention, tomboy Cathy Downs, who was engaged to his brother and owner of the Circle S Ranch; the saddle salesgirl takes him to the grave up in the hills, aware that Gwynne has caught his eye. Later, Cameron is approached by four citizens who offer him the job of town tamer ("This place needs cleaning up. You can do it."), but big Rod ain't interested: All he wants is a bath and a good night's sleep before tackling Hadley and his mob; Hadley has given instructions to shoot the troublemaker in the back—he's much too good in a face-to-face shoot-out, and knows it.

Thanks to Edwards (of *Pink Panther* fame) and Champion's biting screenplay, *Panhandle* becomes a suspenseful game of cat-and-mouse, Cameron prowling the sidewalks on the alert and constantly rubbing Hadley's surly bunch up the wrong way, especially the volatile Edwards. "Can I get you a drink?" asks the cocky gunslinger of Cameron in the saloon. "Sure," is the dry response, "if they'll serve it to you." Rod then gets in a heated smooching session with Gwynne, the couple rolling on the floor in passion before he kisses her, hard. "You *do* get your way," she pants. He kisses her again, harder. "Nice!" she sighs. Back in the saloon, Cameron joins the card table with Hadley, the two eyeing each other like a pair of rattlesnakes about to strike. Baby-faced Edwards, incensed at Cameron's dismissal of his perceived toughness, calls him out, only to be thumped and sent hurling across the floor like a rag doll, the prelude to a three-minute brawl with thug Jeff York, one of the best, and most vicious, you'll ever see in a Western. Cameron's the victor, bloody but not broken, Hadley threatening to run him out of town before an approaching storm breaks, Gwynne having told the viper "No more romance!" As the wind gets up and the rain pelts down in the night, Cameron approaches the Last Frontier, Edwards and two pals in the street. "Go on home little man," challenges Cameron; Edwards, fuming at the insult, fires off a shot (which Cameron allows) then falls, like his two partners, in a storm of hot lead from those two deadly six-guns, a classic showdown, three bodies lying in the rain-soaked dirt. Entering the saloon, Cameron tosses a silver concho onto Hadley's card table; the town boss is missing one from his gun belt, the one that was found near Billy Sand's body, proof of who shot the newspaper proprietor in the back—Hadley! ("There's an empty space in your gun belt. This concho will fill it up."). Relieved of his guns, Cameron is marched out into a dark alley by one of Hadley's confederates; Gwynne witnesses it and tosses a pistol to Rod from an upstairs window. Cameron shoots his would-be assassin, Hadley hears firing, tries to hide behind a door but is brought down by four more shots. "I'm comin' back," Rod tells Gwynne, ambling off down the rain swept main street of Sentinel to put his house in order before returning to carry on with the blonde where he left off.

Cameron in *Panhandle*

Panhandle is an incisive, undervalued Western drama, Rod Cameron's authoritative, rock-solid performance driving the narrative to new heights of macho suspense. He's spectacularly good in his role of the hard-driven, revengeful John Sands, especially in his repeated spats with Hadley; Selander and Champion's remake, *The Texican* (Columbia, 1966), a vehicle for Audie Murphy, was a very poor substitute by comparison. Those Sepiatone views of Lone Pine's rugged scenery, and the characters whose lives are played out in the violent Western frontier towns, transport you back to a distant era, as though filming took place at the time the events unfolded, uniquely different to fans who have never experienced this classic '40s horse opera, ranking as one of Cameron's finest stints in the saddle.

In 1948, Cameron parted company with Universal, going out on a mundane note with George Sherman's *River Lady*. From this date up to 1957, he divided his time mainly between Republic, Monogram and Allied Artists, featuring in a number of traditional low- to medium-budget Westerns in the manner of the four cowboy heroes featured in *Six-Gun Law*, some good, some not-so-good. Like a schoolboy who has blotted his copybook, Cameron, although figuring in practically all of *River Lady*'s scenes, was relegated to third billing behind Yvonne De Carlo and Dan Duryea; ravishing De Carlo (as Sequin!), shot mainly in close-up, was still being promoted as Hollywood's latest hot property while Duryea found himself being pushed further into the limelight by his agents. *River Lady* had a terrific Paul Sawtell score; dazzling exterior photography from Irving Glassberg; and a budget of a million bucks. But it lacked heart, a passionless empty vessel manufactured with the sole purpose of elevating De Carlo up the ladder of movie fame, and very little else. Like most logging/timberjack outings, the plot was simplistic: Cameron (Dan Corrigan) and the independent logging companies are being driven out of business by De Carlo's syndicate, fronted by smarmy bullyboy Duryea who desires De Carlo—but she's in love with Cameron. De Carlo lays her cards on the table to her lover: If he doesn't go wandering off into the woods for months at a time and settles down, she will marry him; scheming behind his back, she arranges for Rod to become head honcho in John McIntire's floundering outfit, thus tying him to a desk job, which is where McIntire's radiant daughter, Helena Carter, enters the frame. Anxious to escape her domineering mother Esther Somers, who calls Cameron "a timber rat," she virtually throws herself at the big, office-bound lug ("I think you're pretty," she tells him), much to De Carlo's horror and Duryea's undisguised glee. Now he can lay *his* hands on the syndicate boss, busy running a casino on board her riverboat, *The River Lady*, and steamroll over the independents without Cameron's pesky interference.

And that's about it, a Western soap opera of the tepid kind. Cameron, furious to discover that De Carlo landed him the position with McIntire ("Don't try to run things for me!" he storms), breaks off his engagement to her and weds besotted Carter instead, while Duryea plans to ambush the next pile of logs floating down river and become King of the Castle. De Carlo struts her stuff on the riverboat, singing a song, and Cameron walks out on poor Carter, leaving De Carlo wondering whether or not there's any chance of her romance with her ex-beau being back on the burner. Sherman finally conjures up a show-stopper to make up for all the tedium and lack of action: Duryea's men converge on a massive log jam, there's a multiple punch-up in the swirling river between rival factions and Cameron blows up the obstruction—and Duryea with it. Much to De Carlo's consternation, he also goes back to Carter, realizing that she's the girl for him, leaving the lass to steam down river in her boat to an uncertain future.

The out-in-the-woods logging scenery is attractive, De Carlo's looks alone light up the screen, Duryea hisses and connives and Cameron treads the boards on autopilot. All in all, *River Lady* is run-of-the-mill fare, lacking in drama and humor, talking of which—where was Fuzzy Knight when he was so urgently needed? Cameron's time at Universal-International was at an end: It had been a rocky ride but a formative one. With the exception of *Frontier Gal*, and possibly the bizarre one-off that was *Salome, Where She Danced*, none of his Universal Westerns matched the magnificent *Panhandle*, and that had been produced by Allied Artists, a sign of things to come. From now on, it would be the lesser film companies that would showcase the best of Rod Cameron as a Western star, something which, by and large, Universal had failed to do.

CHAPTER 8

HAYDEN: TALL MAN RIDING, 1949-1955

Paramount's 1949 release *El Paso* was Sterling Hayden's first appearance in a Western, an over-ambitious, overlong oater produced in Cinecolor on a budget of $1,000,000, John Payne in the lead role. Hayden plays an ex-Confederate officer sent to El Paso from Charleston to seek out judge Henry Hull and get him to sign some legal documents, only to find the magistrate a drunken sap, firmly under the thumb of the town's corrupt sheriff, Dick Foran, and real estate-grabber Hayden (as Bert Donner). Also in town is Payne's ex, Gail Russell, the lass still having feelings for our rather poker-faced hero. When farmer Robert Ellis is brought in for the murder of a deputy (he was only shooting in self-defense), it becomes apparent that Foran, Hayden and their lynch-happy hyenas are out to pinch all that property owned by the poor old defeated Confederates, trampling over their crops on what they term "the State's land." Payne, outraged at the treatment meted out to his former pals from the war, forgets all about returning to law practice, learns from sharpshooter Eduardo Noriega how to be quick on the draw with both left and right hands, discards his fancy duds for a ghastly rainbow-colored shirt and hits the trail with a band of vigilantes, vowing to bring justice to El Paso and end Foran's reign of terror. Bodies swing from trees, Russell pleads with Payne to stop using a gun, George "Gabby" Hayes goes through his bumbling old hayseed routine, Ellis and his wife are killed, their young son joins in the crusade and eventually, during a climactic sandstorm shoot-out, Payne drops Hayden. Foran and his boys are cornered in the Rio Grande River but Payne prevents them from being strung up, allowing the gang to stand trial: Law and order has prevailed over the gun; justice of the legal kind has returned to El Paso, and Russell has returned to the arms of Payne, once more attired in a smart suit.

Why is *El Paso* so substandard on Western entertainment values when, on that budget alone, the picture should have been far more exciting? Perhaps if handled by moviemakers other than low-budget producers William C. Thomas and William H. Pine who, in the words of the *New York Times*, came up with "a third or fourth rehash of a standard Western plot," adding, "it doesn't pack a wallop," it might have worked. In many ways, *El Paso* is a typical whimsical '40s Western, a myriad of semi-comic characters all hustling and bustling and interfering with the action, Darrell Calker's busy, very loud score highlighting their silly antics but becoming an intrusion. True to type, whiskery Hayes, a Wild West salesman of sorts, blunders his way through one jape after another, a string of pots and pans jangling around his neck, two Indian buddies in tow (it's notable that characters like Hayes and his Redskin pals very rarely figured in '50s oaters, deemed too childish for a mature audience) while Mary Beth Hughes' light-fingered Stagecoach Nellie is nothing more than decorative fluff. Even the bad guys look strangely old-hat, Hayden throwing his 6-foot-5 frame around on set with very little conviction. As for Payne, he's as stiff as the shirt he wears in the opening two reels *(not* that rainbow shirt!), his love scenes with Russell the cinematic equivalent of a cold shower. Director Lewis R. Foster tries to cram too much in, the result a noisy, lengthy disjointed muddle that fails to hold the interest and brings on severe indigestion after 30 minutes or so. Good points: Fine location filming around Gallup, New Mexico, lit in Ellis W. Carter's garish color tones; and the finale taking place, quite divertingly, in a raging sandstorm. A big disappointment, then, with Hayden, quite honestly, failing to register or make an impact, brute force taking precedence over acting nuance.

After Hayden's significant movie breakthrough in *The Asphalt Jungle*, he began to receive top billing, headlining his next Western, Paramount's *Flaming Feather*, in 1952, a "spot-the-villain oater" (*Variety*) in which he played rancher Tex McCloud, out to nail The Sidewinder, a black-clad desperado terrorizing the Arizona territory in 1877 with a pack of pillaging, rustling, murdering Ute renegades op-

Hayden romances Barbara Rush while Forrest Tucker looks on in *Flaming Feather*.

erating out of Canyon Diablo; Hayden's spread has been their last target. Forget the meandering plot (script/story: Gerald Drayson Adams), just concentrate on Ray Enright's slam-bang direction (he composes his cast full frame a lot of the time, or from the ground upwards, to add immediacy and dynamics), Paul Sawtell's pumping score and double-Oscar winner (*Gone with the Wind*; *Blood and Sand*) Ray Rennahan's vivid colors, the action filmed around the ancient Indian cliff settlements at Montezuma's Castle National Monument, Camp Verde, and Red Rock Crossing, Sedona in Arizona. Enright's fast-moving oater had two gals vying for hunk Hayden's attention: Tarty saloon singer Arleen Whelan and sassy Barbara Rush, engaged to oily businessman/trading post boss Victor Jory (Lucky Lee). Whelan has money issues with Jory amounting to $20,000 and is jealous of Hayden fancying Rush over her, so employs gambling gunman Richard Arlen to finish Hayden off; meanwhile, Ute lass Carol Thurston (as Turquoise) sulks in the background, in love with Jory and looking daggers at Rush every time Jory cuddles up to her ("Lucky. You won't marry white girl," she warns him). Ian MacDonald plays another gunslinger attired in black, the scenario, taking place in the mining backwater of Fort Savage, haphazard and disjointed, characters' motifs not made all that clear in Adams' convoluted screenplay. To add to the general melee, Lieutenant Forrest Tucker, grizzled, tobacco-chewing Sergeant Edgar Buchanan and their cavalry platoon are also out to capture the elusive Sidewinder, Forrest placing a bet with Hayden of a year's troop salary if he gets to the mysterious killer first.

When evil MacDonald is plugged by Hayden, everyone thinks The Sidewinder has been put paid to. Wrong! It's Jory (who's behind the trap) all along (as if we hadn't already guessed, fully aware of the actor's propensity for taking on the role of arch villains); the chain of events then thankfully moves out of the confines of the town into the spectacular Sedona wilds, the Utes attacking Hayden, Forrest, the cavalry, the two girls (Whelan expires from a bullet, as does Arlen), in fact the entire cast, a furious prolonged shoot-out, the air blue with gunsmoke, contrasting strongly with the red hues of the rugged sandstone cliffs. In an exciting closer, Jory the Sidewinder then drags Rush up a series of near-vertical ladders into an old Indian cliff dwelling, Forrest and company scaling the walls in pursuit. During another blazing gunfight, Jory tussles with Hayden over a circular fire pit: The Sidewinder is accidentally shot in the back by Thurston (she was aiming for Rush) and Rush flings her arms around Sterling's neck. "Saved again, Tex!" she cries, glad to be free of Jory's slimy embrace.

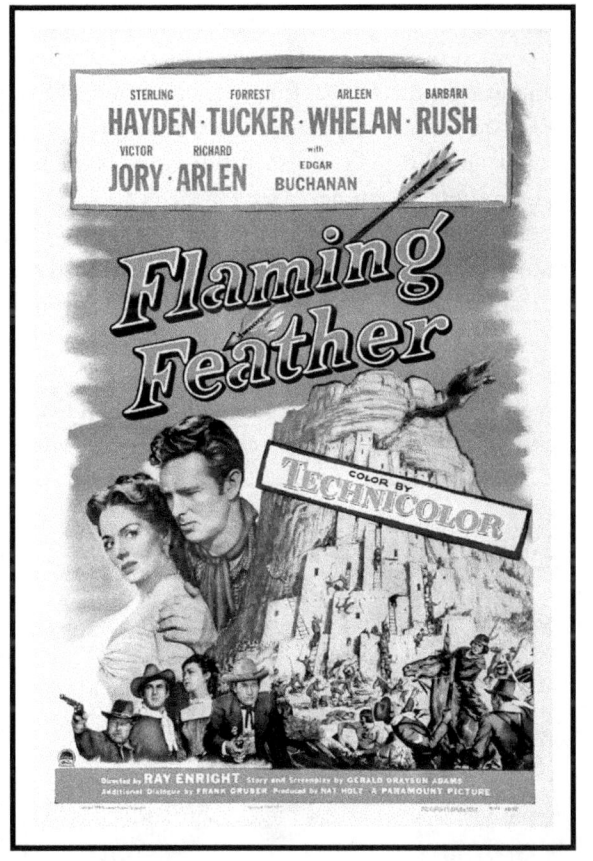

An invigorating outdoor yarn, regrettably containing traces of, to its detriment, standard '40s over-plotting, *Flaming Feather* is noisy and colorful, a huge improvement on *El Paso*, Sterling easing himself into the saddle rather than hitting you in the face with his understated performance. He's a little too laid-back in some scenes, more Joel McCrea than Randolph Scott, relying on his height and muscular frame to push him through the proceedings, looking occasionally as if he was having trouble finding his spurs.

Paul Sawtell and Ray Rennahan were retained in Hayden's next for 1952, Paramount's $700,000 beautifully filmed *Denver and Rio Grande*, located in

Colorado's scenic Durango region and relating the story of the feud between rival railroad builders the Denver and Rio Grande and the Canyon City and San Juan outfit in the 1870s. Roly-poly Edmond O'Brien played the gang boss of the DRG, sour-faced Hayden (as McCabe) driving the other company, determined to sabotage O'Brien's efforts in bringing his tracks into Denver at the expense of his own (in fact, you never see Hayden's crew laying tracks; they're too busy causing mischief). Dynamiting cliff faces to create landslides, blocking the planned route, planting spies in O'Brien's camp (including secretary Laura Elliot, bent on causing maximum damage to O'Brien for killing her brother, even though he's innocent; Hayden was the culprit), stealing a train and lastly commandeering several DRG's depots—these are the underhand tactics deployed by Hayden and slimeball assistant Lyle Bettger to ensure the DRG fails to live up to the promises made to its backers and, as a company, is bankrupted.

Denver and Rio Grande is absolutely stunning to look at, almost like a travelogue of the Colorado Rocky Mountains, thanks to Rennahan's intense color photography, and performances across the board are fine: O'Brien hustles and bustles, bearded Hayden storms around on set, warning his rival, "You throw one stake in the river, and I'll throw you in right after it," Dean Jagger brings gravitas to his role of the DRG magnate, J. Carrol Naish is dependable as always playing the DRG's engineer, Bettger is his usual leering, devilish self and comedy comes in the form of flirtatious couple Zasu Pitts, the cook in a traveling saloon, and train driver Paul Fix. There are shoot-outs and incidents a'plenty, including a literally incendiary head-on collision between two real locomotives which took five days to film at a cost of $165,000. A pair of narrow-gauge DRG trains plus rolling stock, due for the scrapyard, were packed with explosives; director Byron

Haskin instructed his crew to position themselves well away from the track, both trains were set in motion and the resulting terrifying explosion was worth the price of admission alone. Also, credit must go to Haskin for not relying on back-projection in the railroad sequences, a process which grates in many similar pictures; yes, it's used very briefly, but overall is absent, and all the better for it. The climax is a winner as well, Hayden's jackals versus O'Brien's construction crew, hiding behind a tall barricade on the rail lines and pinned down under a continuous hail of bullets (Naish: "Bees have been buzzing around since dawn." O'Brien: "Yeah. Lead bees."). Hayden's mob maneuvers a flatbed carriage onto the tracks loaded with dynamite but Hayden is winged in the back by Bettger who, in turn, is hit by O'Brien. Elliot tells the DRG squad what is about to happen and they quickly run for the slopes; the carriage hits the barricade, with Hayden, wounded, still laying on it, and goes up in a fireball. The closing minutes see the DRG escaping the insolvency courts and O'Brien cozying up to Elliot.

The pace is brisk, the outdoor scenery splendid, but somewhere along those endless mountain tracks, *Denver and Rio Grande* loses its way, becoming simply serviceable, predictable and a little clichéd. It's vaguely unsatisfactory as a whole; the *New York Times* summed this feeling up with "isn't so much a motion picture but a picture with motion," although they did praise Haskin's "galloping camerawork" and "picturesque settings." "Solid oater," stated *The Hollywood Reporter*. Frank Gruber's script doesn't exactly sparkle, while Pitts and Fix's comedy routine belongs to the late '30s/early '40s, not in a new age Western of this caliber. The gaudy, smoke-belching locomotives and eye-catching vistas, plus Sterling's meaner-than-mean turn and that mesmerizing train crash, elevate the movie to must-see status, even if occasionally the momentum and dialogue lapse into ordinariness.

Sterling Hayden's fourth Western could not have been in starker contrast to the three that had preceded it. Charles Marquis Warren directed two mediocre horror movies in his time (*The Unknown Terror*; *Back from the Dead*, both 1957), as well as a pair of first-rate Joel McCrea Westerns, *Trooper Hook* (1957) and *Cattle Empire* (1958). But 1952's *Hellgate*, distributed by Lippert Pictures, may well have been his finest hour in the director's seat. It comes as something of a sensation to those unaware of the film's existence: Tough, uncompromising and downright vicious, Warren's violent prison break drama, filmed in California's Bronson Canyon, showed the Western growing up fast, fitting in with new adult trends beginning to exert themselves in the much-loved horse opera. Sterling was on top of his game, right at home in this *noir*-type format, looking one hard son-of-a-gun, playing veterinarian Gilman S. Hanley who unwisely treats notorious Confederate guerrilla James Anderson (a venomous performance) for damage to his ribs following a fall from his horse. It's Kansas, 1867, and the defeated Rebels are still rampaging through the countryside, refusing to believe that they lost the war. Hayden, an ex-Graycoat officer himself, now leads the quiet life but is arrested for aiding and abetting Anderson and his gang by accepting stolen money amounting to $15,000 found in saddlebags for the Rebs buying allegedly rustled horses. Given a cursory trial, found guilty and treated like a criminal, he escapes execution, only to be sentenced to serve time in a hellhole of a federal prison built inside a vast mine pit in the arid New Mexican desert, presided over by sadistic cavalryman Ward Bond and infamous screen villain Robert J. Wilke, himself an expert in sadism.

Ernest W. Miller's harsh monochrome photography highlights the grim conditions the men have to put up with; crammed six together in underground cells, the "scurvies" are forced to work on the rock face every day with minimal water, choking in clouds of dust. The prison has no natural water source and has to rely on supplies brought in from the nearest town once a month. And it's no good attempting escape: Once out in the desert, Pima braves will hunt any prisoner down, a reward offered of $25 alive, or $50 dead. If brought back in one piece, they're incarcerated in the oven, a huge metal box roasting under the merciless sun. But fellow inmate James Arness has found a possible way out, an old Indian chimney-cum-tunnel in the rocks above their cell; once free, they could steal horses and make it across the burning wastes to Mexico. Trouble is, one of their number, almost completing his term, has squealed to renegade-hating Bond who, on reflection, decides to let them make their break for freedom, then hunt them down like a pack of wild dogs. In the meantime, Hayden's lovely wife, Joan Leslie, is petitioning Washington like mad to have her husband's sentence terminated; he's an innocent man, she implores, undeserving of this life-threatening treatment.

"A few years ago, I used to bayonet that uniform," snarls uncooperative Hayden in Bond's office. "You're not gonna like what happens to you here, guerrilla," Bond spits back, refusing to hand over Leslie's letters to her husband, fully aware that she's trying to get him released. "In this hole, we gotta breathe together to live," states Arness to Hayden, the two involved in a Battle of the Giants to see who's the meanest; Hayden, at 6-foot-5, was a big guy, but Arness, at 6-foot-7, was bigger! After an abortive escape attempt by a half-crazed convict, the man shot down from a scree and impaling himself on spiked logs, Arness, Hayden and three others stage an abortive revolt, then break through the tight passage; scrambling over the pit's rim in full view of a sneering Bond, the informer among them is pushed to his death by Arness and they jump on four horses, heading across the desert where, during a sandstorm, three are wiped out by the Pima trackers (Arness gets an arrow through the neck, shot in gruesome close-up). Bond has an official letter stating that Hayden is now a free man, but still escorts him back to the prison under guard and, suddenly, Warren's riveting, in-your-face showpiece, boosted by a terrific Paul Dunlap score, takes an unexpected twist.

Typhus has hit the compound and men are dropping like flies, the nearby town refusing to issue any water in case of infection. Bond, swallowing his pride, asks Hayden if he will ride to Mexico with a detail and obtain the necessary supplies to combat the disease. Hayden agrees with the proviso of "I go alone," but diverts to the town barricade instead where he reasons at gunpoint with those manning it, saying "fresh water will kill the fever at the prison." To Bond's astonishment, the falsely accused inmate returns with a wagonload of water, the commandant at last pledging that he will stand witness to Hayden, claiming a dying prisoner had confessed that the vet had nothing whatsoever to do with Anderson and his nefarious activities. Warren closes with a moving scene, Hayden trooping over the fields, to be embraced in the loving arms of his tear-stained wife.

"An excellent job," crowed *Variety* of Hayden's glowering star turn, commenting on "the general brutality of prison life." *Hellgate* is a relative obscurity to many Western fans but proves conclusively that low-budget independent film companies could, on occasions, come up with the goods and knock spots off any similar fare issued by the big guns (assistant to Warren was future Western/action director Andrew V. McLaglen). This is such an occasion: Warren's stark prison offering packs one almighty punch, like a Western variation on all those [British] X-rated prison/crime pictures that began to seep onto the circuits during the middle of the decade. Highly recommended, with the whole cast, especially Hayden, Arness, Bond and Wilke, in scorching, unforgettable form.

After *Hellgate*, Hayden took on a variety of roles throughout 1952 to finance his love of boats and the sea: A swashbuckler in Columbia's *The Golden Hawk*, a military man in Monogram's *Eagles of the Fleet* and a slot opposite Bette Davis in Fox's *The Star*. In these, he demonstrated the Sterling Hayden style of acting: Largely impassive with bouts of animation, his macho muscularity and six-foot-five frame carrying the day. Allied Artists' *Kansas Pacific*, his first movie in 1953, is a case in point. You would think that judging by his expression, or lack of it, the actor's mind, in his early scenes, was on his beloved sea and ships and when his next paycheck was due, not focusing on the camera, but he does liven up in yet another railroad yarn that, by a whisker, beats Paramount's far more expensive *Denver and Rio Grande* to the post. Shot in two weeks on a $200,000 budget, Ray Nazarro's tale of the Union-financed Kansas Pacific line, under threat from Bill Quantrill and his Rebels just prior to the Civil War, moves like wildfire, backed by Albert Sendrey and Marlin Skile's first-class score, unusual Cinecolor photography and classy acting all round. It's a good old-fashioned Western actioner, nothing more, nothing less, and Hayden, in the words of *Variety*'s film critic, "impresses," the movie "better than the average AA pix."

Western heavyweight Barton MacLane feels his job as railroad engineer is under threat when Sterling (Captain John Nelson) turns up in civilian duds (not the fresh-faced kid out of college with a slide rule he was expecting); he's been tasked by Washington to bring the tracks into Kansas City on time and put a stop to those villains causing mayhem to the railroad and those running it. A big bold locomotive has been stuck at Rockwood for six weeks and track-laying progress has to be made in order for the rolling stock to begin ferrying ammunition and supplies to the growing Union army in case of hostilities

Italian still for *Kansas Pacific*

breaking out with the South. Frontiersman James Griffith, in buckskins, is hired as a guard, more gunfighters are taken on and work commences in earnest.

Southerner Reed Hadley (as Bill Quantrill) is the man behind the disruptions ("We're going to stop that train and help the Confederacy."), sending out his gun toughs (including Myron Healey and Clayton *The Lone Ranger* Moore) to push boulders onto the line, get signed up and cause trouble among the workers, steal dynamite, buckle the rail tracks and fire on the construction crew, anything to prevent the Union benefiting from that vital rail link. As if all this isn't enough for Hayden to contend with, MacLane's daughter, Eve Miller (the actress committed suicide due to depression in 1973, aged only 50), is giving him the cold shoulder, convinced he's there to oust her dad from his position. Then our lofty hero straps on a sidearm and reveals his true identity and she changes her attitude, going all gooey-eyed! When two cases of dynamite are stolen, Hayden rides into town, gets two of the rogues arrested (he's brought down the third) and begins to suspect Hadley's involvement. Hadley then goes to extremes, blowing up a train using two cannons—in a tit for tat operation, Union soldiers open fire with their own cannon on the next train that shows up, destroying Hadley's artillery. The Rebels are shot to pieces and in a furious fistfight among rocks, Hadley is the worse for wear after receiving a pummelling from Hayden's mighty fists; the train at last makes it to Kansas City. Smartly dressed Hayden departs for Washington to report to his superiors, leaving Miller to wonder why on earth she didn't make more of those manly arms and rugged demeanor; one peck on the lips is all she receives.

Sharply orchestrated by Nazarro, one of the Western genre's unsung directing heroes, *Kansas Pacific* is an entertaining slice of open air action, speeding through its 73 minutes with aplomb, and Sterling is on top masculine form, seemingly enjoying himself. Did he enjoy himself while making *Take Me to Town* (Universal, 1953)? Douglas Sirk's Western comedy-cum-drama-cum-soap opera is one of those films that you start off by thinking "I'm gonna hate this movie," and end up saying, "Well, it wasn't all that bad—or was it?" Buffs might also be forgiven in wondering why Universal ever bothered with such cornball material in the first place. In a plot centered around saloon singer Ann Sheridan, on the run from Marshal Larry Gates, becoming Sterling Hayden's housekeeper and looking after his three young boys while he's working in a logging camp, Hayden looked somewhat bemused but allowed flashes of comedic charm to break through that gruff exterior. And if anyone was expecting another *Denver and Rio Grande* or *Kansas Pacific* as that giant, smoke-belching Iron Horse thundered toward camera in the opening seconds, they were to be bitterly disappointed!

First seen escaping from a train via a shattered window, Sheridan (Vermilion O'Toole), minus crooked boyfriend Phillip Reed, makes her way to Pine Top, meeting mentor Lee Patrick (Rose) over at Timberline where the dame has set up a portable opera house/saloon. Hayden (as Will Hall) is a timberjack as well as Pine Top's preacher; work in a logging camp means having to leave his three young scamps, engagingly acted by Lee Aaker (nine), Harvey Grant (seven) and Dusty Henley (four), to scout around for another partner for their widowed dad. Three pairs of eyes zero in on flashy, sassy Sheridan and decide that she's the perfect mate ("We want a woman," Aaker

Hayden and family romp in the pool in *Take Me to Town*.

tells Sheridan, much to her amusement). When Gates appears in town, Sheridan, against type, takes up the offer of catering for the lads' needs ("Pa wants you to stay—for good."), mainly to escape the marshal's attention, much to the disgust of Pine Top's prim and proper ladies, led by starchy Phyllis Stanley, horrified at the thought of a redhead setting up house with the local pastor, never mind the fact that she fancies him herself. We're now in *The Comedy of Errors* territory: Sheridan sings a couple of ditties and flashes her shapely pins (future screen goddess Anita Ekberg has an uncredited part as a dancer), but has to continually take cover when Gates, busy romancing Patrick, who is trying to get him to quit as a lawman in order to save Sheridan's hide, comes snooping; Reed turns up, running his hands all over Sheridan's fulsome figure; Sheridan doesn't want to know, having set her sights on Hayden's masculine sexuality; and Stanley, as stiff as that collar she's wearing, is determined to get rid of that "devil wrapped in a maiden's form." It all comes right in the end, as you would expect in such sentimental tosh: Sheridan puts on a show to raise funds for the building of a new church, chivvying the unwilling townsfolk (including Stanley) into participating by making props and backdrops and also acting various roles; Reed is waylaid by Hayden after an out-of-context brawl and arrested; and Sheridan, free of all charges, becomes the kid's new mom, and the town's Sunday School teacher. The happy family is last seen dressed in striped bathing costumes, wading into a pool for a refreshing dip, an apple pie-cute closing scene if ever there was one.

The Westerns of Calhoun, Cameron, Hayden and Widmark

"Ponderous dullness ... ethical misfire," sneered the *New York Times*, while *Variety* wrote, "likeable ... good ... folksy." You pays your money and you takes your choice: *Take Me to Town* can't make up its mind whether to be a family picture, a small-town Western melodrama, an unlikely romance between two opposites or something akin to one of Hal Roach's legendary *Our Gang/ The Little Rascals* shorts of the 1920s. It failed to raise much interest at the box-office, an oddity from Universal-International that admittedly has its moments: The mischievous kids are a delight, Sheridan is alluringly glamorous and Sterling slightly more animated than usual. Otherwise, once seen, quickly forgotten.

During 1953/1954, Hayden continued to go where the work called, from family romantic drama in Warner Bros.' *So Big* to war in Allied Artists' *Fighter Attack*, on to crime *noir* (probably the milieu that showcased his talents the best) in Warner Bros.' *Crime Wave* and even indulging himself in medieval pomp in Fox's *Prince Valiant*. But the big guy still didn't go much on the acting profession, judging by his comments on the set of *So Big* when he was allegedly overheard saying to a fellow actor "Let's get this crap over with." Well, at least it made a change from all the preening and posing a great many publicity-mad Hollywood players were up to at the time. Hayden was a rarity in a movie capital teeming with fame-hungry males and female divas, a film star who didn't particularly want to be a film star, and occasionally this nonchalance, a "why am I bothering" attitude, could be glimpsed in some of his screen portrayals.

An example of the man's lackadaisical approach was there for audiences to witness for themselves during the first reel of *Arrow in the Dust* (Allied Artists, 1954), Lesley Selander's action-packed but dramatically redundant wagon train versus Indians oater. Hayden, playing army deserter Bart Laish, ambles into a saloon, asks for supplies, gallops out into the hills and comes across signs of Indian massacres. Reaching Camp Taylor, scene of a recent Pawnee raid, and taking on the identity of a fatally wounded cavalry major, an old acquaintance of his

Hayden and Coleen Gray in *Arrow in the Dust*

from West Point, Hayden, in a fit of conscience after his friend has accused him, with his dying breath, of being a "gambler, gunfighter. Now a deserter. Looks like you've added coward to the list," rides off to lead an immigrant wagon train heading to Laramie, taking over command of the troop detail, much to young officer Keith Larsen's surprise, arousing his suspicions over Hayden's credentials. In this opening section of the movie, Sterling acts the part of a hard-nosed, don't-mess-with-me loner to the best of his ability, but as soon as he becomes top dog, barking out orders by rote, his performance falls horribly flat, even when he's trying on his charms with Coleen Gray, decorative but just as one-dimensional. He literally looks as though he's simply going through the motions to get that paycheck and hang what's going on around him. But what's going on around him makes up for his passionless turn: Shot in lush colors by Ellis W. Carter amid the vivid red and orange buttes and mesas at Burro Flats in California's Simi Hills region, Selander forgets all about plot depth and goes all-out for repeated Redskin sorties, cramming in half-a-dozen Indian attacks led by Apache Chief Rasakura, taking place amid those sun-baked rocky ledges. In between the flying arrows and fusillade of bullets, crooner Jimmy Wakely warbles "The Weary Stranger," strumming on his battered guitar, while wily troublemaker Tudor Owen's freight wagons, overflowing with whiskey and repeating rifles, are attracting those whooping Pawnee and Apache savages like bees to a honeypot. Wise old scout Tom Tully knows who Hayden really is, but he's saying nothing, content to let the fighting "major" get the train out of a whole heap of Injun trouble which, in the end, he succeeds in doing after blowing up Owen's stock of carbines, the dealer in hard liquor and firearms falling to his death from a cliff, Tully's knife stuck in his chest (henchman Lee Van Cleef, in a brief appearance, is clubbed to death). With their prize destroyed, the Indians are repulsed yet again and retreat into the canyons; Hayden reveals his scam and true self, kissing Gray and escorted off to face trial and a light sentence.

A deafening score courtesy of Marlin Skiles adds weight to Selander's quick-fire pacing, making *Arrow in the Dust* a pretty decent B-Western of its type enlivened by several exhilarating shoot-outs, despite Hayden's unenthusiastic show hindering the narrative (his lifeless romance with Gray is perfunctory to say the least). The accusation is there—if only he could have sustained his watchable character interpretation that intrigued in the movie's introductory spell, it might have been a darn sight better than it turned out to be; as it stands, he lets the side down, a distinctly forced, strained and to his fans, odd star turn that jars.

Listed in the *1001 Movies You Must See Before You Die*; misunderstood by the critics; since lauded by film luminaries Martin Scorsese and François Truffaut; rated one of the 100 best American films of all time by *Chicago Reader*'s Jonathan Rosenbaum; and raking in a huge profit (for the period) of $2,500,000 for Republic Pictures: Nicholas Ray's feminist Western to beat all feminist Westerns, *Johnny Guitar* (1954), is a cinematic, and Western, one-off, 110 minutes (105 in the edited version) of sexual repression, personality ambiguities, lesbian undertones, Western B-clichés, plot subtexts, catfights, histrionics, digs at the Joseph McCarthy witch-hunts raging in Hollywood during the early 1950s, full-on violence and reverse gender roles, all wrapped up in Shakespearean-cum-Italian Grand Opera-style Freudian symbolism and acted by two leading ladies who positively despised one another. It could easily have been titled *The Battle of the Bitches*, such was the acrimonious relationship between one of Tinseltown's greatest of all divas, the legendary Joan Crawford (49), and fourth choice (behind Bette Davis, Barbara Stanwyck and Claire Trevor) Mercedes McCambridge (38). The claws came out when these two drink-loving harpies clashed, both on set and off, much to Ray's relish, the director capitalizing on the women's undisguised hatred of each other to boost the plot dynamics. Viewed today, *Johnny Guitar* is strangely reminiscent of an overheated Spaghetti Western, Crawford and McCambridge chewing the scenery to shreds. Boy, did that open hostility and ill-feeling manifest itself on the silver screen!

First, the crew: Multi-Oscar nominated Victor Young's melodic score (he won an Academy Award for *Around the World in Eighty Days*) is delightful, more suitable in a romantic drama (there's little romance in this film; what there is comes across as basic and verbally blunt), especially his leitmotifs when ex-lovers Crawford and Hayden are rekindling their passion; cinematographer Harry Stradling (two Oscars: *The Picture of Dorian Gray* and *My Fair Lady*, plus countless nominations) filled the screen with bright colors, filming taking place in Arizona's Red Rock Crossing region at Sedona; Ben Maddow contributed toward Philip Yordan's biting script, peppered with double meanings, but didn't receive a credit because of his communist blacklisting; and Peggy Lee sang the title song. As stated, McCambridge, battling alcoholism, was fourth choice to play Emma Small, while Crawford wanted either Paul Newman or Robert Mitchum in Sterling Hayden's role of Johnny "Guitar" Logan. Hayden later commented: "There is not enough money in Hollywood to lure me into making another picture with

Sterling strums and Joan Crawford glowers in *Johnny Guitar*.

Joan Crawford. And I like money," her tantrums just one more nail in the coffin, adding to his general disenchantment with the film business and all those in it. Ray shot some of McCambridge's scenes early morning at her insistence, enraging Crawford, who stormed into her rival's dressing room and slashed her wardrobe (Crawford was having an affair with Ray, thus fueling a certain amount of womanly jealousy). She then went on to scatter McCambridge's undamaged costumes all over Arizona's main highway. "A mean, tipsy, powerful, rotten-egg lady," ranted McCambridge after the shoot, claiming sometime afterward that Crawford, out of spite, had blocked any work coming her way for two years (she was the voice

Crawford eyes up Hayden in *Johnny Guitar*.

of the Demon in *The Exorcist*). "I have four children. I do not need a fifth," was Crawford's acid put-down. As for the press, they sharpened their knives. "A fiasco ... color is slightly awful ... Hayden is morose," said the *New York Times*. "Sexless," critic Bosley Crowther opined, *Variety* stating "it never has enough chance to rear up in the saddle and ride at an acceptable outdoor pace." On its 1975 reissue, the *New Yorker* called the film "A very rum Western with cockeyed feminist attitudes."

The movie itself? A cult classic of the very first order. Crawford (as Vienna, dressed from head to toe in black and sporting a gun belt, just like a bad guy) has built herself a saloon/casino in the back of beyond, counting on the new railroad bringing in customers and cash. When McCambridge's brother is killed in a stagecoach holdup, the neurotic cattle queen storms into Crawford's gaudy joint with unsmiling Ward Bond and his men during a sandstorm, accusing the hard-as-nails saloon queen of being behind the robbery ("A railroad tramp! We don't want you here!" she shrieks). Then Scott Brady (The Dancin' Kid) turns up with his three cohorts (Royal Dano, Ernest Borgnine and Ben Cooper) and *they're* roped into the blame game. Meanwhile, Hayden (first seen riding over hills being dynamited by construction teams) lounges at the dinner table minus his six-shooter (he's a gunslinger by trade), strumming a guitar and amusing himself by watching Crawford, a slash of crimson lipstick contrasting with her fine cheekbones and chalk-white cosmetics, go head-to-head with McCambridge, whose own face is contorted into an ugly mask of pure fury. Outlaw Brady is having an on/off fling with Crawford, thinks Hayden is a loser, then changes his mind when the 6-footer thrashes Borgnine in a fistfight. "The name's Johnny Guitar," says Hayden to Brady. "That's no name," sneers The Dancin' Kid. "Anybody care to change it?" counters Hayden, curtly. In the background, John Carradine is, or tries to be, a calming influence on an establishment packed to the crystal chandeliers with clientele all bordering on the edge of insanity.

Brady's cabin lies on a remote hill situated behind a waterfall; he's planning one more job to make up for the grief he's suffered by *not* being responsible for the stage robbery. In the nearby town, his gang relieves the bank of its takings but Brady allows Crawford to keep her money; McCambridge finds out and hits the roof, determined more than ever to hang Crawford from the nearest tree. After Crawford and Hayden decide to marry, the saloon boss, attired in a white dress (McCambridge is now clothed in black and has strapped on a pistol, a case of role reversal!), is waylaid alongside young Cooper (he's besotted with Crawford as well), the saloon burned to the ground by McCambridge and Bond's mob (also dressed in black!). Cooper is hanged, Hayden rescues Crawford from being strung up and the finale takes place in the vicinity of Brady's retreat. Bond's posse, led by snarling, psychotic McCambridge, collects in force at the foot of Brady's cabin. Hayden, now armed, pumps five slugs into Borgnine, the gap-toothed bully still smarting over losing out in that fistfight and having just stabbed consumptive Dano in the back to grab his share of the loot. "We've both done a lot of living," sighs Crawford, dazzling in black pants, canary-yellow blouse and scarlet neckerchief, to Hayden. "Our problem now is to do a little more." The climactic showdown between the two women sees McCambridge shooting Brady in the head (graphic for 1954) and winging Crawford, who dispatches her with a single bullet, McCambridge tumbling down the slope to her death. Now free, Crawford and Hayden embrace under the waterfall to the refrains of Victor Young's lovely music—yes, even that great film fantasist Jean Cocteau's presence can be felt in the closing stages of Nicholas Ray's flamboyantly bizarre, over-the-top, highly melodramatic, wickedly self-indulgent, grossly overacted, utterly compulsive homage to sexual angst and the female psyche triumphing over male machismo. It demands to be seen more than once, in fact several times, if only to confirm that what you sat through in the first place actually existed as a motion picture! Oh, and by the way—Sterling does okay, surmounting the trials and tribulations of working alongside volatile, self-obsessed "I want everything done *my* way" Crawford by presenting us with a hard-boiled character more right in the head than the rest of the cast put together.

It was back to normality for Hayden—but not for long. After scoring a hit as the sheriff in Lewis Allen's sniper *noir* thriller, *Suddenly* (United Artists, 1954) and appearing in two further successes, Universal's *Naked Alibi* (1954) and United

Artists' *Battle Taxi* (1955), he found himself dragged into Republic's *Timberjack* (1955) after John Wayne had turned down the role of logger Tim Chipman. The reason? Vera Ralston, Republic boss Herbert J. Yate's Czechoslovakian-born wife (he was 39 years her senior; she was 35 at the time of shooting, Yates 74). Ralston (née Vera Hrubá) had met Yates in 1943 when he signed her to a lucrative Republic contract, having become fixated with the ice-skating songstress, leaving his wife and children for her in 1948 (his vision was to transform Ralston into the next Sonja Henie, Hollywood's reigning ice-skating queen); they married in 1952. Ralston had co-starred opposite Wayne in *Dakota* (1945) but they hadn't got on; the Duke subsequently blamed her acting inexperience for the failure of 1949's *The Fighting Kentuckian* at the box-office and refused to work with her again. Hayden was hired on a whopping (and enticing) salary of $20,000 plus bonus if *Timberjack* came into profit (it did, even though the average Republic Western cost around $50,000 to produce) and Ralston kept on, enraging the company's shareholders who condemned Yates for being blinded by a talent his wife apparently didn't possess, and of throwing good money after bad (she was once nominated as The Worst Actress of All Time). But this was the woman who, at the Winter Olympic Games in 1936, had had the temerity to say to Adolf Hitler that "I wouldn't skate for the swastika. I would skate *on* the swastika." "The Führer," she later added, "was furious." So the girl had guts, if nothing else: In Joseph Kane's outdoors adventure, stunningly filmed around Western Montana's Glacier National Park, she does her best to be flirtatious, sexy and Marlene Dietrich-like, hampered by a thick accent and questionable ability. Against her, Hayden appears less bored and more patient than usual.

Thank goodness, then, for composer Victor Young's sweet-sounding soundtrack (the title theme is extremely hummable), four catchy songs (one sung by tunesmith Hoagy Carmichael to his pet dog), grim-faced thug David Brian stomping from one situation to the next, Adolphe Menjou's flowery language and Sterling looking fine and dandy in a check shirt. The story? Hayden travels to the Talka River Logging Company to uncover the truth behind his father's death, teaming up with old pal Chill Wills; Ralston is a singer at the Vermilion Belle, romanced by oily Brian; Hayden flies here, there and everywhere on a rail handcar, his crew felling trees on what Brian claims is his land; there are several punishing brawls, mostly involving bruiser Howard Petrie and his toughs, all wielding axe handles; Ralston abhors violence and can't make up her mind over Brian or Hayden as possible husbands, the pair now at loggerheads; Brian's offer of $100,000 to buy Hayden out is rejected; Brian accidentally kills Menjou, Ralston's father, so now has two deaths on his hands (he was responsible for murdering Hayden's father); Hayden commandeers one of Brian's locomotives to transport the logs to the lake ("I owe half of this line and it's legal."); Brian hires eight gunmen to put a stop to his rival's operations; and in a final shoot-out among the lofty firs, Brian is brought down, much to the relief of Ralston who now doesn't have to make a choice; in the last few minutes, she promptly marries Hayden.

Timberjack is entertainingly sturdy enough and glows in Republic's oft-used Trucolor process. The songs are melodious, a solid cast gives the somewhat mundane material their all and the forested mountain vistas are impressive. If you try to ignore the shenanigans behind the making of it, and Ralston's hammy performance, the movie is okay fare for a wet Saturday afternoon, not the greatest flick that Sterling took on, but nevertheless worth your while.

In *Shotgun*, Ben Thompson (Guy Prescott) rides into town with two cohorts; he's just been released from a six-year jail stretch and intends taking revenge on the two lawmen who put him behind bars, ex-gunslinger Clay (Sterling Hayden) and Fletcher (Lane Chandler). Armed with a sawn-off shotgun, he lets Fletcher have it with both barrels, almost cutting the marshal in half, and hightails it out, one gunman brought down by Clay. Ignoring the pleas of his fiancée, Clay arms himself with a similar shotgun and rides into the hills to mete out his own brand of justice on Thompson and his gang. En route, he comes across one outlaw staked out on the ground, a rattlesnake waiting to strike; tethered to a tree is Thompson's feisty woman, saloon goodtime gal Abby (Yvonne De Carlo). The half-dead outlaw (Robert J. Wilke) is cut free but, during a river crossing, shot by Clay after trying to outwit the marshal. Apaches are on a rampage, led by Chief Delgadito (Paul Marion), Thompson supplying the renegades with brand new Winchesters. Clay then rescues bounty hunter Reb Carlton (Zachary Scott) from a horde of Redskins and the three proceed on the trail to catch up with Thompson and his outfit, Reb for the reward, Clay for the anticipated pleasure of killing his enemy. Both men come to blows over the tomboy charms of Abby; meanwhile, Thompson's hombres have tied up the two men manning a stage relay station, waiting for Clay to appear. In a shoot-out, two hit the dust, with a little help from Reb. Clay chases after Thompson, leaving Abbey and Reb to set up camp where they're attacked by Indians. Reb is pinned to a tree in agony, an arrow through his chest, Abby abducted; Clay hands Reb his gun and the bounty hunter shoots himself. Clay rides into Delgadito's encampment and finds Abby there with Thompson. To determine who's the bravest, the pair have to duel with shotguns on horseback. Thompson blasts Clay's horse from under him, goes to gallop away but receives a lance in the back from the Apache chief for perceived cowardice. The Indians depart, leaving Clay and Abby to ride off to Calexico to plan a new life together on a ranch.

Allied Artists' *Shotgun* (1955) is a sparse, tense, character-driven Western reminiscent in some ways of Budd Boetticher's *Comanche Station* (Columbia, 1960); Randolph Scott could quite effortlessly have stepped straight into Hayden's size 12 boots. What the audience is presented with in Lesley Selander's bleak Boetticher-type scenario are two disparate groups trekking over unforgiving territory, one relentlessly pursuing the other, savage Indians lurking in the background an added threat, the dialogue (Rory Calhoun, Clarke E. Reynolds and John C. Champion) short and terse to match each person's mean attitude. And never has Arizona's Red Rock Crossing at Sedona been captured so magnificently on film (cinematographer: Ellsworth Fredericks): Selander's oater is a visual feast for the eyes, breathtaking vistas of mighty red mesas, towering rock faces and deep canyons that, in their own way, are as scenically splendid as anything John Ford conjured up in his John Wayne outings. *Shotgun* was also uncompromisingly brutal for its time: Hayden actually had to shoot a real rattler, not a model, and hated the scene; Wilke's body is pushed into a river and left to float downstream; there are two prolonged vicious fistfights, a feature in most of Sterling's Westerns, but far more overt here; Hayden's horse is hit by shotgun pellets in graphic close-up; and Scott's death is particularly harrowing. And in one short scene in the 49th minute, Selander throws in a nude shot of De Carlo reflected in the river. "What do you two think you're dividing? A sandwich?" spits De Carlo before her jealous rivals slug it out on a riverbank; after the fight, Scott wipes the blood from his battered face, snarling to De Carlo, about Hayden, "He's still more killer than lawman." The interplay between the trio, indeed from the whole cast, is faultless and *natural*: no forced playing here from these professionals, all of who were right at home in this kind of setup. Selander knew it and achieved minor miracles on low funds. From the opening view of Prescott's gang riding through that stunning Arizona wilderness to the closing seconds, Hayden, a lot slimmer and turning in a tough, gritty performance, cuddling up to wildcat De Carlo, *Shotgun* is a taut, underrated masterpiece of Western minimalism, deserving of re-evaluation, a tremendous '50s cowboy drama that pushes all the right buttons. Carl Brandt's vibrant score is also the icing on this riveting little Western's cake.

Next Western in line for Hayden after *The Last Command* (see chapter 11) was United Artists' *Top Gun* (1955). Any movie directed by Ray Nazarro was worth the price of a ticket, and this tidy, no-frills oater was no exception. Nazarro had worked with scriptwriter Richard Schayer on four separate occasions, all George Montgomery Westerns: *Indian Uprising* (Columbia, 1952), *Cripple Creek* (Columbia, 1952), *Gun Belt* (United Artists, 1953) and *The Lone Gun* (United Artists, 1954); their collaboration (Steve Fisher also co-wrote) produced *noir*-type Westerns of outstanding merit, made on low budgets. *Top Gun* (subsequently remade in 1960 as *Noose for a Gunman*, and in the Audie Murphy vehicle, *The Quick Gun*, 1964) kicks off with a lengthy rear shot, much favored by Nazarro, of Hayden (as Rick Martin) slowly riding into Casper, Wyoming. There, he stops at the cemetery, seeking four graves—his mother's and the three Calton brothers, who he shot down in a gunfight. Next to his mother's grave, an empty hole,

Hayden and Regis Toomey take cover in *Top Gun*.

reserved for him. Hayden's a feared gunman and the town doesn't want his menacing presence or his double holsters anywhere on the streets, except for "trigger happy young squirt" Rod Taylor, on the prod and dying to beat the gunslinger to the draw ("The big man's yellow," he sneers). Hayden, a troubleshooter paid to sort out other people's problems at gunpoint, has an ally in hotelier Regis Toomey and has arrived in Casper to inform Marshal James Millican that outlaw John Dehner, with his gang of 15 thugs, is due to ride into town the next day to take control of the place. They're not interested in money; their reputation is such that no town will let them enter to spend it. No, what Dehner and this vicious bunch of no-goods are after is liquor, victuals and women. Hayden's ex, Karin Booth, is due to marry Casper's local land-grabbing rat, William Bishop, the louse responsible for the death of Hayden's mother in a crooked property transaction. When Millican attempts to form a posse to combat the threat of Dehner, the citizens back off, Millican forced to consider asking Hayden, and his guns, for help in boosting his squad of four.

High Noon-ish in concept (the lone lawman versus a pack of polecats bent on mayhem), Nazarro's pared-to-the-bone oater crackles with pithy dialogue. "He looks like a big easy target to me," smirks Taylor, dressed in black, anxious to goad Hayden into a shoot-out. "You'll live by the gun and die by the gun," says Booth to her former lover, who challenges Bishop over his Ma's demise: "I be-

Hayden slugs William Bishop in *Top Gun*.

lieve you killed her. You're gonna pay." Bishop then coerces Taylor into facing up to Hayden, taunting him with the promise of, "I'll set him up for you. Then you'll be top gun." "Get off your horse and draw," barks Taylor to Hayden on the outskirts of town, falling to the gunman's bullet. Hayden is arrested but released when Dehner's raiders, after killing Millican and losing nine men themselves, storm into Casper, the women, children and cowardly menfolk seeking sanctuary in the church. Nazarro then winds up the action with some nifty gunplay: Hayden, made town marshal, sits down with Dehner and thrashes out a deal—help yourself to $50,000 stashed in the hotel and quit Casper. The ruse works; he waylays Dehner's boys in the hotel, shoots them one by one and has a standoff with the unkempt outlaw boss ("May you live until I kill ya," growls Dehner to his nemesis). Bishop sneaks up behind Hayden, pointing a pistol; as Dehner is dropped, Booth blasts Bishop in the back with a rifle. Hayden and Booth ride off together the next day, despite entreaties from the council to stay put and take up the position of Casper's marshal; after all, why should Hayden want to take charge of a town full of spineless specimens after what he's just been through? Another lean, mean '50s Western from the prolific Nazarro, Irving Gertz's thumping score, together with Lester White's stark black-and-white photography, adding to the picture's simplistic, grubby, cold-hearted mood—and Sterling shines as the monosyllabic, tight-lipped gun hawk who won't let anyone push him around.

CHAPTER 9

CALHOUN: GOOD-LOOKER WITH A GUN—THE CLASSIC "Bs" 1954-1958

Now on $8,000 a week (good, but not when you consider that the average shooting schedule for a '50s B-Western was three to four weeks—between movies, many lesser stars were not salaried, paid only when working), Calhoun supplemented his income by using his skills as an electrician, carpenter and plumber to save on the household budget; according to wife Lita, he was notoriously miserly when it came to spending cash on items for the home. Freelancing after leaving Fox, Rory would embark on 12 essential B-Westerns up to 1958 (plus *The Spoilers*, not so essential), establishing himself alongside the likes of Audie Murphy, George Montgomery and Rod Cameron as one of the medium-budget horse opera's most reliable leading men, his movies all making a profit, whether they were support features or not. United Artists' star-studded *The Yellow Tomahawk* (1954) kickstarted this productive period, a long way off from the big-money trappings he was used to in his days spent on the Fox backlot: Now we were getting down to nitty-gritty basics, reflected in Lesley Selander's steely, and at times quite violent, Western set amid Utah's rugged Kanab region (Selander, a master at handling low-budget Westerns, had also directed a fistful of essential oaters starring Randolph Scott, Montgomery, Murphy and Cameron). Unfortunately, the picture, originally released in color, is only available (as of 2016) in black-and-white—a color restoration job on this vital, bleak little actioner is urgently needed.

Calhoun, in buckskin jacket, played scout Adam Reed, a friend of Cheyenne chief Lee Van Cleef (Fire Knife). Holed up in the Wyoming mountains with his braves, hatchet-faced Van Cleef simmers and stews, nursing feelings of hatred toward the Bluecoats, busy erecting a frontier post in a nearby valley under the command of Major Warner Anderson. Van Cleef hasn't forgotten the Sand Creek Massacre of 1864 and holds Anderson, named by the Indians "The Butcher," responsible. By building a fort, Van Cleef reckons the whites are breaking the current peace treaty, so Calhoun, after a meeting with the hostiles, rides down into bad medicine territory to sort matters out and prevent a possible recurrence of hostilities, especially as the chief is on the brink of forming a war party in reprisal for all the wrongdoings meted out to his tribe; to ram home the point, Rory buries a yellow tomahawk in Anderson's shiny desk, a sign that the Cheyenne are on the verge of war, treaty or no treaty. For the first 30 minutes or so, Selander's oater is leisurely paced, introducing the audience to a wealth of characters that will all figure in the action to come: Anderson's martinet of an officer, bent on "eradicating the savage."; likeable womanizer Noah Beery, Jr. and his lovesick Indian girlfriend, Rita Moreno (as Honey Bear); Peggie Castle, engaged to a lieutenant but falling under the spell of Calhoun's twinkling blue eyes; and devious Peter Graves, who has murdered two partners in his greed for gold, blaming it on the Redskins and hiding the precious dust in his saddlebags. Smoke signals are spotted high on the horizon, an attack seems imminent, the women are given the opportunity to take a wagon to Oregon, Anderson and a platoon ride up into the hills to retrieve buried ammunition boxes (they're empty, replaced by tomahawks) and at the 36th minute, all hell breaks loose. The resulting graphic five-minute massacre, backed by Les Baxter's thundering score, is strong meat for 1954, men, women and even children hit with arrows, lances and bullets, and hacked to death by tomahawks, bringing to mind the similar infamous sequence in Ralph Nelson's controversial *Soldier Blue*, made 16 years later. Van Cleef prevents a brave from scalping Calhoun's unruly mop, his only concession to mercy. "You got your massacre," Calhoun snarls to Anderson who returns to a scene of total devastation, more concerned over the state of his ripped-up wardrobe than the scores of corpses littering the compound. The survivors then make tracks for Fort Ellis and safety, meaning a tense trek over rocky terrain where the disparate group encounters Van Cleef and his warriors, determined to wipe them out to the last man.

The drama escalates when, at a powwow with Calhoun, Van Cleef agrees to let the group go free on condition that they leave them The Butcher to be dealt with, Cheyenne fashion. Although Calhoun detests Anderson and his Indian-baiting beliefs, he refuses to go along with his old friend's offer, leading to a series of taut skirmishes in which Van Cleef is the only Cheyenne left alive. Setting a trap with a quiver, Calhoun fires an arrow into the chief's chest without any feelings of remorse, enabling the remaining stragglers to reach Fort Ellis. For saving his life, Beery, Jr. realizes that Moreno (she plunged a dagger into a marauding brave) is the girl for him, the pair riding off to Mexico. Castle hitches her skirts to Calhoun (they've spent a night of lust up in the hills) and the scout walks into the major's office to give evidence against unhinged Anderson; he turns out to have Cheyenne blood coursing through his veins, a secret he kept from the authorities—"You slaughtered the Cheyenne to kill the past," states Calhoun as the door closes and the trial begins.

"Don't run. There's no place to run to," says Calhoun to cowardly Graves as the arrows fly, adding weight to Richard Alan Simmons' succinct script dealing with the old "Indian problem," and seemingly all at ease in the kind of medium-budget setup that probably best suited his marginal virtuosity. *The Yellow Tomahawk*, acted with conviction by the entire cast, boded well for future Calhoun offerings out West in its minimal, hard-hitting approach, the kind of material that Anthony Mann might have considered, using James Stewart in the lead role; there's not an ounce of flab in this riveting Western that, as stated, warrants a digitally restored release in color to appease Western addicts everywhere.

Dawn at Socorro (1954), directed by George Sherman on a budget of $500,000 (the veteran knocked out over 60 Westerns in his long career, mostly "Bs") was the first of five compelling (and one not so compelling) Universal-International Westerns Calhoun starred in up to the end of the 1950s and remains a superlative genre example. Gaining a bit of weight for the role, his dark hair tinged gray at the sides to make him appear older than his 32 years, Calhoun played cold-hearted gambler/gunslinger/classical pianist Brett Wade, a Doc Holliday-type figure suffering from tuberculosis, forever coughing into a white cloth, a result of an old bullet wound inflaming his lungs. A psychological, almost *noir*-ish, scenario containing deep, rich Technicolor photography (Carl E. Guthrie) and a biting script (George Zuckerman), *Dawn at Socorro* showcased not only a strong cast of stalwarts—David Brian, Piper Laurie, Kathleen Hughes, Mara Corday, Edgar Buchanan, Alex Nicol, Skip Homeier, Roy Roberts, James Millican and Lee Van Cleef, among others—but saw Calhoun getting his teeth into the part and making a decent fist of it. It proved that Rory was not just a pretty face—he could act as well; the film is a reminder of just how good he could be.

A wooden sign at the beginning details the infamous shooting at Keane's Stockyard in 1871 and we flash back to that year, the Ferris gang terrorizing Lordsburg and rudely interrupting Calhoun's game of stud poker. In a tense fracas with the rowdy saddle bums, Skip Homeier, the youngest Ferris sibling, is shot dead, leading to the stockyard clash at sunup, three (two law officers plus Rory) against three (shades of *Gunfight at the O.K. Corral* here); two Ferris boys bite the dust, Lee Van Cleef fleeing for his life. The shoot-out is witnessed by Piper Laurie, on her way to Socorro to take up the job of saloon girl in smarmy David Brian's casino; she's been thrown out of her home, classed as a jezebel by her puritanical father (why is never really made clear, although she states that she was accused of bedding all the ranch hands). On the stage to Socorro, Calhoun gets acquainted with the solemn-looking lass, gunslinger Alex Nicol itching to put a bullet in the gambler; Van Cleef, pursuing the stage and bent on blasting Calhoun, is gunned down at a relay station. Arriving in Socorro, Calhoun decides not to take the train to Colorado Springs to recuperate as advised by his doctor; Laurie has aroused his interest, so he stays put, much to the consternation of Sheriff Edgar Buchanan who sees trouble brewing on the horizon, and he's right to be worried, what with Calhoun and Nicol watching each other's backs and Brian wanting rid of the card sharp, seeing him as a threat to his own designs on Laurie.

A great deal of Sherman's well-crafted feature takes place in saloons and casinos (artfully lit in dark browns and reds), but this does nothing to detract from the personal dramas taking place, the director shooting in close-up, *noir*-style, to heighten each character's innermost feelings and agendas. Calhoun, like most gunmen, yearns for a peaceful life, preferably with Laurie, but will his violent past let him go? Predatory Brian also desires Laurie (lovely in a red costume)

Piper Laurie succumbs to Rory's charms in *Dawn at Socorro*.

and won't release his hold on her in a hurry. The tense interaction between the main protagonists culminates in a mammoth nighttime game of two-card stud, Calhoun betting his takings against Brian's casino; if he loses, he'll catch that dawn train to Colorado Springs: "If you lose, you leave town—without her," growls the casino boss. The cards don't fall right for Calhoun; punching Brian to the ground as a farewell gift, he waits for the train, unaware that Brian is willing to give Nicol $5,000 to kill him. Calhoun isn't wearing a gun; a citizen hands him a gun belt, asking "Who's comin' after you?" "My past," Calhoun replies. "Every darned miserable day of it." The resulting explosive showdown, watched by twitchy Buchanan, concerned Laurie, smiling Brian, decorative saloon dames Mara Corday and Kathleen Hughes, plus the entire town, is worthy of inclusion in a Sergio Leone 1960s Spaghetti Western: Sherman focuses on hands hovering over gun butts as Calhoun and Nicol close in on the street; there's the sound of a train whistle, the two reach for their shooting irons and Nicol hits the dirt. It doesn't end there; a few of the townsfolk start firing; Calhoun gets two and puts a well-earned slug into Brian for good measure. Handing his weapon to Buchanan who's mighty relieved that it's all over, Calhoun finally boards that train, Laurie by his side, giving him his alcohol-based medicine, the fitting climax to a top-flight oater given a great deal of thought and attention by all involved; essential Western viewing. Even the critics were kind: "Sleek and efficient … thoroughly satisfying," crowed the *New York Times*, *Variety* chipping in with "a handsome production."

Calhoun rounded off a tremendously rewarding 1954 with his second Universal trail buster of the year, Richard Carlson's *Four Guns to the Border*, based on a Louis L'Amour story. Sex reared its ugly head in George Van Marter and Franklin Coen's taut screenplay in the shape of coltish Colleen Miller, blossoming from tomboy to woman under the rough tutorship of tight-lipped gunslinger Calhoun (as Cully). Calhoun (wearing his customary black hat) and his gang (John McIntire, George Nader and Jay Silverheels) are planning to rob the bank in Cholla ("A big bank—and a big cemetery!"), the black-clad leader also out to settle an old score with Charles Drake, Cholla's sheriff; the two were once partners but fell out years ago over the charms of Nina Foch, now Drake's wife. The scenario is further complicated by Apaches lurking in the surrounding hills and the arrival at Nestor Paiva's desert store, La Tienda, of retired gunman Walter Brennan and his willful daughter, Miller. During a nighttime thunderstorm, the rain hammering down, Miller creeps outside in the wet and unleashes her pent-up lust on Calhoun, a man of very few words, in a scene of uninhibited passion that, for the year, is pretty explicit (as is Miller seductively licking a stick of candy). But surly Brennan's having none of it, threatening to kill Calhoun stone cold dead if he ever dares to lay a finger on Miller again. "You don't want a gunslinger," he warns her as they ride off into the wilderness. "My mother married one," is her tart riposte.

Meanwhile, dark-haired, black-jacketed Calhoun rides into Cholla to slug it out with fair-haired, brown-jacketed Drake (emphasizing the good versus evil aspect of the tale), a cunning diversionary tactic: McIntire, Nader and Silverheels sneak in behind everyone's back, relieving the bank's safe of its takings while the whole population is watching the bruising fistfight (broken up by Foch with a riding crop). The four outlaws hightail it out of town, followed by Drake and his posse; Paiva's store is found burned to the ground, his body lying in the embers under an Apache corpse, a cat and her kittens the sole survivors, a tender touch amid all the machismo

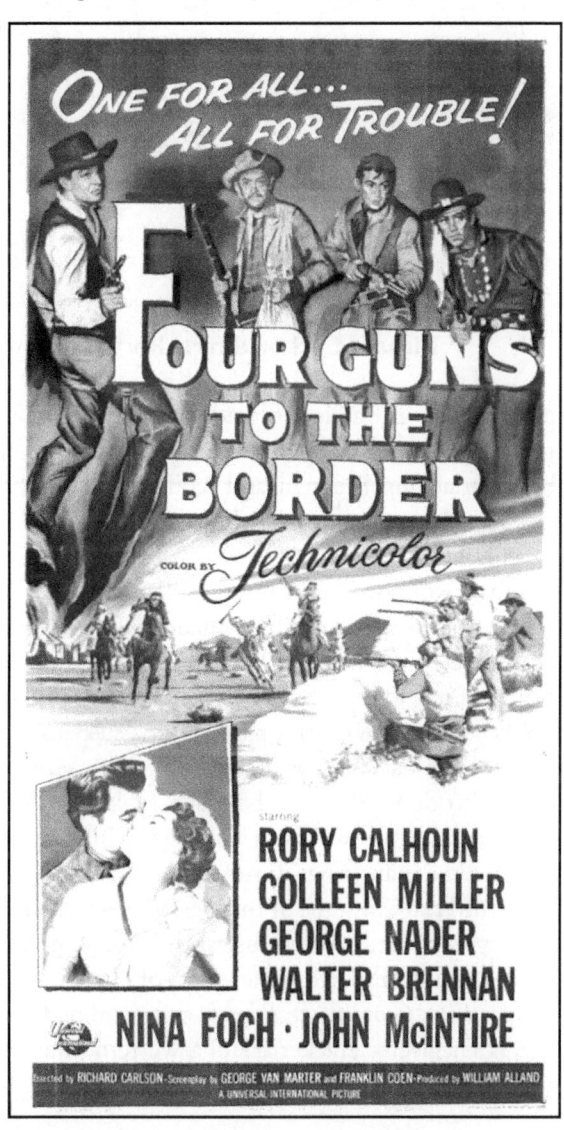

The Westerns of Calhoun, Cameron, Hayden and Widmark

Richard Carlson directs Rory Calhoun and Colleen Miller.

taking place. The action, filmed in California's boulder-strewn Apple Valley (photography: Russell Metty), steps up a pace (not that it needed to), the Apache bucks attacking Brennan and Miller, Calhoun and company charging to their rescue, a fierce shoot-out orchestrated with dash by Carlson (famous for playing Doctor David Reed in *Creature from the Black Lagoon*) which leaves Calhoun seriously wounded and his gang members dead. Against Brennan's wishes, Calhoun is taken to his ranch in Shadow Valley, Miller determined that the taciturn gunslinger is the man for her, dressing his bullet wound and trying to convince Calhoun not to leave before he's mended. Brennan rides to town to get a doctor, Drake and his boys turn up and after a suspenseful face-off, Calhoun, wincing in pain, calls a halt just as Drake goes for his gun. "Alright Jim, I'm whipped. But you didn't do it. She did," he gasps, looking at Miller. Patched up and recovered, he's escorted to town for a fair trial, Miller knowing that at long last, she has grabbed the man of her dreams.

Universal Westerns of this period were the business, in direction, acting, cinematography and score (musical director Joseph Gershenson cobbled together a raucous soundtrack from the works of Hans J. Salter, Frank Skinner and Herman Stein): *Four Guns to the Border*, a streamlined example from the genre's golden age, is a neglected crackerjack of a Western, showing Rory Calhoun maturing into the kind of role he was perhaps destined to play, that of the bad boy come good.

Carrying the weight of the world on his beefy shoulders (the Calhoun torso is on full display near the end) and rarely smiling (but smoking incessantly), he holds the attention in a picture brimming with telling performances and exciting set pieces, 83 minutes of pure Western joy; they knew how to pack it all in under 90 minutes and make it work in those days, as this compact, spiffy actioner, encapsulating all the ideals present in the archetypal '50s Western, proves.

In 1955, Rory's personal life came under the spotlight in the Hollywood gossip columns: His agent, Henry Willson, became aware that *Confidential* magazine was about to print an exposé on the secret gay lifestyle of Rock Hudson, another of Willson's clients, which would have caused a scandal and perhaps torpedoed Hudson's future movie prospects. Willson negotiated with the taboo-busting tabloid, giving them information about Calhoun's early criminal activities and time spent behind bars on condition they dropped the damaging article on Hudson. The deal was made, the disclosure on Calhoun's delinquent years published, but this had no adverse effect whatsoever on his film career or how the public perceived him as a movie celebrity; all the article did was to further promote the actor's "bad boy" image and make him even more popular, especially in the eyes of his adoring female fans.

It was also in 1955 that he had his first stab at film writing, contributing toward the screenplay of Allied Artists' *Shotgun* alongside Clarke E. Reynolds and John C. Champion. Calhoun was to have starred in the picture but changed his mind at the last moment, the lead role going to Sterling Hayden (see chapter eight).

Those adoring female fans weren't to be disappointed with RKO-Radio's *The Treasure of Pancho Villa* (1955), made on a near-two million dollar budget in Mexico and shot in SuperScope, William E. Snyder's vivid photography capturing the harsh, rocky landscapes of Mexico's Morelos area. Set in 1915 during the Mexican Revolution, Calhoun (as Tom Bryan) exuded tough,

Calhoun wields "La Cucaracha" in *The Treasure of Pancho Villa*.

Publicity shot of Calhoun and Gilbert Roland

sweaty masculinity, a mercenary carting around his own Lewis machine gun, named "La Cucaracha," and falling in with old partner-in-crime Gilbert Roland, busy planning to raid a train carrying gold bullion ("One last job, gringo."), the spoils going to help the cause of deposed dictator Pancho Villa. At first, Calhoun is firmly against the idea; he's sick of being a hired gun, yearning for women, men's perfume and the good life. But he joins Roland's confederates for the buzz, along with righteous teacher Shelley Winters; the lady is prepared to get her manicured hands dirty in the name of idealism, even if it means firing a rifle in times of trouble.

After a slow talkative start, director George Sherman ups the pace with an explosive attack on two locomotives steaming over a bridge; the gold is snatched after a lead-filled exchange and slung on the backs of 20 mules, Gilbert making tracks for Villa's hideout and having to pass through mountainous Yaqui Indian territory to reach their goal. People's motives come under close scrutiny: Gilbert trusts no one, convinced that Calhoun wants the gold for himself (he does manage to pocket one coin); two-timing Joseph Calleia (a standout performance) also desires to divide the riches between himself and his men, thinking the revolution all washed up; and Winters, somewhat out of place in this all-male setup, fancies Calhoun but not his money-grabbing ethics ("You're so hard-boiled," she tells him before he treats her to a trademark violent Calhoun smackeroo). The movie becomes a long hard ride for survival, mistrust rampant among the ranks, with intermittent bursts of gunplay when the military catches up, Calhoun creating havoc with his lethal weapon. Finally, the outfit splits; Winters, declaring her love for Calhoun, is packed off to safer climes while Calleia, siding with the soldiers, attempts to claim the gold as his own—he's shot dead by Roland for his treason to the Villa regime. Alone on a ridge, the gold stacked beneath them, Calhoun and Roland battle it out with the militia: Gilbert is hit in the face by a bullet and expires; Calhoun presses a charger and dynamites a cliff face, the gold and soldiers buried under tons of rock. Marking his friend's grave with the cross-like detonator handle, Calhoun wanders off to an uncertain future.

If you can turn a blind eye to that anachronistic Coca-Cola sign on display in the opening reel (although invented in 1886, the Coke sign seems more 1950s than 1915), *The Treasure of Pancho Villa* is a one heck of a thrill-ride, rough around the edges maybe and ably boosted by Leith Stevens' noisy score. It looks hot, dusty and arid (Roland admitted it was an uncomfortable shoot) and, in some instances, is clumsily handled by Sherman, but the authentic, sun-scorched backdrops, together with Calhoun and Roland's villainous double-act, make it a worthwhile trip into another, seldom-filmed locale, perfect fodder for Western buffs needing something slightly different on their menu. "Colorful photography," wrote *The Hollywood Reporter*, the *New York Times* adding that Calhoun had "swagger" in the lead role.

Rory's next, Universal's disappointing *The Spoilers* (1955), came in on a budget of $800,000, made over a million dollars profit in America alone, had the actor on $10,000 per week and starred Anne Baxter, Jeff Chandler, John McIntire and character actor Wallace Ford, who had been knocking around in the film industry since 1929. Yet this fifth version of the old Rex Beach novel, a rehash of the Marlene Dietrich/John Wayne/Randolph Scott 1942 vehicle, was a tired-looking, long-winded effort devoid of any real excitement and screen chemistry between the three lead players. By now, the story was old-hat: Baxter was Cherry, the hard-to-get saloon tart with a heart of gold ("There'll be no brawls here, gentlemen, unless they're over me."), Chandler her poker-faced on/off beau, owner of the Miter Mine; Calhoun, looking flashy but empty, played crafty Alex McNamara, the corrupt

Calhoun, Jeff Chandler and Barbara Britton in *The Spoliers*

Anne Baxter commiserates with Jeff Chandler in *The Spoilers*.

gold commissioner, busy challenging the legalities of miners' claims in Nome, Alaska, 1899 and wooing Baxter; and Barbara Britton turned up as an ice-cool blonde, Calhoun's second-in-command. The inclusion of double-crossing croupier Ray Danton, his crippled left hand hidden in a black glove and nursing an almighty crush on Baxter, did little to relieve the tedium as Chandler sets about reclaiming his mine from Calhoun, retrieving $80,000 of stolen gold locked in a safe, rekindling his romance with the glamorous dame and undoing Calhoun's shady practices, the smartly dressed dude in cahoots with crooked lawyer Carl Benton Reid.

A weak stock Universal score, muddy Alaskan streets, a poorly executed locomotive pileup, a few bouts of desultory gunplay, dancing gals strutting their stuff, grizzled old-timers John McIntire and Ford trying to outdo each other in the curmudgeonly stakes and saloon owner Baxter dressed up to the nines, overacting like crazy and flashing her bosom and legs in a futile attempt to add some spark—*The Spoilers*, more '40s than '50s in outlook, is adequate but forgettable. Director Jesse Hibbs keeps his foot on the brake pedal, not letting loose until the four-minute, climactic saloon-wrecking punch-up between Chandler and Calhoun, orchestrated with verve but coming far too late in an 84-minute Western that would have led to fidgeting bums on seats, even among diehards. Universal had scored a huge hit with their remake of 1939's *Destry* in 1954, Audie Murphy starring in the lead; their latest revamp of a former renowned Western just didn't pull it off and wasn't in the same league. The *New York Times* wondered whether "we will have to go through all this again—in 1965." They needn't have worried—we didn't!

It was back to slam-bang form in Jack Arnold's *Red Sundown* (Universal, 1956), a humdinger of a Western coming between two of the director's most famous horror/sci-fi movies, *Tarantula* (1955) and *The Incredible Shrinking Man* (1957). It marked the screen debut of 24-year-old Grant Williams, who went on to star as Scott Carey in *Shrinking Man* and was also the final appearance of Western heavy James Millican; he died of cancer aged 45 shortly before the film's release. Also in the production was Calhoun's wife, Lita Baron, no doubt wondering whether her tasty husband could manage to keep his wandering hands off blonde Martha Hyer. Arnold was responsible for one of Audie Murphy's most notable Westerns, *No Name on the Bullet* (1959), and admirably demonstrated his spare, economical style in *Red Sundown,* creating the ideal vehicle for Calhoun, the actor now on a Western roll: Universal utilized him the same way they did with Murphy, placing him in a series of B-oaters surrounded by solid co-stars and directed by men of no mean talent. The man was simply getting better and better.

Terry Gilkyson's plaintive tune, "Red Sundown," bookends a picture boosted by a bombastic Hans J. Salter soundtrack, Calhoun, playing gunslinger Alec Longmire, seen riding alone on the wide parched prairie, a lyrical image from

RED SUNDOWN TECHNICOLOR

Starring
Rory CALHOUN
Martha HYER
Dean JAGGER

ROBERT MIDDLETON
JAMES MILLICAN
LITA BARON
GRANT WILLIAMS

Arnold that was used to introduce Audie Murphy's avenging gunslinger in *No Name on the Bullet*. Calhoun's credentials are established in the first 15 minutes: He picks up horseless outlaw James Millican, takes him into town, slugs screen bruiser Leo Gordon in a saloon and pinches one of his horses, the pair riding off, pursued by Gordon's gang. Bunking down for the night in a deserted shack, the two reflect on the role of gunfighters and how little in the way of money and personal worth the whole business brings to their lives; Millican gives Calhoun his signet ring as a sign of respect, bonding with his new buddy ("This is all I got left for being a big man."). During the night, Gordon's men surround the shack, set fire to it and plug Millican in a hail of bullets. Calhoun, concealed in a shallow grave, emerges at dawn, dusts himself down and gallops into Durango, the scene set for part two of this taut-as-a-bowstring drama.

Durango is in the middle of a range war. Cattle baron Robert Middleton, owner of the Triple X Ranch, is erecting fences around his property, edging out rival local ranchers objecting to his bullying tactics. Sheriff Dean Jagger can't cope with all the trouble brewing—he pins a badge on Calhoun despite his notoriety, the new deputy quickly making his presence felt by ordering Trevor Bardette's cowhands at gunpoint to back off from stealing Middleton's wagon-loads of wire, even if he disagrees with the burly rancher's underhand methods. His prowess with his twin pistols (the left has its butt facing outwards) promotes him to folk hero status in the eyes of two adoring youngsters, the street urchins sticking to his boot heels like flies ("He walks like a cat. He's plenty fast!"). But deep inside his soul, Calhoun wants to quit being a gun hawk and settle down. Is Martha Hyer, Jagger's daughter, the one to settle down with, even though she despises men who make a living out of killing? And what about Lita Baron (Mrs. Rory Calhoun), an ex-love and currently Middleton's mistress.

A catalyst arrives in the form of hired gun Grant Williams (Chet Swann), taken on by Middleton to cause maximum damage after Calhoun has rejected a similar job offer from the rancher. Williams, in his movie debut, brilliantly plays Swann to the hilt, a deranged, trigger-happy psycho first seen smashing up Bardette's home and telling him and his terrified wife to get outta town in 24 hours. Jagger hasn't a hope in hell of stopping this blond-haired loose cannon: "If you shoot it out with Swann, you're dead," Calhoun yells at him; his point-blank advice is for Jagger to disable Williams in both legs with a shotgun, fired from a rooftop. In a tense standoff, Calhoun the ex-gunslinger faces Williams the young gunslinger, shotgun aimed at eye level: "Chet Swann! Get outta town! Mount up before I blast you all over the street!" he shouts, Williams reluctantly retreating but promising to return. He does, following a savage saloon fistfight between Calhoun and Middleton ("Triple X will be fencing tomorrow. Interference will be met by gunfire," Middleton brags to the townsfolk), which sees the cattle boss behind bars. Next morning, Jagger bravely squares up to Williams; his gun is shot from his hand, leaving it to Calhoun to take on the role of town tamer and stalk the killer kid through stables, finishing him with a single bullet. Job done, Calhoun hands in his badge, promising Hyer he'll be back when he's sorted out proper (and lawful) employment, riding off into the distance, Gilkyson's melodic theme song reprised once more, a reformed character all alone with his thoughts and plans for the future, with or without Jagger's daughter.

Red Sundown is a standout Western from the Universal-International stable, with Calhoun, still only 34, at the top of his game. It was quickly followed by *Raw Edge* (Universal, 1956), whose bizarre plot centered on one thing above everything else—sex! According to Harry Essex and Robert Hill's heated screenplay, in Oregon, 1842, magnate Herbert Rudley (Gerald Montgomery) has laid down a law, the Law of the Strongest, decreeing that it's a case of "first come, first served" as regards to any unattached female looking, or *not* looking, for a suitable husband ("An unholy doctrine," says the local padre. "Might is never right."). When John Gavin (his screen debut) defies Rudley's puritanical beliefs, he's strung up, wrongly accused of attacking and almost raping Rudley's wife, Yvonne De Carlo, in a barn. Indian lass Mara Corday finds herself a widow and, even worse, has to face a lineup of the West's most plug-ugly suitors, eagerly waiting for a chance to jump into her still-warm bed: Neville Brand, Robert J. Wilke, Ed Fury (future star of Italian peplum; he played *Ursus* in 1961), Gregg Barton and Emile Meyer, mugs more at home on wanted posters than in a lady's boudoir, enough to send Corday galloping like the wind to her Indian lodge in the hills. Wilke ("She's free!

Rory tends to Yvonne De Carlo in *Raw Edge*.

She's mine!") is the lucky man (Corday the unlucky woman), whisking her off to her cabin to force his unwholesome attentions on the girl.

In the 16th minute, tough hombre Calhoun (Tex Kirby) rides into town, a (yes, you've guessed it) notorious ex-Texas Ranger gunslinger and Gavin's brother, determined to mete justice (*his* justice) on those responsible for his brother's brutal demise, having just visited Gavin's smashed-up homestead and seen his hanging body. In one fraught, melodramatic situation after another, Meyer and Brand (father and son) decide to overthrow Rudley's domain, both jealous of the man's success and each having designs on desirable De Carlo; Calhoun becomes involved with De Carlo (the two had a brief liaison at the time); Brand has a rough 'n' tumble with De Carlo in a mountain stream, both toppling over a waterfall; Corday's Indian pals snatch Rudley, delivering his mutilated corpse to the Montgomery Ranch; lecherous Brand, the real culprit who attempted to rape De Carlo, sets his sights on her as *she's* now a widow, shooting rival Meyer, his own father, in the back in a set-to at the ranch, and blasting smooth operator/gambler Rex Reason, also present; and following a vicious punch-up between Calhoun and Brand (two-fisted action scenes in Calhoun's Westerns were always a darned sight more in-your-face than in other oaters), Brand falls onto a cow horn, skewered to death. Come dawn, Calhoun hitches up with besotted De Carlo, the two riding off to San Antonio to play house, on set and off it.

An unusually violent and sexist Western for the time, *Raw Edge* presented women as chattel, there for man's pleasure and nothing else, a rather bleak premise focusing on the darker nature of the male psyche; there's little emotional depth involved between the dysfunctional characters, only when De Carlo shows obvious relief when deadpan Calhoun invites her to join him at the end. But it's organized with panache by Universal second unit director John Sherwood, the first of only three features he would make, the other two being *The Creature Walks Among Us* (1956) and *The Monolith Monsters* (1957); Maury Gertsman's gorgeous Technicolor photography is a delight, as are the wooded Californian San Bernardino National Forest locations. A Western Shakespearean-style offering, somewhat unpleasant at times, *Raw Edge* is something of a once-only affair, Terry Gilkyson's warbling of the tuneful title theme at odds with the movie's sexier, racier content.

From medium-budget Universal oaters to a low-budget Columbia oater—*Utah Blaine* was a typical "King of the Quickies" Sam Katzman-produced B-feature of the day, made in black-and-white for around $200,000 and released in early 1957. But it had verve, dash and style, thanks to Fred F. Sears' greased-lightning direction and professional gunslinger Calhoun, striding through the pulse-racing action with a three-day growth of beard, twin guns smoking like crazy (he wore the same gun belt that he had sported in *Red Sundown*). If *Utah Blaine* sounded odd as a title, the rest of the character's names were just as bizarre: Gus Ortmann, Rip Coker, Rink Witter, Russ Nevers and Lud Fuller. Robert E. Kent's screenplay, adapted from a Louis L'Amour story (as many a '50s Western was), concentrated on bully-boy Ray Teal's underhand efforts to lay his thieving hands on two profitable ranches, the 46-Connected (30,000 head of prime beef) and the Bar-B, run by Susan Cummings and Angela Stevens. Both girls' fathers have recently been murdered by Teal's land-grabbing range wolves, led by Steve Darrell and gunman George Keymas, although at the start, Calhoun (as Utah Blaine, fresh out of Mexico after having played a key role in a revolution) saves Ken Christy, dual owner of the 46-Connected, from throttling at the end of a rope; Christy, in gratitude, tells the stranger to report to his partner and, as a reward, to be given the job of ranch foreman plus the promise of 1,000 head of cattle if he puts a stop to Teal's reign of terror; Christy is later found dead, shot by Keymas.

A plethora of incidents and chases tends to overwhelm the senses at times, but basically, the plot boils down to one thing—Calhoun, shotgun-toting buddy Paul Langton and ex-heavyweight boxing champion Max Baer, plus the two women, determined to end Teal's despotic rule by enlisting the aid of the downtrodden citizens of Red Creek in exposing the tyrant for what he is. In between umpteen bouts of hard riding, fistfighting and gunfire (Keymas, like Calhoun, wears a double holster), busty, leather-clad Cummings goes all weak at the knees every time Rory strolls into her room, panting with desire (yet another female who despises Calhoun for being a hired gun, but can't resist those dark good looks), while man-giant Baer, wounded, lies up in her basement (he gets shot in the face), Langton longing to put his treasured shotgun to good use, lovingly caressing both barrels. When it becomes clear to everyone that Christy legally left half his ranch to Calhoun for saving his life, Teal rounds up all available guns for a climactic showdown in Red Creek. In town, Calhoun and Langton inform Teal that they have already recruited 50 new ranch hands, a ruse; seething at seeing his twin prizes slipping through his fingers, Teal prepares to order his self-proclaimed vigilantes to open fire but finds himself boxed in, the townsfolk poised with rifles on the rooftops. In the ensuing furious gun battle, Teal is brought down and Keymas, after a tense standoff with Calhoun, expires in a hail of lead. The final scene has couples Calhoun, Cummings, Langton and Stevens waltzing off to play house on their respective ranches, the finale to a very rowdy, very satisfying small-scale Western with a big heart from Columbia, Katzman, Sears and Calhoun.

In 1957, Calhoun, in collaboration with partner/Hollywood talent scout Victor M. Orsatti, formed his own production company, Rorvic, the aim being to test his talents in the sphere of film writing and producing. In 1958, Rorvic, in conjunction with Desi Arnaz and Lucille Ball's Desilu Productions, came up with the idea for a television series, *The Texan*, starring Calhoun as Captain Bill Longley, a Civil War Confederate who roams the countryside like a Western version of Robin Hood, righting the wrongs of the people. Budgeted at $40,000 per 30-minute episode and networked through CBS, *The Texan* ran for 78 episodes over two seasons, from September 1958 to September 1960. A third season was scrapped when Calhoun, who was no stranger to the world of the small screen, announced that he wanted to concentrate on feature films, mainly B-Westerns. A 10-disc set containing 70 episodes is currently commercially available.

The first Rorvic production, MGM's *The Hired Gun* (1957), was a modest effort compared to the glossy studio's usual lavish budgets, coming in at $323,000 and filmed in black-and-white, the running length a short 64 minutes. Those were the minus points. On the plus side, CinemaScope was utilized to capture in all their glory the eye-catching vistas at Lone Pine, stunningly photographed by Harold J. Marzorati, while Albert Glasser, known for his incredibly noisy horror soundtracks (*Giant from the Unknown*; *Indestructible Man*), knocked up a pretty noisy score here. Director Ray Nazarro, a '50s B-Western specialist, had made four great George Montgomery oaters among others, so was perfectly at home in this medium-budget enterprise, the first of three he would participate in with Calhoun. Above all else, Rory was back in his favored role, that of a tight-lipped, mean as hell professional gunfighter charged with bringing Anne Francis back to Texas from New Mexico to be hung; she's been falsely accused of murdering her husband, the real culprit Vince Edwards, her brother-in-law; he shot Regis Parton in a drunken scuffle to get his hands on his father's inheritance, blaming the shooting on Francis. Can Francis convince Calhoun (Gil McCord) that she's innocent, particularly as the taciturn gunman has been offered $5,000 to bring her in alive?

"They're going to hang a woman. An innocent woman," intones Francis over an opening view of the hangman's noose, but soon, Chuck Connors, disguised as a priest, has sprung her from jail, taking her to a ranch in New Mexico. When Calhoun, having been assigned to bring the gal to justice, turns up, ostensibly to find work as a ranch hand, Connors' suspicions are aroused, particularly as his romantic overtures toward Francis are rudely rebuffed

Calhoun and Anne Francis in *The Hired Gun*

("I don't have any feelings. I'm an escaped murderess."), the blonde lass locking her eyes on the new quiet-but-deadly dude on the block. Lone Pine's panoramic mountain scenery comes into its own when, out in the rocky wilds, Calhoun makes his play, forcing Francis, even though she's no pushover, to return to Texas pronto, unaware that a circuit judge has already cast doubts on the verdict and has turned down an extradition order. At a waterhole, Connors and two men catch up; Connors foolishly goes for his gun, shot dead by Calhoun. Following a skirmish with Indians, the gun hawk delivers Francis to Edwards and John Litel across the border, collects his fee but then takes her back to New Mexico under the safekeeping of Salvador Baguez; he now believes her story, turning the screws (by torture; tied up with wet rawhide which constricts in the sun will loosen any man's tongue!) on Guinn "Big Boy" Williams, a witness to the shooting, getting him to spill the beans to a judge. Back in Texas, Calhoun confronts Edwards, who has snatched Francis, and Litel, now having serious reservations over Edwards' version of events. A standoff between Calhoun and Edwards sees the dishonorable brother hitting the dirt, Francis cleared of all charges. The "fugitive hellcat" (as the posters proclaimed) and her knockout-looking gunslinger ride off together ("You said I was in your custody," she coos), no doubt to play naughty games among the splendors of Lone Pine.

Sixty-four minutes doesn't go much quicker, or get any better, than in Nazarro's tight, gritty Western, Calhoun and Francis bouncing off each other with consummate ease, spitting out writers Buckley Angell and David Lang's pithy one-liners through gritted teeth, a dream partnership set against a dream landscape. And Western fans must have been asking themselves at the time—is there a better-looking gunslinger on celluloid than Rory Calhoun in his prime? On this showing, the answer was probably no, there wasn't! He was undoubtedly one of the handsomest of actors ever to strap on a gun belt in an age when audiences expected men to look like men. Calhoun had scored again!

Columbia's *Domino Kid* (1957) followed *The Hired Gun*, Ray Nazarro retained at the helm, Rorvic producing and Calhoun contributing toward Kenneth Gamet and Hal Biller's taut screenplay. And taut is what this revisionist *noir* Western was all about: In the opening sequence, a man in a saloon has three slugs pumped into his guts, the gunman backing off toward camera; the back of that gunman is next seen slowly cantering into town where he dismounts, Nazarro maintaining that rear shot as the stranger ambles into a cantina, demanding a coffee. After lighting a cigar, he converses with the owner, Don Orlando ("They say this Domino is a very bad one." Calhoun: "Don't believe everything you hear about me." Orlando: "Domino! Caramba!") before getting down to business, shooting his second victim in a blazing street set-to. The cigar-chomping, spurs-jingling gunman is Calhoun (Cort Garand), known by all as Domino; he returned home from the Civil War to find his ranch, the Double-Six, taken over by land-grabbers, the cattle gone, his father murdered. Five men were responsible—this tall, mean-looking avenging angel in black has despatched two; three more to go, two of them known to Calhoun, but *who* is the fifth man? That's the conundrum facing the detached gun hawk as he steamrollers over Sheriff Robert Burton's protestations to let things be, attempts to stoke the fires of his faltering romance with Kristine Miller, owner of the Littlefield Stage and Freighter Line (bar girl Yvette Duguay also desires him), and ward of the predations of Andrew Duggan, intent on claiming both Miller and the Double-Six Ranch for himself.

Shot in stark black-and-white by Irving Lippman to impart a moody, atmospheric air (it plays almost like a detective movie of the period), Nazarro composes many of his scenes in close-up, *noir*-fashion, adding punch to the sudden gunplay and gravitas to Calhoun's understated, pitch-perfect star turn, *not* wooden as some critics suggest, just Calhoun being Calhoun, the director capitalizing on the actor's quiet strengths, not to mention his swarthy, brooding persona. He's a man who can't let go, the need for revenge driving him on: "I got one more to go," he informs Miller after gunning down Roy Barcroft in a saloon and James Griffith in his own home. "I got to get that last man." "You're turning into a professional gunman and outlaw," sobs Miller, unable to get through to his cold resistance. "Killin's gotten into your blood." Calhoun, shunned by the town's women (but not the men who think he's a hero), is convinced that Duggan may be his final target (and so are the audience): The financier has refused Calhoun a loan to refurbish his ranch, stating, "I'll buy you out if you leave Pradera," and has also ordered the damming of a river on public land, cutting off the Double-Six's water supply. In a seemingly unrelated incident in the town's cantina, Eugene Iglesias is assaulted by hulking ruffian Peter Whitney who's knocked to the ground by Calhoun; coming to, Whitney and two gorillas drag the Mexican off to the stables to be thrashed by a leather-clad chain; Calhoun intervenes again, and told by grateful Iglesias that the fifth killer on Calhoun's wanted list is Whitney. The next day's showdown sees a double standoff: Duggan, rifle in hand, faces up to Calhoun while Whitney, lurking behind a tree, waits for his chance. In the resulting crossfire, Calhoun is hit in the leg, hauling himself through the dust under a hail of gunfire to finish off Whitney and receiving another bullet in the shoulder. As Miller plugs up his wounds, Duggan hovers over the pair, realizing that Calhoun was on the side of right all along, albeit on his own terms.

Mischa Bakaleinikoff's sparse incidental music underscores a Western that is just as minimalistic in its approach to well-worn themes of Western revenge. Produced on very low finances, *Domino Kid*, in its unassuming way, features the best of Rory Calhoun, now quite adept at playing mysterious, monosyllabic gunslingers, a forerunner in many ways to the Clint Eastwood "Man With No Name" antihero that was to appear on screen so successfully during the 1960s. And in this picture, Ray Nazzaro's sheer bravura and creativity behind the camera might well have been one of the many influences that gave birth to Sergio Leone's *Dollar* trilogy, such is the artful positioning of his lens in many of the scenes; that, and the underlying threat of violence, is what makes Rorvic's second production a little-remembered gem.

The 1950s saw the rise of the "pro-Indian" movie, filmmakers imbuing their productions with a certain amount of sympathy toward the plight of the Native American Redskin, turfed out of his native habitat and forced to live on guarded reservations. United Artists' *Ride Out for Revenge* (1957) was one such picture, albeit made on a lower scale than most. Lloyd Bridges played a racist, alcoholic cavalry captain stationed in Sand Creek, 1868, forever cursing the Cheyenne, viewing them as nothing more than troublesome dogs to be persecuted at his drunken whim. On the other hand, upright lawman Rory Calhoun (Marshal Tate) thinks the opposite, carrying out a romance with delectable Indian lass Joanne Gilbert (Pretty Willow), sister of Vince Edwards (Little Wolf). When Edwards and his father, Frank DeKova, enter town (a sublime opening scene of the two trekking over the wide expanse of Sonora's prairie), running the gauntlet of sneering, bigoted townsfolk ("They're walkin' pretty tall for beggars, ain't they.") and asking Bridges for food and supplies before winter arrives, the bully sends them packing ("No more charity. Get out!"), even though they attempt to trade with a gold nugget. Trooping back up the street (a lengthy tracking shot by Bernard Girard, his first major feature film), DeKova is gunned down from behind; Richard Shannon is the killer, but Bridges ignores the fact. After all, who cares about one dead Injun? Stern-faced Calhoun does, that's who. "They'll be back," he warns Bridges, adding, "You're scared of them, Captain," a true-enough statement; Bridges is a coward of the first degree, getting others to do his dirty work for him. Sick of all the prejudice, Calhoun hands in his tin star and heads for that wooded glade in the hills to play house with Gilbert; Bridges, meanwhile, plans to infiltrate the Cheyenne camp, get rid of them by fair means or foul and lay his hands on the gold.

Producer Norman Retchin's careful screenplay packs it all in over a 78-minute running time: Calhoun is lodging with Gloria Grahame, an Indian-hating widow hungry for his manly affections; and Calhoun's nephew, young Michael Winkelman, also loathes Indians, his family wiped out in a raid. In a tense night attack on Sand Creek, made even more suspenseful by Leith Stevens' ominous drum-laden score, the lad is shot in the back by Edwards and dies. Calhoun's loyalties are now put to the test; he *has* to kill Edwards for the crime, even if it means jeopardizing his relationship with Gilbert—"I've got to murder to protect all of you from being murdered," he tells clueless Bridges, blonde Grahame turning nasty by siding with the unhinged army boss, furious at Calhoun's rejection of her busty charms. Gilbert, aware of what Calhoun plans to do, tries to stab him to death, relenting when he tells her he had Edwards lined up in his rifle sights but couldn't pull the trigger. Bridges and his platoon ride up into the hills, come upon Calhoun and Edwards fighting in a pool and open fire; Edwards is brought down in a hail of lead, as is Calhoun, or so Bridges thinks. He survives, and in a final confrontation outdraws Bridges who's about to grab more gold nuggets for himself. The Indians gather together their belongings and begin the long march to their reservation in Oklahoma, watched by Calhoun and Gilbert from a ridge. "Things change," says Calhoun, resigned to the fact that the Redskins have once again been press-ganged into moving from their beloved hunting grounds on orders from the white man.

Leisurely paced, *Ride Out for Revenge* is a thoughtful exercise in racial intolerance, more social Western drama than gung-ho action; it works because of decent acting all round, an intelligent script and idiosyncratic directorial touches from Girard, who concentrated more on television shows than the cinema. It's also blessed with pin-sharp black-and-white photography courtesy of Floyd Crosby, winner of an Oscar for *Tabu: A Story of the South Seas* (1931) and a Golden Globe for *High Noon* (1953). Yes, the film may lack gun-blazing set pieces, but once in a while, that's no bad thing; in its own quiet way, Girard's little-seen oater manages to get its message across without resorting to histrionics and umpteen rough 'n' tumbles, an underrated guilty pleasure: "Solid ... worth a look," commented *Variety*.

During 1958, Rory put in one-off performances in a number of television series such as *The Schlitz Playhouse*, *Telephone Time* and *Suspicion*, all non-Westerns. It was also the year that saw him starring in his final oater for Universal-International before he parted company with them, playing the title character in Richard Carlson's *The Saga of Hemp Brown*, a colorful narrative centered on revenge set amid the wooded backdrop of California's Conejo Valley Thousand Oaks area. Shot in CinemaScope and rich Technicolor by Philip Lathrop, the tale, or saga, told of Lieutenant Hemp Brown's attempts to bring to justice cocksure villain Jed Givens (played with bags of smarmy relish by John Larch). Ruthless Givens and his gang have just waylaid a wagon containing an army payroll strongbox, brutally killing three troopers and a woman passenger but sparing Brown who is subsequently court-martialed for cowardice. The top brass claims that Givens died on the battlefield, so how could he be responsible? He didn't, the deranged soldier planted his papers and insignia on a corpse to enable him to escape the army's rigid regime and low pay. Brown is determined to clear his disgraced name by bringing in Givens alive rather than dead ("I'll prove Jed Givens is alive," he tells the court); how he goes about achieving it forms the crux of the story, written by Bernard Girard, the director of *Ride Out for Revenge*.

"You should have killed me too, Givens, for your own good," snarls Calhoun to Larch at the beginning, after the robbery and shootings, eventually, in the final reel, beating his enemy to pulp (there are a lot of prolonged, savage fistfights in the film) and getting him to confess to the crime in front of San Juan's lynch-hungry mob. This leaves Calhoun free to take up Beverly Garland's offer of a warm bed for the night, or perhaps forever. She's a two-bit artist living in Fortunio Bonanova's caravan (the Bolanos Traveling Show), having met horseless Calhoun, half-dead from exhaustion, on the road and taken him in, much to the consternation of her boss. "What an adorable guy—such a cutie. I couldn't take my eyes off him," Garland later cooed in interviews, and this adoration shows in her feminine tenderness in treating his abrasions and bruises, the two engaging in lip action come morning; the girl has become smitten in a flash! Like many actresses of that time, she was bowled over by Calhoun's strikingly handsome features (and never has he looked more ruggedly handsome than in this picture), although declining the chance (she stated) to become one more notch on his bedpost (in an early sequence, starlet Yvette Vickers also throws herself at him with wild abandon).

When Larch and his cohorts murder rancher Tom London's wife and steal her jewelry box, fans might be forgiven in thinking that there's going to be one hell of a shoot-up, Rory versus six gunmen and coming out on tops. It fails to materialize, although he brings down one in a stable gunfight, yet the movie doesn't fall flat, as some have said. Carlson's moody opus opts for an atypical slant on the traditional revenge Western, and thanks to Calhoun's menacing presence, plus the obvious chemistry between him and Garland, it succeeds. *The Hollywood Reporter* gave the *The Saga of Hemp Brown* guarded praise: "A one-plot Western, but classed as an 'A' … divertingly offbeat … Calhoun plays it mostly taciturn." As usual, Universal's musical supervisor, Joseph Gershenson, included his name on the credits, but keen-eared soundtrack buffs will pick up refrains from many of the company's horror/sci-fi scores in the incidental music, including *Tarantula*,

Carolyn Craig, Tom Pittman, Rory and Barbara Bates in *Apache Territory*

Revenge of the Creature and even *Man Made Monster*. The composers who wrote these scores—Hans J. Salter, Herman Stein, among others—were not given a mention, a criminal omission, some might say.

Calhoun rounded off 1958 with Columbia's *Apache Territory*, as good a B-Western as they can get. First, the statistics: It was the third Rorvic/Ray Nazarro collaboration; it was the 17th Calhoun Western to come in at under 85 minutes (proof that less was best); it was the last Western he would make for five years; and three of the cast became members of Hollywood's long roll call of tragedies: Tom Pittman in a car crash only weeks after the film's release in September 1958, aged 26; Carolyn Craig from suicide in 1970, aged 36; and Barbara Bates from suicide in 1969, aged 43. These last facts give the movie an added poignancy—combined with Calhoun's virility, Leo Gordon's bull-headedness, John Dehner's cowardly cad, Myron Healey's anxious family man and Frank DeKova's friendly Pima, Nazarro's tough little cowboys versus Injuns yarn is potent stuff, vividly filmed in one location, California's Red Rock Canyon, the cast dwarfed by those towering striated walls of pink sandstone.

Calhoun's a lone drifter, Logan Cates, first spotted riding through the harsh rocky landscape (photography: Irving Lippman) and attacked by renegade Apaches. Fifteen minutes into the action, he's boxed in a clearing beside a waterhole with unexpected company, the Indians hidden among boulders. The assorted ensemble comprises Dehner and Bates, an ex-love of Rory's; Craig, quivering in a catatonic state due to her family being wiped out; Pittman, sole survivor of a bunch of cowpokes minding their own business; Sergeant Francis DeSales and his troop detail; and DeKova, an amiable Indian but deadly with a knife if crossed. Nazarro focuses on this small disparate group as they fight for survival and among themselves. Calhoun is looked upon as *de facto* leader, which bruiser Gordon objects to; he knows how to get out of a tight situation, even if all around him don't, as summed up in this piece of crisp dialogue (Charles R. Marion; George W. George; Frank L. Moss, from Louis L'Amour's story) between him and Bates:

Bates: "Well, I'm afraid, Logan. We're all afraid."
Calhoun: "There's nothing against being afraid, Jen."
Bates: "You're not afraid." Pause. Then, "You're not, are you?"
Calhoun: "Man's not afraid of what's ahead of him, only what's behind him. Things are worth livin' for he's afraid of losin'. Me, I got nothin'."

To Dehner's utter dismay, Bates is turning her eyes on the man she used to love, although at one point she spits at him, "You're like a rock—immovable!" But at least he *is* a man; she admires the fact that, against type, he alone has taken responsibility for their life-threatening predicament, unlike her fiancé who wants nothing more than to run like hell, regardless of the safety of others. One by one, they fall to Apache arrows and bullets (there's a tense interlude where Calhoun, having infiltrated the Apaches' camp to find food, nearly falls afoul of an inquisitive Gila monster lizard), Healey caught and tortured; Calhoun has to sneak out and put a bullet in him to end his agony. With only seven whites left, the Indians are eventually eliminated by canteens full of gunpowder tossed into their

Six-Gun Law

camp. Pittman and Craig head toward California to buy a ranch on the proceeds of the gold given to them by DeKova, while Bates hitches her skirts to Calhoun, the pair galloping off to Yuma to resume their previous romance, spineless Dehner having expired in the dust.

Apart from the TV series *The Texan*, mentioned earlier, there were to be no more Western adventures for Rory Calhoun in the 1950s. He wouldn't strap on a gun belt until 1963, in Allied Artists' *The Gun Hawk*. What he had left behind were at least 16 essential sagebrush sagas (this includes 1949's *Massacre River*) that proved conclusively that the '50s were the genre's finest hour, with actors like Calhoun contrib-

Publicity photo from *The Texan*

uting to the rich, diverse Western tapestry of that particular decade. Rory may not have been the greatest of Hollywood players on the backlot and would have been the first to admit it, but in the sphere of the medium/low-budget Western, he generally came up trumps. Watching him again in *The Yellow Tomahawk, Dawn at Socorro, Four Guns to the Border, Red Sundown, Utah Blaine, Domino Kid, The Saga of Hemp Brown* and *Apache Territory*, you can begin to appreciate just how darned good he was in the saddle and how great a lot of his Westerns were, easily the equal, in their own tightly knit fashion, to those made by Randolph Scott, Audie Murphy, Rod Cameron, George Montgomery, Jeff Chandler and a host of other cowboy stars. Tall, sexy-looking, mean, terse and quick on the draw, with a hint of a darker side to their nature and taking no bullshit from anybody; that's how fans liked their Western heroes to be presented on the big screen in a darkened auditorium and in this respect, Rory Calhoun very rarely disappointed.

CHAPTER 10

CAMERON: 1948-1957

Republic Pictures' supremo Herbert J. Yates signed Rod Cameron to a lengthy contract in 1948 on $10,000 a picture, hoping that he could do for him what he had done to John Wayne. It didn't come off quite like that, even though Cameron made some highly respectable Westerns with the company in this nine-year period. Rod didn't possess Wayne's mighty box-office clout or swagger; the Duke was one of Hollywood's major, most popular A-listers, while the likes of Cameron were content to sit on the perimeters of all-out fame, relegated to the "B" arena and taking on whatever was offered, giving the project their all. That first Republic project was 1948's *The Plunderers*, set in the 1870s and directed by Joseph Kane, the first of seven Westerns he would make with Cameron, filmed in the company's frequently favored Trucolor around California's Vasquez Rocks and Kernville areas (cameraman: Jack A. Marta). Rod played Major John Drum, assigned by the military authorities to infiltrate Forrest Tucker's gang of renegades who are causing a nuisance by stealing ore shipments from the Martin Mine and generally running riot. To hoodwink smart "you don't fool me" Tucker, Cameron "murders" Sheriff George Cleveland (a setup) and then enters a sham marriage with the outlaw leader's intended, Adrian Booth (aka Lorna Gray), to prevent the law from following her on her frequent trips out of town, all the way to Tucker's hideout. Cameron, a fake $1,500 reward on his head from his fictitious exploits in Texas, thus enhancing his reputation as a wanted killer, strikes up a brittle relationship with gun-happy Tucker, and it's this mistrustful pairing that gives *The Plunderers* its edgy appeal, both actors in fine fettle, the one-liners coming thick and fast.

Elsewhere, though, the movie gets bogged down in a second fraught relationship, that of Cameron and Hungarian born actress Ilona Massey. First meeting at the gaudy Palace of Chance, Massey singing (and talking) in a thick European accent, the decorative lass takes a shine to Rod after his by now familiar trademark rough and ready chat-up technique: "Anyone tell you you're a handsome heifer?" he grins before chased out of town for that supposed sheriff slaying by Grant Withers' posse. Massey, close buddies with Booth, is jealous of her liaison with Rod, even though it's not legal, so we have plenty of bitchy banter courtesy of Gerald Geraghty and Gerald Drayson Adams, Massey hopping mad that Cameron is going to shop lovers Tucker and Booth when the occasion arises, threatening *not* to go to California with him to play house on his Fork River Ranch. Tucker, devilish henchman Paul Fix and their coyotes rustle a herd of horses,

Rod and Forrest Tucker tackle the Sioux in *The Plunderers*.

almost selling them to the cavalry before a survivor of the robbery spots Tucker and the detail gives chase; Tucker and Fix are ambushed by the resurrected Cleveland, placed in handcuffs and escorted to an army outpost. Saved from a necktie party, the pair are shoved into an outbuilding outside the fort. The Sioux, led by Chief Red Cloud, attack to the sound of war drums (and R. Dale Butts' pounding score) and Kane at last livens up the pace with a slice of thundering-good action: The outbuilding containing Tucker and Fix is set ablaze, Booth receives an arrow in the back, the stockade's foundations are dynamited, Tucker and Fix perish in a flurry of hand-to-hand fighting and the cavalry appears on the scene to save the day; haughty Massey finally agrees to follow Rod to California.

The Plunderers proved to be vaguely unsatisfactory, too talkative and static in the middle section, Massey out of her depth in a Western (she was more believable as Baroness Elsa Frankenstein in Universal's 1943 memorable monster-fest, *Frankenstein Meets the Wolf Man*); the *New York Times* got it right, saying the film was "old-fashioned and pallid." However, matters would improve hugely with *Stampede* (Allied Artists, 1949); before that, Cameron featured as Bob "Bittercreek" Yauntis in 20th Century Fox's *Belle Starr's Daughter* (1948), part of a loan-out agreement he had had written into in his Universal contract, billed third behind George Montgomery and Ruth Roman. The 1940s saw a lot of Westerns of the "famous outlaws' territory" variety, and Lesley Selander's efficient outing was one more for the pot, okay in parts but ruined by a distinctly non-cowboy (more family drama) score from classical Hungarian composer Edward Kilenyi. Cameron played a smiling, psychopathic ambitious thug in this one, shooting Isabell Jewell, Belle Starr, the Bandit Queen of Cherokee Flats, and Ruth Roman's uncle, Kenneth MacDonald, in the opening minutes after murdering Antioch's marshal, shattering the peace treaty forged between Starr's outlaw enclave and the town. Cameron has his beady eyes on Roman, Belle Starr's feisty daughter, and embarks on a stagecoach-robbing spree while Antioch's new marshal, Montgomery, also falls for Roman's tomboy charms. Now calling herself Rose of Cimarron, equipped with check shirt and hefty gun belt, she joins Cameron's bunch under the impression that Montgomery killed her mother and uncle, not knowing that brutal Rod, her new lover, is the murderer. Old-timer Wallace Ford knows the truth behind Belle Starr's slaying but is blasted by Cameron in a saloon before he gets to tell anybody; it's left to fatally wounded William Phipps, sick of Cameron's wicked methods, to reveal the real facts to Roman. After a couple of saloon standoffs, a great deal of charging here and there on horses and repeated bursts of gunplay, Montgomery's posse eventually shoots it out with Cameron's gang; the two big guys square up, the marshal gets the drop and the outlaw boss bites the dust. Montgomery decides to wait for Roman as she begins a five-year prison term for robbery.

No-nonsense "Gorgeous" George ("Take those guns off and get outta town!" he orders the heavies, a much-treasured Montgomery line) versus vicious Rod was a major drawing point to cinemagoers in a formulaic '40s horse opera that is a passable time-waster; Cameron was a tad more over-the-top than usual, good-looker Montgomery the lead star still finding his feet in Westerns but just as energetic. Reasonably entertaining frolics, the utterly strange soundtrack at odds with what's taking place on screen, and proof that Cameron wasn't averse to playing bad guys; most of his good guys were very rarely all that "good" anyway!

When reviewing a motion picture, one judges the result on acting performances, direction, script, music, production values, cinematography and plot, and how the whole package is put together. *Stampede*, released by Allied Artists in 1949 in Sepiatone (current DVD issues are monochrome only) is a tremendous Rod Cameron Western where every constituent in the above categories falls absolutely right into its proper place, the outcome a hard-bitten, grim yarn of homesteaders (nesters) impinging on land owned by cattleman Cameron (as Mike McCall) in the 1880s. What you have here in Lesley Selander's mini-masterpiece is a meaty, adult, straight-to-the-point drama produced on the cusp of the '40s Western morphing into the more violent, psychological framework of what followed in the 1950s; no frills, just honest-to-goodness hatred and confrontation, Rod in commanding form, an antihero before the term was coined and overused in the 1960s. Bearing all this in mind, how then could Bosley Crowther of the *New York Times* go on to describe this riveting nailbiter as thus: "Cheaply manufactured horse opera ... labored ... grade C Western ... no cow would be foolish enough as to sit all the way through this film ... actors treated with less consideration and less respect for their intelligence than the cows ... and the same for the producer's regard for the audience." Film critics sometimes get on their "high horse" and find faults that don't exist; on this occasion, this unjust critique totally warrants a put-down in itself. Let's see why.

Due to the land-grabbing laws of 1887, Steve Clark's settlers arrive on extensive land run by cattle rancher Cameron and his brother, Don Castle. Castle tags along incognito with the wagon train, eavesdropping on their plans and Cameron, furious, turns up, riding roughshod through Clark's camp. Cameron lays claim to the only source of water in the bone-dry North Valley area, Spirit Lake, and he ain't gonna relinquish his rights to anybody, not to Clark, corrupt Blackwell town banker John Miljan, crooked land developer Donald Curtis, Curtis' devious representative John Eldredge, and certainly not to pint-sized Gale Storm, Clark's wildcat of a daughter. The firecracker spits, kicks, claws and snarls, storming into lawyer Jonathan Hale's office during a meeting with Cameron. "Go back home," Rod bellows, lifting her up

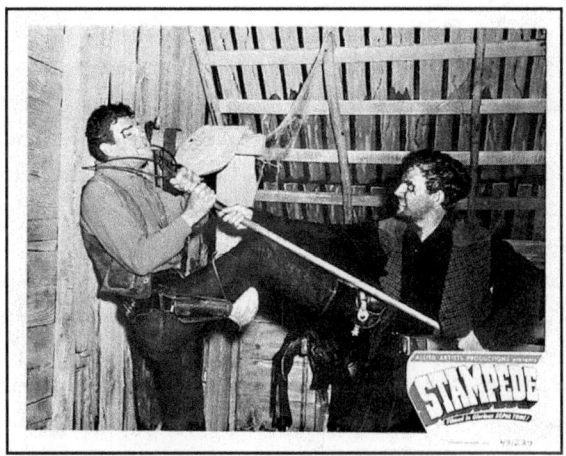

Stampede **was superb Western fare.**

and receiving a slap in the face. To her shouts of protest, he looks her square in the eyes.

"Oh, I don't know. Man gets a little tired of looking at nothing but cattle."

"I'm surprised you know the difference, McCall."

"It's *Mister* McCall. And it's easy. You haven't got any horns."

Three great lines that ably demonstrate John C. Champion and Blake Edward's numerous sharp exchanges peppering a terse script.

Cameron owes the bank $30,000; Miljan, under Curtis' thumb, says he'll tear up the demand note if his client hands over water rights to the settlers. "Nothing doing" is Rod's brusque response, so Curtis, who wants the settlers to remain in order to boost his own expansion plans, organizes a robbery to clear the bank of funds, therefore piling more pressure on beleaguered Miljan. During the fracas, Cameron accidentally shoots an innocent bystander; handing his gun over to Sheriff Johnny Mack Brown, he rides into the hills to meet up with happy-go-lucky Castle, the two fired upon by Storm from rocks; she's grabbed and receives a spanking from Castle. "You talk mighty big for a small girl," Cameron barks, emptying her rifle's magazine and tossing it back to her. "Hey. Wait a minute. Forgot your crutch." At the cow punchers' camp, one of Cameron's men is shot and killed, and the cattle boss heads back to Blackwell to investigate, caught in an iconic shot by Lesley Selander and photographer Harry Neumann; cantering and searching for tracks, Cameron pauses and lights up, mountain ranges shimmering in the distant heat haze, the big man looking swell astride his steed. In a faultless production all round, Edward J. Kay's resonant score is used sparingly, punctuating the narrative flow where necessary but absent in many scenes, cementing the belief among film music buffs that sometimes, "less is more."

Thwarted Curtis, getting more evil by the minute, arranges for two hitmen to tail Cameron to the livery stables after a nester dance, resulting in one shot dead, the other unconscious after a terrific, five-minute fistfight. Next day at the inquest, Rod is cleared of murder ("A cowboy gunman," sneers Eldredge) and free to leave: Curtis ups the ante, instructing one of his men to murder Castle; the deed carried out, storm clouds gather as Cameron walks up Blackwell's main street, Castle's body draped over his steed, threatening retribution. Miljan, high on whiskey, is then shot in the back to stop him squealing, Curtis intending to blow up Spirit Lake's dam ("You'll have all the water you want," he tells Eldredge and Clark) and stampede Cameron's steers over a cliff. This harrowing scene, ending with the cattle baron staring down at hundreds of twitching bodies at the foot of a ravine, wouldn't make it past the censor's scissors these days, and it's still upsetting to watch, even now. A climactic shoot-out sees Eldredge and his cohorts biting the shores of the lake, Curtis drowned by Cameron. Storm gallops up to Cameron. "Your people wanted water, right?" He presses his foot on the plunger and the dam goes up in a ball of flame. "There it is." As the curtain closes, the 6-footer lifts up the five-footer and plants a smacker on her lovely face.

Bleak, uncompromising and doom-laden, *Stampede* saw the standard '40s Western, often over-populated by whimsical characters and too much half-jokey chat and general tomfoolery, growing up. Underserving of that *NYT* review, Selander's little beauty deserves re-evaluating for the classic it truly is.

Stampede was superb Western fare—and the same can be said of Cameron's next, Republic's tough, formidable *Brimstone* (1949), featuring an outstanding performance from Walter Brennan as Brimstone "Pop" Courteen, father of three very different sons: Favorite (but a dishonest waster) Jim Davis; dimwitted Jack Lambert; and greenhorn James Brown, the youngest. Brennan was famously adept at playing curmudgeonly characters; here, he excels himself, his Brimstone Courteen one of the Western's all-time venomous villains, a mean, lowdown ornery critter without an ounce of good in his body. Why so? Embittered Brennan is incensed at nesters barging in on his territory and setting up home on his land. "I'll bankrupt 'em, every one of 'em, like they did to me," he snarls, staging one robbery after another to relieve the homesteaders of their hard-earned savings, breaking into their ranches and rustling their steers, in between verbally and physically abusing his three sons ("I'll nail your hide to a barn door" is his frequent threat, spat out through clenched teeth). Fatherly love doesn't figure in Brennan's world: He's out to whip his three offspring into shape, whether they object to his methods or not. But then the Ghost appears, a mysterious black-clad outlaw, turning up at the scene of Brennan's holdups and relieving *him* of the stolen loot, disappearing into the night ("That was a ghost! We gotta find out who he is—fast!"). In the town of Gunsight, the Courteen gang (minus Brown, deemed too inexperienced to be in on the action) blow up the bank and hightail it out, richer by $15,000, the outraged citizens calling Sheriff Forrest Tucker "incompetent" and baying for his dismissal. A new marshal (Jack Holt) is imminent, so Tucker had better get his act together, pronto. Outside of Gunsight, the Ghost snatches the bank loot from fuming Brennan and, in the 16th minute, reveals himself to be Cameron (Johnny Tremaine); he's a federal marshal, working undercover to expose Tucker for what he is, a crook in league with Brennan; he's also charged with curtailing the Courteens' activities. After robbing an express train depot, Rod trots into Gunsight, meets Tucker and is deputized on a promise that he'll find the missing money from the train holdup, located somewhere in the Wolf Creek area. Leaving Tucker's office, he sees a young boy bullied in the street by Lambert, forever trying to live up to his father's expectations. Cameron makes his presence felt and gets the drop on the coyote; Lambert backs down, much to Brennan's annoyance. "I'll give you one more chance, Luke. You let one more man beat you to the draw and I'll bust your skull wide open. Maybe let you in a new set of brains," he rages.

The Ghost makes another appearance, holding up a stagecoach, although this time, it's Brown committing the act; he's romancing nester filly Adrian Booth behind his nester-hating father's back and needs the cash to set up house. During the robbery, he wounds Marshal Holt and receives a bullet in the arm, later telling Brennan that he accidentally shot himself. Tucker reckons that Cameron, evasive about his whereabouts, pulled the job and wants him locked up; meanwhile, the furrows on Brennan's grizzled brow grow ever deeper when he learns that Brown is carrying on with Booth behind his back. "You're not marrying a nester," he growls, and Booth's brother, David Williams, is then blamed for being the Ghost.

Yes, Thames Williamson's intelligent, if a might complex, screenplay twists and turns like the trails these dudes cross, but he isn't finished with the surprises just yet. In nearby Cottonwood, womanizer Davis is busy getting drunk in a saloon, pretending to be under-suspicion Brown, an alibi to throw Cameron off the scent. In walks Rod, fights Davis and shoots him. Williams, the second contender for the Ghost's title, faces a stiff 10-year sentence for robbery and armed assault; Booth knows he's innocent and that Brown robbed the stage, so she's caught in a dilemma. Cameron has a bruising encounter with Brennan and his two surviving sons in a saloon brawl, whipping all three, and eventually, Brown is arrested, confessing to holding up the stage; he receives a light one-year jail term in Riverton's territorial prison; the circuit judge willingly marries Brown and Booth after the trial. Brennan, Lambert and Tucker lure Cameron to Cottonwood's Four Aces saloon to finish him off ("Like a man to a piece of cheese.") but deputy Guinn "Big Boy" Williams blasts Tucker in the back as he gets a bead on Cameron. Escaping through a trap door, Brennan and Lambert emerge from a cave and chase after Booth and Brown, on the stage to Riverton ("My son married to a nester? I'll see him dead first."). Lambert is brought down by Cameron, followed by Brennan, the words "I'll nail your hide to a…" on his dying lips; Brown and Booth can now map out a future together without the interference of patriarchal Brennan.

Expertly pieced together by Joseph Kane, *Brimstone* is like *Panhandle* insomuch that it brings the Old West to the viewer like the pages of a faded picture book, a glimpse of violent times long past. Jack A. Marta's Trucolor photography paints the picturesque Kernville rocky wilderness and Lone Pine's Alabama Hills in pastel hues (the opening rustling/stampede sequence is in Sepiatone), Nathan Scott's evocative, somewhat somber score used frugally, imbuing the movie with a melancholy, almost fatalistic, air. All this, complemented by solid performances

George Montgomery under arrest in *Dakota Lil*

from the entire cast that do full justice to Williamson's crisp script, elevates *Brimstone* to B-Western greatness; it's almost a blueprint of how to make a celebrated horse opera work on minimal finances. And, as stated, deranged Brennan ("Terrific," said *Variety*) is galvanizing in every scene he's in, the Western father from hell!

Cameron crossed over to Fox to end his Universal loan obligation in 1950, starring for a second time beside George Montgomery in Lesley Selander's *Dakota Lil*. Like *Belle Starr's Daughter*, Cameron was billed third behind Montgomery and Marie Windsor *and* was cast as a psycho, vicious strangler Harve Logan, aka Kid Curry, throttling his enemies with a riding strap wrapped around his wrist. Montgomery played federal agent Tom Horn, on the trail of the infamous Hole-in-the-Wall gang down Matamoras way on the Mexican border in 1897. Cameron is first seen strangling a train guard during a $100,000 heist; the unsigned treasury notes are expertly forged by the silver screen's most glamorous counterfeiter, singer Windsor, to legalize them for the outlaws' use. Montgomery, Geronimo's large war knife strapped to his back, follows Windsor's trail to Red River, Wyoming (lovesick pianist John Emery accompanies her), infiltrating the gang led by Walter Sande (Butch Cassidy). Cameron isn't the only unhinged criminal around; grinning Jack Lambert fires off dumdum bullets, paralyzing his victims, hence his name, Dummy. Aided by law officer Wallace Ford, Montgomery arrests Lambert and handcuffs the loony to him; during a fracas, Ford is captured by the outlaws and Lambert killed. Inept sheriff Larry Johns thinks Montgomery is a bad 'un, especially when he's shown around the outfit's camp by Sande, but when Windsor discovers that Montgomery is a Secret Service agent, she decides to fall in with him after witnessing Cameron garrotting Ford, a sight that disgusts her—anyway, handsome George has caught the lass' eye (arousing jealous Emery's suspicions) and he's promised to go lenient on her if she cooperates in bringing the Hole-in-the-Wall bunch to justice. As a ruse, she sets up her forging equipment but wily Cameron has figured out what's going on; he strangles Emery and tries the same on her but she breaks free and, after a chase, Rod gets Geronimo's knife squarely between the shoulder blades courtesy of George, his corpse dragged away in the dust by his horse; Montgomery and Windsor ride off together to play house.

Boosted by a super Dimitri Tiomkin score, it's a shame that existing official DVD issues of *Dakota Lil* come in black-and-white, not in the original Cinecolor (these are available on gray market copies). The picture is fast-moving and crammed with exciting incident; although Cameron plays second fiddle to Montgomery, he burns up the screen when he appears, albeit in an unsympathetic role not usually associated with his other Westerns. And he was still persevering in the Western milieu to the exclusion of everything else, only Allied Artists' 1949 comedy *Strike It Rich* and Republic's 1951 mystery drama *The Sea Hornet* creating the odd diversion.

It was back to top billing in Columbia's energetic *Stage to Tucson* (aka *Lost Stage Valley*, 1950), Cameron competently playing yet another agent, Grif Holbrook, ordered by the Union (and President Abe Lincoln!) to carry out an investigation into the disappearance of 10 stagecoaches owned by the Butterfield Stage Line just prior to the outbreak of the Civil War. Initially, Rod is against the idea, wanting to settle down in the Californian sun after a lifetime of adventure—and he's owed $2,200 back pay! But he soon changes his mind, taking up a position in Tucson. En route to Tucson via the Apache Pass Relay Station, Cameron is joined on his stage by blonde vixen Kay Buckley and, out on the trail, they're attacked by the so-called Phantom Stage, a bullet-proof vehicle constructed of sheet iron run by Roy Roberts' Southern sympathizers; Cameron grabs a gun and jumps from the metal contraption after being nabbed, wounding the driver, an old pal, and disappearing among rocks. Roberts, boss of the Maroon Freight Company, and his followers are out to break the Yankee-held East-West line of communications, converting the captured stagecoaches into war wagons; Cameron, reaching Tucson on foot, sits on the fence, his loyalties divided, besides which his mind is on other matters, having started a romance with feisty Buckley in his office, much to driver Wayne Morris' frustration; *he* wants to marry the gal and reckons Cameron is far too old for her. Director Ralph Murphy focuses on the Cameron-Morris friendly rivalry at sporadic intervals, fairly amusing at times, involving verbal slingshots and slugging one another senseless (Cameron to Morris: "We're getting married in two weeks." Morris: "Did you say marrying or adopting?"). To add to Cameron's overflowing urgency list, ex-flame Sally Eilers (her last movie) runs the town's saloon and she's married to oily Roberts, although, judging by the expression on her mascaraed face when Rod's broad frame enters the establishment, she still holds a candle for her former beau. Whiskey-sodden doc, Carl Benton Reid, treating the bandit hit by Cameron upstairs, is in cahoots with Roberts and out in the street, a motley group of citizens are training for possible warfare.

A hard-drivin' B-movie mix from director Murphy, displaying the new decade's more dynamic approach to the horse opera, *Stage to Tucson* is embellished by one in a long line of just-right scores from Paul Sawtell, while Charles Lawton, Jr.'s bright Technicolor photography vividly showcases Lone Pine's Alabama Hills, and Red Rock Canyon, to their best advantage (scenic backdrops that were a major viewing experience in dozens of '50s Westerns), notably in the rampaging finale, several stages-cum-wagons full of Roberts' hijackers (including the armor-plated model) pursuing Cameron's carriage across salt flats, ending in a spectacular pileup. Before that, Roberts shoots Harry Bellaver's dog for being too exuberant, an act he will regret later, and Benton Reid ponders whether he should throw in his lot with the Unionists when war is finally declared. Morris worms his way into Roberts' hideout to flush out the renegades, leading to Buckley becoming so worried about his welfare among this den of vipers that she declares her love for him; the wedding to Rod is off! Robert Creighton Williams, Frank Burt and Robert Libott's over-plotted narrative tends to get a bit higgledy-piggledy at times, but entertaining all the same, before that thrilling climax, Roberts receiving a well-deserved slug in his guts from Bellaver for killing his beloved pooch. As for Rod, mission done and dusted, he's now hitched to Eilers, the pair plus Morris and Buckley heading off in a stage, everyone still bickering; Morris is now a Union sergeant but, unfortunately for him, he has to take orders from Cameron, a Union officer of much higher rank!

The *New York Times* enthused: "Bristling with action," Western fans getting a "fast, rough ride for their money." Cameron was getting better and better, but the best was yet to come. Lesley Selander's superlative *Short Grass* (Allied Artists, 1950) was the culmination of everything you could now expect to see in a Selander/Cameron Western: A tough, no-nonsense antihero (Rod), short on words, long on gun/fist action; scenic backdrops (Albuquerque, New Mexico); a headstrong heroine (Cathy Downs); a downright nasty baddie (Morris Ankrum); a direct, to-the-point screenplay (Thomas W. Blackburn, from his novel); tense shoot-outs; and, as with most Cameron oaters, a plot dense enough to stand your spoon up in. Shot in stark black-and-white by Harry Neumann and containing a spare, menacing Edward J. Kay score, *Short Grass* is 84 minutes of B-Western perfection; after years of languishing in the vaults, this essential purchase is now available on pristine DVD copies. Go grab yourself a copy, pronto!

First, a word about Lesley Selander. Born in Los Angeles, 1900, Selander directed 145 movies in his long career, commencing in 1936 with Universal's *Ride 'Em Cowboy* and finishing up with Paramount's *Arizona Bushwhackers* in 1968,

Lesley Selander

after which he quit the business. Almost his entire repertoire consisted of B-Westerns (Republic's 1945 long-forgotten horror outing, *The Vampire's Ghost*, was an offbeat exception.), but in all other respects, Selander was a filmmaker of "A" class quality. His low-budget horse operas were strong on characterization, plot and atmosphere, smooth pacing handled with true professionalism, coaxing solid performances from his cast of B stalwarts. He was steeped in Western dynamics and lore, of how, in plain language, to nail a narrative and keep an audience on their toes for 70 to 80 minutes without resorting to fluff and padding. A recent list of top Western directors included (as expected) John Ford, Anthony Mann, John Sturges and Howard Hawks, among others. Selander was nowhere to be seen, a criminal oversight. *Short Grass*, scene-for-scene, is as good as anything Ford could have come up with in the '40s and '50s, as are *Panhandle* and *Stampede*, two other must-have Selander/Cameron classics. Let's applaud men like Lesley Selander, overlooked by the masses in favor of the giants, who worked tirelessly on minimal funds to present fans with a gritty, down-to-earth vision of the Old West perhaps not experienced in those higher-budgeted, glossier but more vacuous, Westerns produced by the major studios. We salute him and all that he stood for.

Cattleman Morris Ankrum and his bunch of drovers are hankering after short grass country on which to graze their beef, moving cattle into territory earmarked for land development, regardless of any objections raised by homesteaders. Ever cautious, he advocates a "softly softly" approach; hotheaded younger sibling Riley Hill doesn't. "Play it quiet. My way," says Ankrum. "And if I don't?" spits Hill. "I reckon you'll just die," is the blunt response. To lay his hands on extra funds, thus enabling him to spread out into the coveted fertile Willow Creek Valley, the cattle baron instructs two heavies, Jack Ingram and Myron Healey, to rob Bissel's Trading Post. Trouble is, inside, drifter Cameron (Steve Llewellyn) is having a quiet whiskey with proprietor Jonathan Hale and in no mood for interruptions. Ingram does just that, hand on holster; Cameron beats him to the draw but Healey shoots his partner in the back. Healey slugs Hale, pinches $3,400 from the safe and heads into the hills with Cameron, whistling merrily, something which his new partner rapidly tires of listening to. "You're so happy, why don't you try singing? Couldn't be any worse than your whistling." Healey, desperate to start a spread

Cameron and Cathy Downs share a tender moment in *Short Grass*.

of his own, pulls a gun on Cameron and wounds him; Rod brings Healey down with a single shot and grabs the cash, Selander seguing from blood dripping onto banknotes to water dripping onto rocks: Cathy Downs is bathing naked in the river just as Cameron rides up and falls from his horse after calling her "Beautiful!" Downs drags him back to her ranch where she and her dad, Stanley Andrews, take care of Cameron, whose rugged charms captivate the girl and set her pulse racing; soon, they're hugging and kissing. However, she yearns for a town life, far away from the hardship and lonely rigors of a frontier existence; Cameron, on the other hand, appreciates the wide-open spaces and the freedom that goes with it. "If you stay," pleads Downs, "you'll have to fight it out with the Fentons." "Men aren't all Diamondbacks," he says, countering her hatred of the use of guns. "Some are," she shrugs. Resigned to sleeping alone in the bunkhouse because of Downs' apparent indifference to their relationship, Cameron has a tense set-to with Ankrum and Hill out on the prairie when marking fencing lines in the soil.

"I want this land," snaps Ankrum to Cameron who tells him he's guilty of trespass and being covered by two compadres hidden in nearby rocks armed with rifles in case of trouble. Hill, furious, reaches for his gun.

"Put that iron up," orders Ankrum.

Cameron stares Hill out. "Remember something kid. There never was a fast enough gun that there wasn't a faster one somewhere. Don't ever punch a gun in my belly again."

The two gallop away, taking their steers with them; back at the ranch, Downs is worried sick over a possible bloody range dispute, wanting Cameron to leave Willow Creek and take her along with him; she abhors gunfighting and knows that the money Cameron gave her father to purchase his strip of land was stolen from Hale's store. Cameron, in love with Downs, goes out to Ankrum's ranch in one last attempt to keep the peace with a deal on the table: Buy the land off Andrews they so urgently require to avoid bloodshed. But the boss isn't there, and Hill, sneering, says he'll take the land *without* paying a single cent. Going for his gun, he's shot dead by Cameron, who then gives half his share in Andrews' stake to Hale, hangs up his pistols and rides off to pastures new.

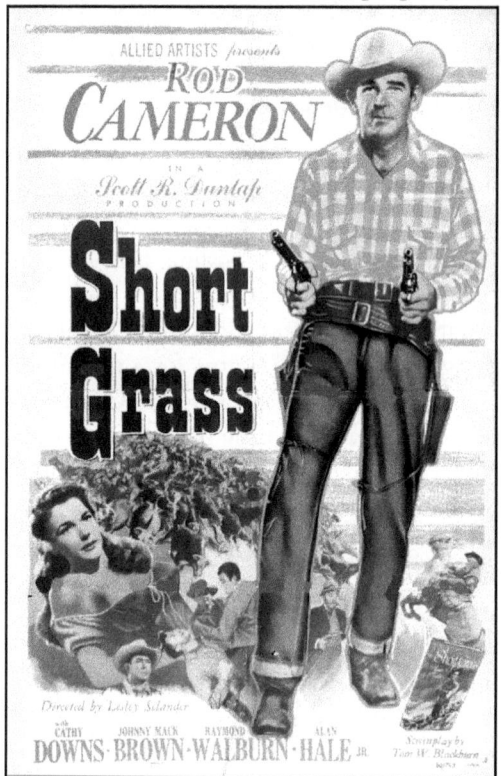

Five years later, in Silver Spur, New Mexico, Hale owns the town saloon and Downs has married alcoholic newsman Tristram Coffin. Ankrum is still stirring up trouble, enraged when he walks into Hale's joint and spots Cameron lounging against the bar minus his guns; he wants vengeance over his brother's killing, but refuses to draw on an unarmed man. When Downs tells Cameron that her father was found with a bullet hole in his back, and local farmer Rory Mallinson has been burned out of his property, burly Rod straps on his double holster, Marshal Johnny Mack Brown and Doctor Raymond Walburn by his side. In a tense saloon confrontation, Cameron against four of Ankrum's toughs, one is shot dead, three wounded, Mallinson expiring in the fracas. A throng of settlers, angry at Ankrum's herds taking over the precious grasslands ("He's bought every acre over 40 miles."), converges on the marshal's office, demanding that Cameron is deputized as marshal, fast losing faith in the current incumbent. Over at his own ranch house with new neighbor Alan Hale, Jr., Cameron metes out further justice two-gun-style to four of Ankrum's boys who are stupidly moving in—one dead, another wounded, one surrendering and one biting the dust care of Hale's fists. Next it's Jeff York's turn, the animal beaten to a pulp by Cameron over a brutal two minutes (as he was in *Panhandle*) for molesting Mallinson's distraught widow, Marlo Dwyer. "I want you to use them now—for me," cries Downs to Cameron, referring to his six-shooters, after her sot of a husband has been murdered, leading to a terrific nine-minute nighttime action-packed set piece among Silver Spur's darkened streets, Cameron, Hale, Johnny Mack and Walburn versus Ankrum's jackals. Guns blaze, bullets whine and ricochet, bodies hit the dirt, Hale finishes off Ankrum inside the saloon and his chief henchman, Harry Woods, gets both barrels of a shotgun straight in the belly; Cameron, injured, staggers out into the street and hands his holster to the saloon's owner. "Hang these up again Charlie—for good this time." "Steve's held me up," smiles Downs, helping her man keep to his feet. "He always has. He always will," she adds, kissing her dazed, bloodied hero, the closer to Selander's slow-burning cracker of a Western drama that rewards, as all good motion pictures do, on repeated viewings—and Cameron, eyes narrowing, features set in stone, tossing out short one-liners (answering questions with his own sharp question) and throwing his considerable frame around, is in domineering form.

Rod's first for 1951, Republic's *Oh! Susanna*, momentarily ended his run of classics, the *New York Times*, for once, hitting the critical nail on the head: "The scenery is lovely in Trucolor. Nothing else is." Scriptwriter Charles Marquis Warren must have spent too much time engrossed in John Ford's colorful cavalry sagas, *Fort Apache* in particular, and then decided on cobbling together his own recipe based around the antics of the boys in blue, or "Dogfaces" as they are called by irate townsfolk in this baffling mishmash of conflicting ideas, erratic direction and wobbly presentation. Maybe because of the carefree title, audiences of the day were expecting to see a Western musical of sorts. Not a chance; no one sings "Oh! Susanna," although composer R. Dale Butts uses the leitmotif constantly throughout and Adrian Booth warbles a solitary tune. Taking place in 1875, the storyline is minimal: Cameron (Captain Webb Calhoun), patrolling the Black Hills of Dakota (cue for a Doris Day song, but not here, where it was probably needed!) for signs of "gold rushers" upsetting the peace treaty with the Sioux, clashes with his superior, Forrest Tucker, the mean-spirited cur not only romancing Cameron's fickle gal, Booth (looking tasty in a shimmering green gown), but refusing to object to the miners heading for the hills, Indian war or no Indian war. In Dawson City, Redskin-hating saloon boss Jim Davis and Tucker are in collusion, so Cameron has his hands full dealing with dithering Booth, objectionable Tucker, smart-ass Davis and Al Bridge, a "rusher" who can't stop hauling his family into Sioux-infested territory in search of the yellow dust. Thank goodness that rambunctious Sergeant Chill Wills is along for the ride, although even his usual "grizzly bear with a sore head" star turn fails to bring a smile to Rod's immobile features.

Oh! Susanna, for much of the 84-minute running time, can't make up its mind whether to plump for knockabout laughs, romantic entanglement (Davis also flirts with Booth) or just good old-fashioned cavalry versus Injuns thrills and spills. Like Booth's capricious character, the narrative dithers, teetering on the edge of disaster by refusing to come off the fence and get on with it. Worse still is Tucker ("I hate sergeants!"), gray hair and iron-gray lines etched into his face, behaving like a self-obsessed slob, criticizing every single move Cameron makes out of a deep-rooted jealousy; Rod is West Point trained while he's had to rise through the ranks on the backs of corrupt politicians. It's an unpleasant, unsympathetic part to take on and, to his credit, Tucker makes a fist of it, but his sheer miserableness and bad temper, combined with an unconvincing Cameron-Booth love angle, lowers the tone, leading to a feeling of disappointment that won't go away. Davis is busy selling repeating rifles to the settlers in the hope that the Sioux will lay their hands on them, Dawson City's residents, feeling aggrieved that they're being prevented from hunting for gold, shouting to Cameron's troop "Dogfaces! Go play in your toy fort. We'll take care of the Indians." Cavalry ex-boxing champion Douglas Kennedy is a new replacement, siding with Tucker and then changing allegiance to Cameron, John Crompton plays the obligatory young greenhorn officer, there's a dance plus a couple of saloon face-offs and at last, in the 65th minute, things get serious, director Joseph Kane placing his foot firmly on the gas pedal. Chief Pactola and his bucks are on the warpath; to rout the Sioux and bathe in all the glory, Tucker heads a troop to engage the warriors, ordering Cameron's platoon to stay in the garrison, which soon comes under attack from Pactola's whooping braves. Dawson City is set on fire and, too late, Tucker realizes he's been led into the hills as a decoy to enable the Indians to besiege the undermanned outpost. "A mule-brained fool," he moans, knowing he's trapped. After savage fighting, Rod rides out to meet the Sioux chief who allows the survivors plus women and children to leave; up in the wooded slopes, Tucker's entire regiment has been massacred to a man, the officer dying in Cameron's arms. Rod, promoted to colonel, goes on to win a string of famous conflicts, becoming a national figurehead out West. He probably married hesitant Booth in the bargain; after all, he's showered her in enough kisses!

That climactic 15 minutes more than makes up for what has gone before, a real firecracker of a battle, but oddly, it appears to belong to a different movie altogether and therein lies *Oh! Susanna*'s shortcomings: It's a cavalry outing that is neither one thing nor the other, a John Ford–type clone disjointed in mood and construction, too many characters milling around in a plot deficient in depth. As for our leading hero, Cameron's flat, monotone delivery, stilted playing and severe expression says it all. (Booth quit the movie business soon after the film was completed.)

Cavalry Scout (1951), the first of three low-budget Monogram Westerns Cameron made in a row (before the company became part of Allied Artists in 1953), was a definite improvement on *Oh! Susanna*, due largely to Lesley Selander's firm hand on the tiller. Whipped up in two weeks on $85,000 finances, Selander's cheapo was a solid, talkative and basic yarn set in Dakota, 1876: Calvary scout Cameron (Kirby Frye) collaborates with Lieutenant Jim Davis, their job to run to earth James Millican's gang who have stolen three lethal Gatling guns, hundreds of rifles and 100,000 rounds of ammunition to sell to Chief Crazy Horse's Sioux in exchange for animal pelts. One of the deadly weapons mows down stagecoaches and trains in a series of holdups, prompting (and forcing) the Union hierarchy, against their wishes, to hire the ex-Confederate officer, one of the best Indian

Cameron takes aim in *Calvery Scout*

scouts in the territory, tasking him to pay a visit to Red Bluff and investigate the matter before it escalates into a full-scale Indian war. Clad in buckskins, our rangy hero ambles into the town's saloon, orders a whiskey and meal and meets owner Audrey Long, treating us to one of his blunt (but effective) chat-up lines:

"You wanna see me?" asks the blonde beauty.

He lingers over her curves, licking his lips. "Why yeah, now that you mention it. Mind if I take a good look?"

Snag is, Long's dating Davis, not that it makes a blind bit of difference to Rod; he knows a good thing when he sees it, and pursues the lass with a vengeance; his rival is *not* amused.

Cavalry Scout meanders this way and that without doing very much, but somehow, by the skin of its teeth, manages to sustain the interest. Smooth operator Millican is the lowdown crook behind the theft, secreting the guns inside his wagons and taking them through one army checkpoint after another without detection, that is until Long is abducted; she's tumbled to the fact that Millican is a rat, and he wants her silenced, sticking her inside one of the wagons where she eventually breaks loose. After three soldiers have been murdered by Millican's boys and scalped at an inspection point, to fool the army into thinking that Indians were responsible, the one real piece of action occurs in the final few minutes: The Redskins blaze away at the soldiers among rocks using their prize new toy, but Long and Cameron detonate a wagon packed with explosives, decimating the Indian camp. Crazy Horse surrenders, Davis expires, Millican is knocked unconscious and Rod is free to plant a big wet kiss on delectable Long; she left the movie industry in 1952 after starring with George Montgomery in Columbia's *Indian Uprising*.

Marlin Skiles' marching music livens up a standard second-billing oater featuring James Arness in one of his earliest roles playing Millican's main henchman. It's nothing special but canters along merrily enough, the cast giving the formulaic material everything they've got, a testament to the hard graft that went into minor-league productions such as this; everyone knew that they weren't appearing in a future classic, but what the heck—the end result was okay fare for the punters, and that was all that mattered.

Cameron's opener for 1952, Monogram's *Fort Osage*, turned out to be his final Western outing with the reliable Lesley Selander. As we have previously seen, Selander was an expert (and a massively overlooked one at that) at conjuring up an efficient, interesting-to-look-at horse opera on minimal funds over a short running time, in this case 73 minutes, at the same time eliciting the very best from his players. At this stage of his career, it was quite obvious that Cameron wasn't going to hit the big time, or the big money; his marginal acting talent served B-oaters like *Fort Osage* well enough, but costly budgeted movies were beyond his scope. However, we had the Rod Cameron Western during this period alongside the Randolph Scott Western, the Rory Calhoun Western, the Audie Murphy Western, the George Montgomery Western, the Jeff Chandler Western and a host of others, so his name by now was familiar to fans of the genre. As second-features, they filled seats and most made money; Cameron seemed perfectly happy enough starring in them, once quoted as saying that "acting was fun," and he had undoubted screen presence in a rough 'n' ready kinda way, due to his height, strapping physique, rugged demeanor and brusque vocal delivery. In his own particular performance sphere, as narrow as it could be, he was his own man, and in this respect, Rod Cameron very rarely let his target audience down.

Fort Osage was made back-to-back with *Cavalry Scout*: same group of technicians, a pithy Daniel B. Ullman script and a similar $90,000 budget. Again, Rod, in buckskins, played a scout (Tom Clay), turning up in the town of Fort Osage, Missouri, recruited as wagon master to escort settlers to California through friendly Osage Indian territory, although thanks to Morris Ankrum and Douglas Kennedy's machinations, it isn't so friendly now. The duo have not only been hiking up prices of supplies, leaving most of the settlers broke and famished, but reneged on a deal with the Indians whereby food and supplies are issued to them as part of a government peace treaty; his own mob has pocketed the cash instead, intending to rake in a profit of $15,000. Chief Francis McDonald ain't happy, his braves reaching for the war paint and attacking a solitary wagon, killing all three occupants. Big Rod, after witnessing the attack, wants to get to the bottom of the trouble before he takes on the job of guide, Ankrum's delectable daughter, Jane Nigh, catching his attention—in true Cameron tradition, two kisses are followed by a slap (well, he's only known the girl for 10 seconds, so what can he expect!). Kennedy has his own underhand agenda, especially when Ankrum shows unmistakeable signs of having a fit of conscience over the whole scam; he knows Cameron could be trouble and arranges for two of his hoods to ambush the burly scout out on the trail. Rod drops one, then plays possum; in the town saloon, he announces his presence to a startled Kennedy by engaging in a savage knuckle fight with hired killer Fred Graham (a customary extended barroom brawl scene included in most Cameron Westerns), shooting the gunman when he goes to reach for his pistol. John Ridgely, an official from Washington, then attempts to persuade Cameron, having second thoughts, to take command of the wagon train, without much success. "California's goldfields are more trouble than Fort Osage," Rod informs Dane Myron Healey, only to be told that the emigrants want to farm, not search for the yellow metal. Rod decides to visit the Osages in their encampment and have a powwow with his old pal McDonald ("Why wagon burned?") where he discovers the truth behind the Indians' discontent with the white man, promising to sort matters out, thus allowing the wagons to proceed in safety across their lands.

The picture's latter half takes place in what today forms part of the Keen Camp wooded area bordering on California's San Jacinto Mountains, shot in highly attractive shiny Cinecolor by Harry Neumann, a splendid area in which to stage a barnstorming finale. Kennedy rounds up his followers and charges into a smaller Osage camp, massacring the Redskins to, in his own words, "scare them." Back in Fort Osage, Ankrum reveals everything to Cameron, admitting the treaty supplies were never delivered to McDonald and handing over a wad of cash to the

158   **Six-Gun Law**

scout, who instructs the disgruntled settlers to fill up their wagons with much-needed goods. On his return, Kennedy confronts Ankrum and puts two slugs in his back for ratting on their deal, bashing Nigh over her blonde head with his gun butt (a nasty moment that will make you flinch) and galloping out of town with his boys toward California. Cameron organizes his own posse which includes Nigh (where's the sheriff in all of this?) and arranges to meet the Osage war chief, hopefully to smooth things over, stating that Kennedy was responsible for the slaughter, not the settlers. McDonald agrees to accompany Cameron with his pumped-up warriors and waylay Kennedy's pack of dogs; if his friend, however, is talking with a forked tongue, Rod's bunch plus Nigh will be shot. Selander piles on the excitement, backed by Marlin Skiles' thrilling score, the Indians pursuing Kennedy's gang through forest glades, culminating in a five-minute shoot-out among rocks, Kennedy collapsing dead in the melee. The treaty goods at last on their way to the Osage tribes, McDonald shakes Cameron's hand in acknowledgement that he was true to his word and it's a case of "Wagons roll!" as the pioneers head off for California, Cameron and Nigh going with them to set up house, the end to a streamlined minor Western admirably handled by Selander and his team.

Man plus boy and dog: A charming opener to Ford Beebe's *Wagons West*, the last of Cameron's three Monogram outings, released in July 1952. The boy was played by 16-year-old Michael Chapin, the lad first appearing in front of the cameras in Fox's *The Sullivans* (1944), aged seven. Chapin and Buzz, his pet pooch, befriend Cameron (as Jeff Curtis) who's relaxing

Cameron and Castle in *Wagons West*

by a lake, tucking into a plate of beans, a cozy scene, a prelude for the mayhem to come. Rod, in buckskins for a third time, has been assigned as wagon master to steer pioneer families through potentially hazardous Cheyenne territory; at present, they're holed up in the Missouri backwater of Joplin, awaiting his arrival and being bossed about by wagon train organizer Frank Ferguson and his two loutish nephews, Henry Brandon and Riley Hill. Cameron arrives in town and starts laying down the law—his law. Ferguson and his boys are to back off: "I'm in charge here," barks Rod, an ex-gunslinger, getting on the wrong side of Brandon who whacks him in the back of the neck, cue for a saloon brawl even before those wagons have started rolling. To make matters worse, the hunky guide makes, in typical Cameron style, an immediate play for Chapin's pretty sister, Peggie Castle (you have to hand it to the big man; he doesn't hang around), steam coming out of Brandon's ears—he's romancing Castle and wants to marry the lass himself. Noah Beery, Jr. and his pregnant wife (Anne Kimbell) join the train at the last moment, Beery behaving strangely, looking over his shoulder and appearing distinctly on edge. Personal vendettas laid out for all to see, the wagons embark for California, Cameron repeatedly kissing Castle ("An irresponsible roughneck," she calls him, grinning) right under the nose of enraged Brandon, almost goading him into using his fists (and gun), while with every lurch and bump over the tortuous trail, Kimbell gets ever nearer to giving birth.

Fair enough, there's not an overabundance of full-blooded action in Beebe's oater, but the director keeps things moving at a fair pace over 70 minutes; Daniel

B. Ullman's script is blunt-edged (suiting Cameron's acid delivery at times) while Harry Neumann's garish Cinecolor tones are at least different from the norm (filming took place in and around California's Simi Hills). It's an amiable, enjoyable trip, enlivened by Cameron, Ferguson and Brandon's antagonistic stance toward one another. When a small group of friendly Indians is encountered (Rod makes them a gift of fishhooks), Brandon shoots the chief in the back out of pure malice. "You killed him. You murdered an unarmed chief," thunders Cameron, unaware that when they cross Cheyenne country, a heap more trouble will loom on the rocky horizon courtesy of argumentative Ferguson and his scowling nephews; the renegade gun runners have been selling rifles to the tribes, a quantity in a box discovered by Rod and junior partner Chapin in Brandon's wagon. When Ferguson fails to deliver the goods to Chief Black Kettle in exchange for animal furs, the furious Redskins attack the circled wagons in force. Amid the fury of battle, Chapin jumps on Brandon's head just as the weasel is about to pump Cameron full of lead from behind; an Indian bullet brings him down, one arrow dispatching Ferguson. The Indians draw back, Cameron cantering over to meet the chief (John Parrish), explaining that unfortunately, he won't be having any rifles—they're going up in smoke as they speak. "I must have the guns," growls Parrish but, no guns in the offing, he shrugs, agreeing to allow the settlers safe conduct through his territory on return of the pelts plus a wagon and team of horses. Kimbell produces twins, husband Beery, on the run from his outlaw family, hence his nervy disposition, shouts with joy, Rod smooches with Castle, Chapin rolls his eyes ("Roughneck! Huh!") and the wagon train continues on its long journey west to the sound of Marlin Skiles' noisy soundtrack; small-time Western offerings such as this don't come any sweeter. Cameron's trio of hokey but entertaining cheapo Monogram oaters can be found in color on *The Monogram Cowboy Collection volumes one and two*; elsewhere, prints are in black-and-white only.

North East Minnesota, 1890—the setting of *Woman of the North Country*: Christine Powell (Ruth Hussey), scheming owner of the Powell Iron Mine Company, tells spineless brother David (John Agar) that she's running the show on her terms, even though he's the inherited head of the family. Steve (Jim Davis), her second, more wayward, brother, has just masterminded a train holdup, a reward of $25,000 posted on the heads of his band of outlaws. Christine, after kicking out gold digging fiancé Andre Duclos (Stephen Belcassy), is busy negotiating ore-shipment terms with Pittsburgh steel boss Henry S. Chapman (Grant Withers) at a gathering of wealthy businessmen in her plush mansion when news comes through that someone is prospecting for iron in the heavily forested Mesabi Range; Christine plans to move into the area to add to the riches brought in by the Broken Mountain Iron Mine and wants to know the identity of the unknown intruder. The prospector turns out to be geologist Kyle Ramlo (Rod Cameron) who has struck 60% pure iron at surface, spread over thousands of acres. To warn him off, Steve and his gang ride out and set fire to two of Kyle's cabins and, after

a shoot-out, leave a note stating "Keep off Mesabi." Spent German cartridge cases are found, a gunsmith confirming that they've come from Steve's pistol. Kyle meets Christine in town, much to his girlfriend Cathy Nordlund's (Gale Storm) displeasure, explaining that he's got $20,000 in his wallet to cover the Mesabi lease and challenging her over her brother's German-made gun, but she gives nothing away; in a moment of passion, he kisses the attractive but devious diva. "Alright, now you got what you've been asking for. Satisfied?" "Not till you get what you've been asking for," she replies. In his hotel room, Kyle is robbed of his lease money; he then singlehandedly attacks Steve's hideout in the woods, forcing a boulder onto the cabin and smashing it to matchwood. The bandits emerge battered and bruised, Steve is shot dead, Kyle retrieves his cash and collects the $25,000 reward on the train robbers. Victorious, he's now basking in riches, his opencast New Era Iron Mine Company reaping healthy dividends while Christine's dynasty suffers a marked decline in fortunes, her town office closed. But the Jezebel, burning with revenge over the loss of her company and brother, isn't finished with him yet, conniving with banker John Mulholland (J. Carrol Naish) to plot her rival's ruination. Perpetually intoxicated O'Hara (Barry Kelley), once sacked by Christine, gets involved in a fight with Kyle at a dinner; the mine boss is hit on the head with a whiskey bottle, ending up in hospital where Christine visits him and professes that, in him, she has met her match. Kyle recovers, succumbs to her charms and falls into her honeytrap, the two starting a romance and getting married. On their return from a European honeymoon, Kyle finds his workforce in disarray, stirred up by O'Hara; the ruffian (along with selected agitators) has been installed by Christine behind her husband's unsuspecting back as the owner of a traveling saloon, his remit to cause maximum damage to Kyle's concern. Kyle lays down the law to his unruly miners, production is doubled and a $1,000,000 railroad is constructed to enable ore to be delivered to Chapman's barges on time—Mulholland has agreed to the huge loan on condition that he marries Christine once she divorces Kyle. As the first locomotive loaded with iron ore approaches Chapman's barges at the Duluth docks, a trestle on the main bridge is destroyed, Cathy spotting O'Hara among the perpetrators. Convinced that Kyle's company will now collapse, Christine smugly spills the beans, saying that she has conspired to bring about his downfall ever since marrying him ("I'll take back what's mine."), that Mulholland will foreclose on the loan in 48 hours and that she demands a divorce. But Cathy's Swedish father, Axel (Jay C. Flippen) and his men quickly repair the bridge, enabling the ore to reach their destination on the specified date. "A milestone! May I congratulate you," enthuses Chapman to Kyle, Christine, realizing that her husband has won the day and is, perhaps, a safe bet, adding her own congratulations, grabbing the hunk for a kiss and whispering "Come home with me" into his ear. Mulholland spots them; seething with jealousy, his hopes of marrying the vixen dashed, he shoots her in the back, the schemer dying in Kyle's arms. Cathy has now got her man to herself, the pair seen romping in the snow as the end credits come up.

As of 2016, Joseph Kane's *Woman of the North Country* (Republic, 1952) is only obtainable from gray market dealers in a murky, monochrome print (not in Trucolor), and this doesn't help its cause. An overblown exercise in period histrionics, Hussey is Hussey by name, hussy by nature, a highly decorative she-devil twisting men around her finely manicured fingers; Rod blunders his way through the few action set pieces, his grim features set in granite; Storm is gorgeous but vacant (her final movie before embarking on an extensive career in TV work); horror/sci-fi fans' favorite Agar is utterly wasted in his role of the milksop brother; and R. Dale Butts' incessant soundtrack works

Publicity portrait for *Woman of the North Country*

in the old Civil War refrain of "Aura Lee" (better known as "Love Me Tender") in moments of twee romance. Full marks to Republic for concocting the speediest bridge repair in screen history, as well as adding a train heist that doesn't make sense—Davis is so well heeled, he doesn't need the money, so what is the point? Old-fashioned in conception for a '50s Western, *Woman of the North Country* is loud, overly melodramatic and somewhat tedious, having little appeal to Western buffs or even lovers of drama; Hussey in all her resplendent glory carries the day, while those around are simply reduced to bit players going through the motions.

Rod Cameron, Brian Donlevy, Barbara Britton, Ella Raines, Chill Wills, James Bell, J. Carrol Naish, Forrest Tucker, Jim Davis, Taylor Holmes, Paul Fix, Roy Barcroft, Chris Pin-Martin, and Jack La Rue—a great cast that populated Republic's late 1952 $500,000 production *Ride the Man Down*, adapted by Mary C. McCall, Jr. from Luke Short's *Saturday Evening Post* novella. Donlevy in fact topped the star list, even though he had far less screen time than Cameron, director Joseph Kane steering the audience through a labyrinthine storyline introducing perhaps one character too many and let down by a hurried ending. More for adults than cowboy-mad children, *Ride the Man Down* is a talkative, very well acted Republic Western just missing the classic mark by an inch; there's not a huge amount of action to be had, and that climax is both muddled and slightly disappointing.

It's 1892, and the owner of the extensive Hatchet Ranch has died from a heart attack in a blizzard prior to the spring roundup, leaving his tomboy daughter Raines, her weak-willed uncle Bell and determined foreman Cameron (as Will Ballard) in charge to combat the imminent threat of range wolves closing in for the kill; cattlemen Donlevy, Davis and Douglas Kennedy desire large slices of the ranch for themselves, as does Tucker, engaged to Raines but siding with Donlevy who has town sheriff Naish in his pocket. All four want smart-shooting Cameron out of the picture; he's determined to hang on to the spread, whether it leads to a range war or not, a real thorn in their collective sides. Back in Boundary, Rod is romancing vain Britton, her father, Holmes, also up to his neck in shady deals with Davis involving moving steers onto Raines' property. Moreover, Raines secretly fancies Cameron and all that he stands for, Tucker realizing this midway through the movie, thus stoking the embers of hatred toward the dogged foreman who simply won't take "no" for an answer. When Bell is shot in the back by Fix, another of Donlevy's minions, Rod, accompanied by Wills and two young rawhiders (Al Caudebec and Roydon Clark) dynamites grassland and water supplies at Indian Springs, an area Donlevy covets, and do their utmost to thwart the range-grabbers at every given opportunity, setting things up for one almighty showdown.

Unfortunately, that "almighty showdown" doesn't really happen, but before that, Kane keeps us all involved in one melodramatic vignette after another: "I've known Will Ballard since I was 10 years old," says Raines to mistrustful Tucker.

Belgium poster for *Ride the Man Down*

""You're not 10 now," replies her frustrated fiancé, spotting the warning signs; Donlevy starts to move his beef onto Hatchet land and bullied off by Cameron, the tough hombre setting fire to his chuck wagon; Fix's girlfriend is bribed $100 to admit that he murdered Bell; Rod smashes up Davis' saloon in a fit of rage; Britton begs Cameron to quit Hatchet; "I've got something to do and you're in the way," snarls Rod before slugging Tucker's jaw in another all-too-realistic fistfight staged without music; Cameron pursues Fix on horseback, the killer's neck broken when he collides with a tree branch; Naish changes sides, deciding to act like the lawman he's supposed to be; Raines informs Tucker their relationship is at an end, receiving a brutal punch in the face, Tucker ranting about Cameron, "I hate him. I'm gonna kill him."; Britton's relationship with Cameron also grinds to a halt ("If you go back to Hatchet, you'll never see me again."), the hussy telling Donlevy the whereabouts of her ex-fiancé, hiding out in Fix's cabin; Kennedy and his pack of dogs decide to bow out gracefully, concerned more for their own safety than encroaching on Hatchet property and being plugged by Cameron; Naish, calling for assistance from Santa Fe's marshal, is wounded in the back by Donlevy, the corrupt cattle boss falling to the ground, a bullet in his belly; Davis is shot dead in an ambush; and in a night scene, Tucker gets it from Cameron, now free to run Hatchet with Raines by his side; she's declared her love for the hunky foreman who has saved the day, and her ranch.

Composer Ned Freeman's use of "Oh Shenandoah" as a recurring leitmotif gives the picture an evocative appeal and the Utah location work is faultless, glowing in Jack A. Marta's Trucolor tones. Everyone plays it to the hilt with elan, a shot at all those critics fond of deriding B-movies such as this and the actors who appeared in them; Cameron, Donlevy and Tucker are on fire, and even minor players catch the eye (Caudebec, one of the young rawhiders, disappeared without trace after making this picture). An all-guns blazing finale would have topped *Ride the Man Down* off beautifully, villains Donlevy and Tucker deserving of much more than a single bullet apiece but, notwithstanding the lack of punch in the "kill the baddies" department, this is one Republic '50s Western deserving of an official release; as at 2016, it can only be obtained through gray market dealers.

In late 1952/early 1953, Cameron started appearing in various television series to broaden his horizons, the first as Ashley Cummings in two episodes of *Chevron Theater*. His next Western, Republic's *San Antone* (1953), failed to match the invigorating *Ride the Man Down*, being one of those motion pictures where everything appears to have gone haywire in its ideas and presentation. In fact, the production is a $400,000 disaster for several reasons, least of all being shot among the splendors of California's Red Rock Canyon and Vasquez Rocks areas in dingy black-and-white, not Trucolor, and an annoying predilection for finishing exterior scenes back at the studio using back-projection images; why couldn't Joseph Kane have composed and completed his shots at the locales they took place in without resorting to reshooting in the studio? In an over-ambitious rambling narrative poorly scripted by Steve Fisher, Cameron played Carl Miller, a civilian adventurer caught up not only in the Civil War but the conflict between rebel leader Juárez and emperor/dictator Maximilian in the fight for Mexican independence. The film opens at Arleen Whelan's ornate mansion where a ball is in progress; the lass, an outrageous flirt, is engaged to Lieutenant Forrest Tucker but teases Spanish worker Rodolfo Acosta when he threatens to leave her service to join the Mexican revolution. She kisses him, he pushes her away, tearing her dress, she screams and soon, he's in danger of being strung up by a group of lynch-happy Confederates. In steps Cameron, Acosta's buddy, stops the necktie party from having their way, engages in fisticuffs with Tucker and gallops off.

Cameron, now promoted to colonel by the authorities, is then tasked with driving a cattle herd to Mexico, escorted by Tucker's troops. "You're no good. You don't know how to be good," says Cameron to Whelan, shoving the sex-crazed floozy off him as she tries to worm herself into his affections (and trousers) before he departs. Tucker, incensed at having to call Cameron "Sir," deserts the scene when Union soldiers ambush Rod's cattle; the trail boss is incarcerated in a

Cameron consoles "sick" Arleen Whelan; Bob Steele isn't impressed! *San Antone*

military prison for a year. Kane chucks in footage of a Civil War battle, Cameron rides into San Antone, meeting up with singing pals Bob Steele (Bob), Harry Carey, Jr. (Dobe), and James Lilburn (Jim), discovers that his German father was murdered in a raid instigated by Tucker and is informed by girlfriend Katy Jurado that Acosta, her brother, leads a group of Mexican rebels: It turns out that Tucker and 49 of his Texan followers have been imprisoned by Acosta; 500 head of cattle is the ransom, and vengeful Rod intends on delivering the steers so that he can personally kill the Graycoat officer. Whelan tags along, much to Jurado's seething anger; she's Cameron's girl and doesn't trust the scheming bitch an inch. Whelan, overacting like crazy in Scarlett O'Hara mode, flaunts herself morning, noon and night, rolls her eyes and grins maliciously on the trip, a trip punctuated by a batch of mournful songs warbled by Bob, Dobe and Jim (sounding drunk at times), the vixen calling on all her feminine wiles to fasten her claws into Rod's broad back, even feigning sickness to grab his attention. Whelan and Jurado have a long-awaited catfight, the infamous Battle of Monterrey, an Alamo-type skirmish, crops up (out of context; it took place in 1846) and Apaches object to Rod's steers using their waterhole, staging an attack, broken up by Acosta's rebels. The ransom is agreed; in Tucker's cell, the two sworn enemies fight with knives, but after punching Tucker to the ground, Cameron demurs from stabbing him to death, allowing the subdued Confederate to ride off with Whelan, a fate worse than death anyway! The picture closes limply with Cameron and the lovely darkhaired Jurado in each other's arms.

"Routine ... lacks inspiration," commented the *New York Times* correctly. Republic and Kane probably opted for an epic sweep on non-epic resources, cramming too much into the plot and coming up in the process with one of the 1950s most lethargic, uninteresting cattle drives, the lazily paced narrative crawling through the rocky wilderness like a snail nursing a hangover. Tucker spits and snarls (although absent for most of the proceedings), Cameron looks stern, rarely smiling, Whelan is one hyperactive Southern belle while Jurado glows and emotes, mouthing trite words of love to Rod. Even the songs are as doleful as the action. The picture sits on too many fences, neither one thing nor the other; lack of color, a flat climax and those repeated back-projected studio shots kill it stone dead.

San Antone may have been one of Rod Cameron's biggest of all Western letdowns; *Southwest Passage*, released by United Artists in 1954, is the exact opposite, a little-seen Cameron gem that can at last be obtained from dealers in color but not in its original 3-D format. Rod was still making forays into television during this hectic career period, starring in *The Pepsi-Cola Playhouse* (1954) and as Detective Lieutenant Bart Grant in 64 half-hour episodes of *City Detective*, from January 1953 to May 1955. In fact, his days of appearing in Westerns, in this decade at any rate, were coming to an end, Republic's *Spoilers of the Forest* his final '50s offering, released in 1957. The actor was concentrating more and more on lucrative small screen work; *City Detective* would be followed by Lieutenant Rod Blake in the successful *State Trooper* series in 1956-1959 (104 episodes), six appearances in *Laramie* between 1960 and 1963, playing Detective Dan Adams in *Coronado 9* (39 episodes, 1960-1961) and guest slots in *Bonanza* and *The Virginian*.

Southwest Passage (aka *Camels West*), set in 1866, concerns Cameron's (as Edward Fitzpatrick Beale) expeditionary force, crossing limitless wilderness and parched desert with a team of camels and their Arab guardians to California; he reckons the ships of the desert measure up to the job because of their unique inbuilt water-storing capabilities and can shorten the journey time. Director Ray Nazarro prefaces the experimental trek by introducing John Ireland, Joanne Dru and Darryl Hickman, pursued into the hills by a four-man posse after the trio have robbed a bank of $20,000 in gold. During a shoot-out, Hickman is seriously wounded; having shaken the posse off, Dru, his sister (and Ireland's girlfriend), returns to town in a dress and forces Doc Morris Ankrum to go with her to patch up Hickman. Trouble is, intoxicated Ankrum ("The fool's as drunk as a coot," storms Ireland) is a veterinarian, used to tending sick animals, not sick humans ("Even a horse doctor is better than none," Dru retorts), but he roughly extracts the bullet from Hickman for a $100 fee, gratefully collecting a further $150 in exchange for his outfit and medical bag; Ireland plans to join Cameron's wagon train posing as a doctor, instructing Dru and Hickman to catch up with him later when the heat of robbery has died down. Ireland enlists in Cameron's group which includes a cavalry detail commanded by Stuart Randall; meanwhile, a larger posse has discovered Dru and Hickman hiding among rocks. Dru, a crack shot, orders two of the posse to "Git!" and Hickman falls off his horse, dead from his festering wound. Quickly making a decision, she heads off for the expedition and boyfriend Ireland.

An exciting opener, then, Nazarro refusing to let up on the pace and intrigue by having mule-skinner John Dehner eventually exposing Ireland's ruse and stipulating that he has half of the loot to prevent him from turning informant. His suspicions have been aroused when four outlaws, led by snarling Douglas Fowley, turn up at Rod's waterhole, demanding food and water at gunpoint; Ireland brings down two and rescues his horse (and its valuable saddlebags); how can a doctor be so handy with a six-gun, Dehner ponders? Dehner is an unshaven brute (he excelled in this kind of role-playing in the '50s), forcing pork down an Arab's protesting throat during dinner and whipping another before big Rod lands him a hefty whack. Dru turns up, Dehner drools over her bathing nude in a pool, she warns him off with two shots and Ireland knocks him senseless—it's no wonder the mule-skinner wants half of that stolen cash. But Ireland's un-doctor-like actions are even causing Cameron to raise his eyebrows, and is the beefy adventurer casting his beady eyes over Dru's wholesome figure?

Cameraman Sam Leavitt takes full advantage of Utah's rugged Kanab rock formations, a superb example of high-grade photography in a medium-budget Western, Arthur Lange and Emil Newman's stomping score coming into its own as Cameron sets up his surveying equipment overlooking a line of low hills, the ultimate plan to construct roads over the desolate area, Dru admiring him because "He's not looking for glory. He's doing this for other people," Ireland wondering where her loyalties now lie. Apaches are the next problem, but the braves look upon the camels as gods, that is until one beast gets a busted leg and has to be shot; buried deep, the Indians dig up the corpse and realize the camel is just like any other animal, so they continue the chase, stealthily and unseen. Cameron's major task is to get his train across 100 miles of desert on minimal water supplies. It's here that scout Guinn "Big Boy" Williams (a Western veteran, his first dating back to 1920) is bitten by a Gila monster; Ireland scoops out the poison but when it boils down to amputation, Dru intervenes; Ireland isn't up to the operation, and she knows it ("Clint. Stop it! He's not a doctor."). Outside the medicine tent, his cover blown wide open, Ireland is belted by Cameron for pulling the wool over his eyes and told to clear out, Dehner at his side, not wishing to see that gold disappear over the shimmering horizon. The pair discovers a waterhole high in the rocks; Ireland kills Dehner after the mule-skinner pulls a gun on him, galloping back to the wagons with canteens full of water (Dru has cured Williams' arm), Cameron now viewing him in a more friendly light. Approaching the rocky slopes to obtain more water, Apaches open fire in force, Cameron's men taking cover under a heavy fusillade of lead. Ireland, acting as decoy, drives the ammunition wagon loaded with dead bodies into the desert; the Apaches follow, allowing Cameron's wagoners and Randall's troops to clamber up into the rocks and refill their canteens ("I reckon we're all in for a short haircut," says one, watching the warriors massing for another assault). A second noisy, smoke-filled slice of action sees Ireland wounded, the ammunition wagon retrieved and the Indians falling and retreating under a hail of bullets. Ireland tells Cameron to return the bank takings to town, thereby redeeming himself in the eyes of Dru ("You can't start a new life on dirty money.") and the wagons roll westward to California, Rod, for once, *not* getting the girl of his dreams.

A tremendous outdoor oater vigorously directed by Ray Nazarro, *Southwest Passage* was the last-but-one truly outstanding Western Cameron would appear in during the 1950s. It's overloaded with roughhouse performances (Ireland comes out tops in the acting stakes), eye-catching scenery and a pithy script (Harry Essex and Geoffrey Homes); no fluff, nothing superfluous to requirements, just 75 gritty minutes of hard-hittin' dramatics ending in an all-guns-blazing finale, those '50s glorious Western ideals that fans wax lyrical about embodied in every single spot-on frame; Nazarro's picture is classy, eminently watchable and comes highly recommended.

Republic's *Santa Fe Passage* (1955) is the equal to *Southwest Passage* in every way, being yet another yarn involving a long arduous trek through hazardous Indian territory, filmed around Utah's stunning St. George region, its evocative canyons, cliffs and mesas forming a magnificent untamed backdrop to an incident-packed trip out West. William Witney's oater was fashioned around good-looking leading star John Payne, Cameron billed third behind Payne and Faith Domergue. Rod played humorless hardman Jess Griswold, leading a train of pack animals carrying rifles and munitions over 600 rough miles to the Mexican army, an unsympathetic part: The gruff loner loves partner Domergue, a half-breed sharing a wagon with her Indian mother, Irene Tedrow, planning on marrying the dark-haired beauty when they reach Santa Fe. But when Domergue casts her big green eyes on new scout Payne (Kirby Randolph), especially when she enters his tent and sees him attired only in long johns, lust replaces any thoughts of a future with Rod and very quickly, she's indecently flinging herself at Payne in wild abandon. Cameron doesn't like it one bit, informing Payne that Domergue is a "Kiowa breed," putting the scout off the scent—the man hates Indians and is deeply prejudiced against them; why is explained in Witney's lengthy prologue.

Payne is a disgraced character, wrongly blamed for allowing a wagon train to enter Cottonwood Pass, the Kiowas massacring every man, woman and child. While this slaughter was taking place, Payne and pal Slim Pickens were supplying George Keymas (as Chief Satank) with faulty rifles, a music box and a keg of whiskey, their plan to get the Redskins drunk and avoid a possible mass killing. Unfortunately, Payne was unaware that Keymas' main raiding party was waiting at the pass to murder the settlers, but that matters not; in the eyes of everyone he meets, he's guilty of negligence and the deaths of those settlers. Cameron has given him a second chance, much to bruiser wagon boss Leo Gordon's displeasure, feeling his trust has been betrayed when buckskin-clad Payne shows obvious signs of interest in his woman once out on the trail:

"Mr. Randolph. Something I think you should know about."

"Such as?"

"Such as this. I'm planning to marry Miss St. Clair."

"Congratulations. Why tell me?"

"Because you're a man. Because this is a long trek for men to be without women."

Having fired a warning shot at Payne, the journey continues, R. Dale Butts' tuneful score and Bud Thackery's crisp cinematography showcasing those rocky wastes, a feast for the ears and eyes; as in many a '50s Western, the jaw-dropping topography was as enjoyable to savor as the action taking place within it, nature in the raw, unblemished and untainted by human hand.

A sequence featuring a huge herd of wild horses that stampedes down a narrow canyon, Payne instructing the wagons to form a barrier, thereby avoiding disaster, is a thriller, and it's not long after that Payne and Domergue roll in the dust, Cameron, puzzled by Domergue's non-response to his kisses and marriage proposals, catching the pair at it on the second occasion, the gal straightening her skirt as she heads for her tent. In the morning, traitor Gordon is shot by Cameron for planning to set up a deal with Keymas regarding the rifles. Payne and Cameron decide to set a trap, Gordon's corpse, strapped to a wagon, used as bait to lure the Indians out of cover. In a furious river skirmish, Payne partly scalps the chief and blinds him in one eye, getting an arrow in his chest. "He not forget you took his hair," intones Tedrow, digging the arrowhead out of Payne who, intoxicated, kisses Domergue right in front of Rod. That's quite enough for Cameron: "She's not for you," he growls to Payne. "Would you marry a squaw? Aurelie's a breed. Ask her." "Nothing like whiskey for a broken heart," he grins, handing over a bottle of the liquor to his dismayed rival. Payne, horrified at the news of

Domergue's true heritage, subsequently gives the lass the cold shoulder, ignoring her when, days later, he's back on his feet: "When I get married, I don't want my bride to be a Kiowa half-breed," he callously tells her and at sunup, knowing that the Indians are on their tail, rides out to check on a spring of fresh water, finding himself promptly surrounded by Keymas and his greasy buzzards; Cameron's second-in-command, Anthony Caruso, has arranged this little meeting to get rid of the scout and his romantic overtures toward his boss' intended. Keymas, however, has no time for backstabbers, shooting Caruso stone cold dead: "Don't like him. Stink too much like buffalo," he snaps, turning on Payne. "You die slow."

Witney winds up his dusty saga in feverish style: Payne escapes from his Kiowa captors, rejoining Cameron, who aims a rifle at his back; the two fight, Cameron falls and breaks his leg and enraged Keymas goes on the warpath. Rod, lying injured, knows he hasn't got a chance in hell, ordering Payne, Domergue and Tedrow to hightail it, receiving a lance in the guts from Keymas. After more shooting and mayhem, the scarred chief is stabbed in the back by Tedrow; she dies in her daughter's arms from an arrow wound. At their journey's end in Mexico, second scout Pickens puffs out his unkempt chest, pleased to be best man at Payne and Domergue's wedding.

A round of applause for Witney and his team for going to the expense of creating an authentic Western street, a paved surface replaced by several inches of clinging mud: It's details like this that add to a production's values and make a film all that more worthwhile. There's not a dull moment in *Santa Fe Passage*; performances are top-notch across the board, the scenery is wonderful, Lillie Hayward's screenplay touches on racial issues without overly stressing the point to boredom level and Witney directs with purpose. This is a great-looking, unmissable '50s outdoors B-Western, one of Republic's finest: Any Western movie novice watching this in tandem with *Southwest Passage* (what a double bill that would have made!) will have some idea why buffs continue to hold these pictures in such high esteem 60 years after they were first conceived—they really are too good to be true!

Cameron only made one Western in 1956, Allied Artists' *Yaqui Drums*, a low-grade effort rustled up in three weeks on a $200,000 budget. As Webb Dunham, he looked older than his 45 years and heavier-set, not smiling once, perhaps mirroring his growing disenchantment with the whole Western deal. In a dispirited picture leadenly directed by Jean Yarbrough, the man behind two classic 1940s B-horror potboilers, PRC's *The Devil Bat* (1940) and Universal's *House of Horrors* (1946), Cameron played a drifter whose brother has been killed attempting to wrest control of his inherited ranch from land-grabber Roy Roberts and his gutless son, Robert Hutton, married to Rod's ex, Mary Castle. The movie opens with a stage robbery, bandit J. Carrol Naish (Yaqui Jack) and his cohorts fleeing the scene as lawmen ride up, guns blazing; two are brought down, Naish wounded, tended to by Cameron at his campfire, the pair forming a quirky relationship. "How d'ya get shot?" asks Rod. "With a gun," replies Naish, grinning, a lip-smacking, over-the-top performance from the 60-year-old which tries its damnedest to lift the movie out of a rut, as does Edward J. Kay's flamboyant score; a good portion of the budget must have been spent on his flowery arrangements but, in the long run, the composer's sterling efforts amounted to nothing.

Roberts is the smarmy villain of the piece who arranged for gunslinger Denver Pyle to get rid of Cameron's brother, claiming that a large parcel of Arizona territory belongs to him under old Spanish land grants that he supposedly owns but which no one, including ineffectual sheriff Ray Walker, has ever seen—and rumor has it that they could be forged. In town, Castle sings "Frankie and Johnny," Rod slugs Roberts in one of several extremely brutal fistfights on offer and crafty Naish, busy forming a Mexican revolutionary force over the border, wants the tough, close-mouthed gringo to "work with me, and we cause plenty of trouble, eh?" After 40-odd minutes, everyone ends up a captive (except Rod) at Naish's hacienda on the Mexican border, the walls under attack from both Indians and the Mexican army. Roberts is held for a ransom of $50,000 and a promise he'll hand back Cameron's property on his release; Pyle confesses to the murder of Cameron's brother and is shot in a tussle with Rod after molesting Castle; Cameron almost strangles Roberts to death in a fit of rage; Roberts thumps spineless Hutton, who dies after hitting his head on a stone hearth; Yaqui drums are heard in the distance; Naish asks Cameron to show his men how to use a stolen Gatling gun; and the Mexican army attacks, Naish expiring in the assault. Cameron, Castle and Roberts leave the hacienda for Arizona in a carriage to sort out their futures, the insurrection having ended.

If only that Gatling gun had been allowed just a few minutes of screen time; it might have brought a bit of firepower to a damp squib of an oater that, notwithstanding Naish's lively, entertaining star turn, comes across as a desultory exercise in Western non-thrills. Rod, grimmer than usual, looked as if he wanted to be somewhere else, while Yarbrough's handling of D.D. Beauchamp and Jo Pagano's formulaic material was dull and lifeless. Teetering on the threshold of outright boredom, *Yaqui Drums* is a Rod Cameron Western to forget; only that juicy piece of acting from Naish is worth 71 minutes of any fan's time.

Rod's very last Western of the 1950s, Republic's *Spoilers of the Forest*, released in April 1957 and directed by Joseph Kane, saw him teamed with Republic boss Herbert J. Yate's Czechoslovakian wife Vera Ralston, her second lumberjack film of the decade after Republic's 1955 *Timberjack* with Sterling Hayden in the lead, also directed by Kane. Produced in Republic's own variation of CinemaScope, Naturama, current ragged gray market DVD issues don't come with the benefit of letterbox presentation, meaning that actors on either side of the picture are missing in a lot of scenes. As for what once must have been photographer Jack A. Marta's colorful Montana forest hues, these are reduced to a blurry red/green mix, not the best of conditions in which to view a relatively short (68 minutes) outdoors yarn containing one or two environmental issues in Bruce Manning's spare screenplay; the setting is modern-day as well, quite a few movie compendiums omitting the fact. Cameron, after this one, wouldn't make another Western for six years, focusing on his *State Trooper* television series and heading for the Continent in 1964 to star in *Bullets Don't Argue* after appearing alongside Rory Calhoun in 1963's *The Gun Hawk*. *Spoilers of the Forest* is okay fodder for Cameron devotees, if just to see not only the picturesque wooded scenery but the hilarious sight of 67-year-old, 5-foot-8 1/2-inch Ray Collins almost flatten 46-year-old, 6-foot-4 Cameron with a couple of ill-timed punches!

Edgar Buchanan narrates the opening sequence, a forest fire decimating the town of Flathead, Ralston (an infant) losing her parents in the fire. Flash forward 15 years and Ralston lives with her adoptive parents, Carl Benton Reid and Sheila Bromley. She also owns 64,000 acres of prime timber land in the Flathead Forest, and crooked lumber baron Collins lusts after those acres, not content at signing a contract with Benton Reid, who doesn't trust the shrewd operator an inch, stipulating that only a single section of timber be felled at a time to preserve the forests for future generations. Solution? Get hunky second-in-command Rod (as Boyd Caldwell) to romance Ralston over the next couple of weeks and reach a point where the gal's so besotted and in seventh heaven that she'll sign a second contract over to Collins to enable him to carry off all her trees at a huge profit, whether Benton Reid objects or not. Rod jumps at the chance: Ralston's flashing smile and curves (but not her thick accent) are a welcome change from cutting timber and ordering the workforce about, but what he hasn't reckoned with is falling for the dame and when he does, his loyalties to Collins come under scrutiny ("Everything I've done is wrong."), as do Ralston's own loyalties with her adoptive parents.

"You like the ways of others now. The new things are not better," bemoans downcast Benton Reid as Ralston, back from partying in San Francisco with a brand new house in town, a new car and Cameron on her arm, accepts a marriage proposal from her man but stubbornly refuses to sign Collins' contract for fear of upsetting her family, who she wants to share her new home with. Director Joseph Kane throws in bags of logging activity and scenes of heavy machinery at work, plus a runaway lorry [truck] crash in which Buchanan is killed, and a rather limp Rod Cameron fistfight, to remind us all that this is supposed to be an action adventure with a message rather than an extended fling between Rod and Vera; he wraps it all up in fairly satisfactory manner when Benton Reid's son (John Compton), driving a lorry loaded with timber, finds the brakes don't work. Cameron and Hank Worden fly to the rescue in a Jeep, averting a serious accident when Compton leaps into their vehicle just as the lorry veers off the road and smashes to a halt. Rod's bravery wins the day with Benton Reid, who philosophizes about good winning over evil; the big man in the check shirt drives away with Ralston into the forest to play house, Collins and his men slinking off to lick their wounds in defeat.

Cameron is sturdy and dependable, Ralston, hair rinsed blonde, rolls her eyes and overacts like there's no tomorrow (but puts in a believable turn, defying to a certain degree her legions of critics who, to a man, stated she *couldn't* act) and a cacophonous stock soundtrack keeps things on the move (glamorous Hillary Brooke, playing Collins' decorative wife, called it a day in the movie industry after shooting finished, stating that Cameron was "relaxed around set and easy to get on with.")—*Spoilers of the Forest* is an undemanding way in which to end one's '50s Western roll call, Rod delivering his standard "Rod Cameron" performance in a film that certainly demands nothing more from him, and nothing less, a pleasant but noisy time-waster of the average-to-good variety.

CHAPTER 11

HAYDEN AT THE ALAMO, 1955

In 1954, John Wayne approached Republic Pictures' boss Herbert J. Yates with the idea of making a picture about the legendary siege of the Alamo mission in San Antonio, Texas which took place over a 13-day period in 1836; in the final assault on March 6, 1836, 189 defenders, both Texans and Tennesseans, were slain to a man under the onslaught of Generalissimo Antonio López de Santa Anna's crack Mexican army of around 2,000 (5,000 in Republic's subsequent version of events). Wayne's proposed budget came in at $3,000,000, with the Duke directing, producing and taking a leading role—in other words, he would assume total control. A rough script had been drafted by Patrick Ford, son of John Ford, but after weighing up all the factors, Yates rejected the project—at first. He objected to both the high cost and Wayne's dominant involvement over himself as president of the company; negotiations broke down, Wayne quitting the table and later going on to partly finance *The Alamo* in 1959/1960, dealt with in chapter 12.

However, Yates decided to go ahead with filming the story, titled *The Last Command*, racking up a budget of $2,200,000, ironically not far short of Wayne's initial estimation. Frank Lloyd was hired to shoot what would be his very last movie. The technically skilled director (he won an Oscar for Warner Bros.' *The Divine Lady* in 1929) was the man behind a stream of 1930s Hollywood classics, including *Cavalcade* (Fox, 1933), *Mutiny on the Bounty* (MGM, 1935), *Under Two Flags* (Fox, 1936), *Wells Fargo* (Paramount,

Hayden squares up to Richard Carlson in *The Last Command*.

1937) and *If I Were King* (Paramount, 1938). Hayden stood in for the departing Wayne, playing Jim Bowie, lured by a big payday ("I need the money to refit my boat," he joked to friends). At 6-foot-5, he was just one inch shorter than Bowie's reputed height of 6-foot-6, so fitted the part to a tee. Richard Carlson, fresh from his success in Universal's classic monster yarn, *Creature from the Black Lagoon*, took on the role of William Barrett Travis, while Western jack-of-all-trades Arthur Hunnicutt was buckskin-clad Davy Crockett. A fine cast also included J. Carrol Naish as Santa Anna, elfin 19-year-old Anna Maria Alberghetti (once touted as Italy's Audrey Hepburn) as Hayden's love interest, Ernest Borgnine, John Russell, Virginia Grey and Ben Cooper. Composing maestro Max Steiner, as one would expect, drummed up a rousing score, Gordon MacRae sang the title theme and highly experienced cinematographer Jack A. Marta (225 films to his credit dating back to 1926) drenched the production, located around Brackettville, Texas, in sun-bleached colors. Scriptwriters Warren Duff and Sy Bartlett took a few ideas from Pat Ford's draft and embellished the narrative by presenting the true facts behind the conflict, or as true a dramatized screenplay would permit to a paying audience looking for old-style entertainment.

A solid roll call of players then, augmented by one of the company's biggest-ever budgets. How, though, has it weathered over the past 60 years and, just as

The Alamo's gallant defenders prior to the Mexican assault

important, how does it stand up to Wayne's $12,000,000 blockbuster released five years later? After a brief history of Texas circa the 1830s, we are plunged straight into the action, Hayden, riding into town, spotting Richard Carlson, hands tied behind back, arrested, to face charges of speaking out against Santa Anna's despotic reign. Hayden's off to see his Mexican wife and children; he owns extensive pieces of real estate in Mexico, a country in turmoil, one of the reasons why, on his release, hot-tempered Carlson accuses the big man with the nine-inch knife of protecting his own interests at the expense of the downtrodden populace ("We will not passively resist to injustice," he rants). Following a knife tussle with burly "oblige me with a fight" Ernest Borgnine, who receives a slashed arm for his pains, Hayden is frog-marched into Santa Anna's office under guard to have a drink with his on/off friend. Hayden informs the dictator (a terrific, strutting peacock of a performance from J. Carrol Naish) that he's undecided about the growing revolution, accusing Naish of being intoxicated on power. Naish later has the unpleasant task of notifying Hayden that his wife and children have died from the plague epidemic, at the same time issuing standing orders that all Texans must surrender their arms under penalty of death. After a secret meeting with freed political agitator Otto Kruger, Hayden attends a gathering of dissidents where Carlson states that "We must load our guns and assert our rights," vowing to oppose Mexican rule to the bitter end and refuse to take what's on offer. Delightful

Anna Maria Alberghetti (Consuelo) enters the frame, a young Spanish Senorita totally smitten by Hayden's masculinity and his sadness over the loss of his family; poor Ben Cooper, her would-be beau, hovers in the shadows, unable to compete with Hayden in the machismo stakes. In the 42nd minute, having laid out his stall, Lloyd introduces a sizzling skirmish across a wide river, 25 riders versus 100 Mexican militia; then, in San Antonio, at a dance, Hayden, absent through mourning, turns up and pinches Alberghetti from under the nose of Cooper ("You remind me of her," he says to the demure girl, talking about his wife). With reports filtering through of 1,000 troops sighted in the hills, Hayden engages in another verbal spat with stuffed-shirt Carlson which almost leads to a punch-up. Hayden refutes Carlson's suggestion that General Sam Houston (Hugh Sanders) is amassing a force large enough to deal with the encroaching Mexican army but decides to join the volunteers with his men, especially when Arthur Hunnicutt (Davy Crockett) and his 29 Tennesseans arrive ("There's a lot of colonels around here."); Hayden ignores Naish's pleas to "Ride away from here, Jimmy, and convince your people to lay down their arms and come out." The defenders encamp in the old mission known as the Alamo, Hayden attempting (unsuccessfully) to persuade Alberghetti to stay at his home two miles distant; they embrace and kiss. Under a flag of truce, women and children are allowed safe conduct, leaving the fort as Cooper is sent to find out when they can expect Colonel Fannin's help. Three giant siege guns are destroyed, Hayden badly injured in the clash, the reason why he passes the reins of command over to Carlson, even though the small army of volunteers has voted him *de facto* leader. Cooper brings the bad tidings that Fannin's forces will not be turning up to support the Alamo; there are no more hopes for extra reinforcements. In a rainstorm, Carlson asks those who don't wish to fight to leave; none do, everyone stepping over the line as a sign of their willingness to stay and fight. Hayden hands Cooper two letters to give to Sam Hous-

Anna Maria Albergetti cuddles up to Hayden

Sterling discusses battle tactics with Arthur Hunnicutt and his men.

ton, knowing that next day, the final assault will commence and none of the defenders will survive the outcome. On the morning of March 6, the Mexican army raises the red flag of battle and swarms toward the Alamo, wiping out the defenders in a bloody confrontation. Houston is given the tragic news ("Their fight will be remembered down through the ages.") as Cooper announces the arrival of the weary, tear-stained ladies from the Alamo, consoling Alberghetti, grief-stricken over losing Hayden in the conflict, Hayden's letter saying that she should now find herself a new life with Cooper.

Comparisons between *The Last Command* and *The Alamo* (*not* the insipid 2004 version) are inevitable, given any fan's interest in the subject and the way both productions came across in a packed auditorium. Hayden, although not in Richard Widmark's acting league, made an impressive Jim Bowie, topping Widmark; he had the height, strapping build and the rough-hewn presence to go with it, one of his most telling, and commanding, star turns. Likewise, Arthur Hunnicutt's Davy Crockett was a lot more believable, and probably a sight more accurate, that John Wayne's portrayal of the backwoodsman; the Duke was simply being himself in buckskins, while grizzled Hunnicutt brought a folksy appeal to the part. Carlson, although creating a stubborn, argumentative William Travis, wasn't a match for Laurence Harvey on full throttle—no contest there. The romance between doe-eyed Alberghetti and tough guy Hayden is underplayed but sweetly intimate, heightened by Max Steiner's moving leitmotifs; Wayne's similar relationship with Linda Cristal appears, in some instances, heavy-handed and forced. And J. Carrol Naish's Santa Anna strides through the scenario with gusto, a juicy display that adds immensely to the movie's artistic values; in Wayne's film, the Mexican dictator doesn't figure until the climactic battle commences. And as for that battle: Wayne went for the sweeping spectacular; Lloyd opted for quickly edited, furious, in-your-face blood-and-thunder. The noisy, show-stopping closing engagement, lasting seven minutes, seems almost without choreography, as if the director positioned his cameras and yelled "Action—just get on with it!" It's fast, ferocious, raw and explosive, bodies hurtling over Lloyd's lenses (the stuntmen certainly earned their pay), death quick and instantaneous, a terrifying sense of being right there in the thick of the fighting, a sequence, in hindsight, years ahead of its time; a monumental tour de force in any Western buff's book, even though it lacks the sheer pomp and majesty of Wayne's showstopper.

Overall, Lloyd's vigorous, spirited and well-acted historical Western, an "A" production teetering on the edge of being a "B" production, has faded from memory, overshadowed by Wayne's enduring three-hour blinder, but, to its credit, the facts presented are far nearer to the real truth leading up to the siege. It's not as flamboyant as Wayne's epic, more down-to-earth and personal in scope. Moreover, it's emotionally draining in places where, perhaps, *The Alamo* wasn't. As a testimony to this aspect of the film (and to Lloyd's directorial expertise over Wayne's lack of deftness), my wife sat through *The Last Command* in August 2016, from beginning to end. After the battle had finished, Carson speared on a bayonet, Hunnicutt, fatally wounded, igniting gunpowder and Hayden hacked down by soldiers, followed by Cooper escorting the surviving women away from the ruined mission and clasping weeping Alberghetti's hands, Steiner's music tugging at the heartstrings, she was moved to tears. The climax to *The Alamo* failed to have that effect. What better recommendation can there be for elevating Frank Lloyd's memorable Western to near-classic status?

CHAPTER 12

WIDMARK AT THE ALAMO, 1960

Sometime around 1945, John Wayne had made up his mind to produce a film depicting the events leading up to one of America's most famous of all conflicts, the Battle of the Alamo at San Antonio, Texas on March 6, 1836, where a force of 189 Texans and Tennesseeans were defeated by a Mexican army of 2,000 commanded by Generalissimo Antonio Miguel López de Santa Anna (in the movie, it became 185 versus 7,000). The story of the fight for Texas independence, a decisive episode in American history, appealed to Wayne's Republican ideals, his fervent patriotism and all-embracing view on Americana, a flag-waver to beat all flag-wavers. To reiterate the facts laid out in the previous chapter, John Ford's son Patrick was hired to draft a rough script and by 1954, Wayne was involved in talks with both Warner Bros. (who showed little interest) and Republic Pictures, whose president, Herbert J. Yates, balked at a possible top dollar figure of $3,000,000; he also objected to Duke supervising the project in preference to himself—after all, he ran the company and made all the major decisions. Wayne walked out on Republic over the collapsed deal; ironically, portions of Patrick Ford's dialogue were used by screenwriters Warren Duff and Sy Bartlett in Republic's 1955 version of events, *The Last Command*, coming in at $2,200,000, not far short of Wayne's proposed budget. Frank Lloyd's movie (see chapter 11) focused more on Jim Bowie's exploits than Davy Crockett's (played by Sterling Hayden and Arthur Hunnicutt respectively) and was a fairly accurate presentation of the circumstances surrounding the legendary 13-day siege, making a profit at the time. But despite the release of Republic's picture, Wayne hung on to his obsessive dream; with producer Robert Fellows, he formed his own production company, Batjac, determined to bring his vision to the big screen regardless of cost (their first production under the Batjac Production banner was Warner Bros.' *Hondo* in 1953, itself budgeted at $3,000,000, followed by the $2,000,000 *Blood Alley* in 1955). In 1956, Duke struck a deal with United Artists, who would finance the project up to a certain point *if* Wayne, because of his undisputed box-office clout, would star in the picture as well as direct it (up until then, Wayne's only experience at directing had been as second unit director on John Ford's 1952 production *The Quiet Man*, and as co-director alongside William A. Wellman on *Blood Alley*). Wayne agreed to this stipulation, securing financial backing from several wealthy Texan landowners and oilmen, bankrolling $1,500,000 of his own money to a budget that eventually escalated to $12,000,000. ("Every last dime I have in the world I tied up in this thing," he complained to *Limelight* in October 1960, just prior to the film's premier at the Woodlawn Theater in San Antonio.) Wayne's backers also insisted the movie be shot in Texas (Sonora, Mexico was originally envisaged for location siting, and some building work took place, but this would not have gone down too well with the over-sensitive Mexicans), so a detailed replica of the Alamo mission and outlying buildings was put into construction near Brackettville, on the 22,000-acre ranch of James T. "Happy" Shahan, one of the most authentic sets ever erected for a Western, or any other film, to date, taking nearly two years to build at a cost of $2,000,000 (ironically, some of the buildings left over from *The Last Command* were also utilized). An extensive village was also constructed to house the crew and technicians, not to mention those hundreds of animals taking part.

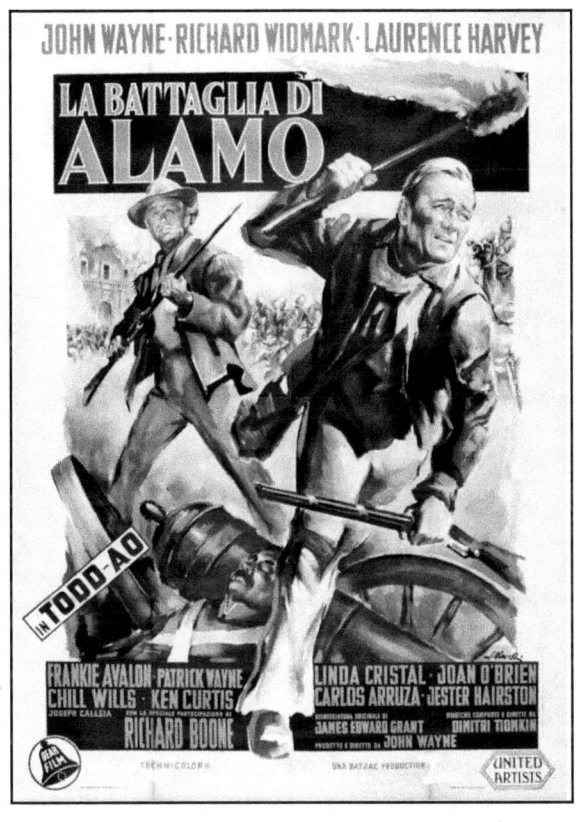

The crucial business of principal casting then got underway in earnest. Duke took on the role of Davy Crockett after bowing to protestations by United Artists and his investors that the part of General Sam Houston, which he had earmarked for himself, was too small-scale for an actor of his stature (Richard Boone was given the part over James Arness). Richard Widmark was also in consideration for playing Crockett (Marlon Brando entered the frame somewhere down the line) but took on Colonel Jim Bowie's character after Charlton Heston, Wayne's preferred choice for the role, had turned it down. Six-foot-two and a half-inch Heston, suffering from exhaustion after spending months filming *Ben-Hur*, wanted a break and doubted Wayne's prowess behind the camera (in later years, Heston admitted that he had made a career mistake). Wayne chose Lithuanian-born actor Laurence Harvey (raised in England) as William Barrett Travis, commander of the mission, following Clark Gable's refusal to participate (Gable, then 58, thought he was a little on the elderly side to play a 25-year-old). Wayne deeply admired English actors ("They had class," he said) and had been impressed by 31-year-old Harvey's portrayal of ruthless social climber Joe Lampton in Jack Clayton's *Room at the Top* (Romulus, 1959). RADA-trained Harvey, who had also performed in several Shakespeare plays on the London stage, turned in a powerhouse performance in that film; Wayne wanted that powerhouse performance replicated in *The Alamo*, to bring fire to his pet production's belly, and he got it, in spades, Harvey turning in arguably the movie's best display of acting virtuosity. Wayne and the volatile Harvey hit it off, Duke amused at Harvey spouting lines of Shakespeare in a Southern twang off set, which is more than can be said about Wayne and Widmark's relationship. Matters were less than cordial between the pair: Widmark thought himself too short (at 5-foot-10) to star as

A battle scene being set up in *The Alamo*.

Bowie (reputedly 6-foot-6) and objected to Wayne calling him "Dick," leading to Duke patronizingly shouting out "Oh Richard, are you ready for the next take, Richard?" Their political beliefs clashed: Widmark was a liberal Democrat, supporting the civil rights movement and gun control; Wayne, a lifelong Republican, opposed both. Widmark didn't think all that highly of Wayne's directorial skills and motivation of actors (and neither did fellow actor Ken Curtis) and had movie writer Burt Kennedy go over his lines of dialogue, altering passages of the script, much to screenwriter James Edward Grant's acute irritation. At one stage, "Dick" announced his intention to quit the project, but a threat of legal action brought him back. He also disagreed with Wayne not hiring Sammy Davis, Jr. (the all-round entertainer had wanted to play a slave), on account that Davis, a black man, was dating May Britt, a white actress (Davis revealed that Wayne had been upfront about the whole situation).

It's down to their innate professionalism that this ill-feeling doesn't manifest itself on screen, the pairing of two of America's best-loved folk heroes a sometimes tetchy, forthright but believable one, thanks to Widmark and Wayne putting aside their differences and getting on with the job at hand. Location shooting began on September 9, 1959 on a $60,000 per day budget and ended December 15, the production plagued by excessive temperatures, rattlesnakes, crickets and short-tempered horses, as well as a certain amount of acrimony between everyone involved and, from Wayne's point of view, an unscheduled (and unwelcome) visit from old mentor John Ford, the famed temperamental director blithely announcing that he would like to contribute a few shots of his own. He did, and they

Richard Boone as General Sam Houston

ended up on the cutting-room floor. During the scene where Harvey fires a cannon in retaliation to a Mexican surrender demand, the recoil caused the cannon to slam down on the actor's foot, breaking it—Harvey chose not to cry out in pain until Wayne had yelled "Cut," mightily raising his esteem in the eyes of Duke, who applauded Harvey's perceived machismo stance. To add icing to the cake, soundtrack maestro Dimitri Tiomkin, Wayne's favorite composer (they had worked together on *Rio Bravo*), was taken on to score the finished film, which finally came in at a whopping 202 minutes, including overture, intermission and exit music.

Premiered on October 24, 1960 in its roadshow length, *The Alamo* was subsequently trimmed down to first 192 minutes (the overture, intermission, and exit music were gone), then re-edited to 167 minutes on theatrical release after reports were sent to Wayne indicating audience restlessness; versions shown on British television these days stick to the 167-minute running time. The picture was nominated for seven Oscars, winning one for Best Sound despite intense (and expensive) lobbying by Wayne and his partners to up the awards quota, which annoyed many Hollywood insiders. Chill Wills' aggressive campaign to grab the Oscar for Best Supporting Actor, whereby the Alamo's defenders appeared to be praying for Wills to win the award rather than praying to defeat the Mexican army, infuriated the Duke, who brought out his own advertisement to counteract the possible damaging effect to the film's relentless promotion; Wayne claimed that Harvey, not Wills, should have been nominated and in this he was right—Harvey's perfectly judged performance as the waspish Travis was ideal Oscar material. Wayne also blitzed the media with an advertising campaign to underline the picture's "Republican Principles," one ad costing $152,000, becoming involved up to his neck in unprovoked political backlash as a result, the campaign viewed as a direct attack on the Democrats, left-wing activists and communists, all of which Wayne abhorred.

"Dick" Widmark and his six-barrel volley gun

Historically inaccurate in some quarters it might well have been (most films based on historical fact are), but Wayne's blockbuster (banned in Mexico for obvious reasons) was very popular with audiences of the period, recuperating its initial losses on repeated successful reissues (the author caught the picture for a third time at the Odeon, Redhill in July 1968 where it played to a packed house). DVDs transferred from the VHS/LaserDisc 202-minute version of 1993 can be obtained, but a full digital restoration job to bring the extended cut to pristine life appears unlikely as existing 70mm celluloid prints, discovered by Canadian buffs

The battle commences!

Bob Bryden, Ashley Ward and Don Clark in Toronto, have deteriorated in storage to the point of non-usage.

Critical reaction at the time was mixed. The *New York Times* admitted that *The Alamo* possessed "dazzling graphic arrangements of the Mexican army," but went on to say that the film was "long and dull … rather sticky Western clichés … a beleaguered blockhouse Western." The *New York Herald* enthused "A magnificent job … top-flight," while *Time* called it "as flat as Texas." The *Chicago Daily News* voiced what many buffs right across the filmic board now think of *The Alamo*: "A rough-hewn masterpiece … emotionally potent enough to make all hearts beat with pride." Most critics, in fact, complained about the film's sheer length and various historical anachronisms but, to a man, praised the stirring battle sequences, especially the blistering final assault, which involved over 7,000 extras and remains a bone-crunching, heart-pounding aural and visual experience, one never bettered, showing that in this one sequence alone, Wayne had triumphed over adversity and his snipers (the *MFB*'s critic, Peter John Dyer, summed up the climactic confrontation thus: "Its sole redeeming feature lies in one of those crushing climaxes of total massacre which Hollywood can still pull off thunderingly well."). Whatever one may think about a movie described as "John Wayne's political platform," its faults, its lulls, its verbose dialogue, its occasional clumsy editing (evident in the 167-minute release), its political ideology based on Wayne's firmly held Republican convictions, its speechifying, its lapses into sentimentality and the controversy surrounding the making of it, the Duke's monumental piece of work remains a damn sight more vibrant, uplifting and entertaining, even after 56 years, than John Lee Hancock's 2004 revamp, budgeted at $107,000,000 and about as dull as Western fare can get; and Billy Bob Thornton (Crockett) and Jason Patric (Bowie) are no substitution for legends Wayne and Widmark, whether the two got on or not.

Five decades on from its initial release date, how does *The Alamo* stand up as a movie per se and not as John Wayne's bank-busting vehicle to laud Republicanism? Has it worn well in the eyes of the fans? Let's have a look at, and compare the differences, in the Director's Cut (DC) with the Theatrical Release (TR), 35 shorn minutes separating the pair, and using character names. First, the music to the Overture, Entr' Acte (after the intermission at 96 minutes; DC) and Exit account for around nine minutes. The remaining 26 minutes in the DC is spread over 23 extended scenes and a number of scene changes, some lasting a few seconds, others several minutes. Notable lengthy examples of what you *didn't* see in the movie in the 1960s include the following:

(a). Following the arrival of General Sam Houston, the scene between Jim Bowie and old manservant Jethro is longer by over two minutes; in the DC, Bowie's character is, overall, given far more depth by the inclusion of many such scenes trimmed in the TR.

(b). After Juan Seguin's warning to Travis about Mexican troop sightings, the DC has the mission commander ranting to Captain Dickinson about Bowie's rebellious nature, Dickinson's wife Sue entering the room, thus curtailing a possible disagreement between the two close friends.

(c). In the TR, the audience is left wondering what happened to merchant Emil Sande, the lowlife who has designs on attractive Mexican widow Graciela Carmela Maria "Flaca" de Lopez y Vejar: Davy Crockett, Beekeeper and company investigate a church basement where a hoard of ammunition, gunpowder and arms is hidden, and there's a sudden ham-fisted fadeout. In the DC, Sande enters the building and is killed when Crockett hurls Bowie's knife at him. Crockett then visits "Flaca" and tells her that she has no more worries about a forced marriage to Sande because he's dead and buried.

(d). The conversation between Crockett and "Flaca" beside the pool before he sends her on her way contains additional dialogue in the DC, including the girl's admission that she loves him.

(e). After the intermission, over four minutes has been trimmed in the TR, including Crockett's men constructing the mission's defenses with logs; a heated row between William Travis and Bowie (one of many) in which Bowie is threatened with a charge of insubordination if he leaves the fort with his men; parts of dialogue between Travis and Captain James Bonham who has galloped in to give a report on Fannin's forces; and Sue Dickinson (Travis' cousin) taking exception to Travis' stubborn, God-like method of command.

(f). Perhaps one of the lengthiest removed sections of all commences after the night of drinking. A patrol comes across a Mexican camp, spotting cattle and being pursued back to the fort, with two defenders killed in the skirmish, the incident ending with Travis stating, "There will be no more patrols." In the TR, Travis' declaration (very brief) is shown, but what leads up to it isn't, another noticeable jump in continuity that can lead to audience puzzlement (although one could argue that this sequence is superfluous to plot requirements as the lengthy sequence where the defenders raid a Mexican camp for much-needed beef follows hot on its heels). Also missing: a further acidic exchange between Travis and Bowie; and segments of Sue Dickinson's daughter Lisa's birthday party: a combined total of around nine minutes.

(g). Following the first major Mexican attack (three-plus minutes in both versions), Parson dies in the hospital, Crockett, against type, saying a prayer; this scene is not in the TR.

(h). During the night before the final assault, several scenes in the TR have been altered or shortened.

(i). The battle itself, 13 minutes from the opening dawn shot to Sue Dickinson screaming at a Mexican soldier, has a couple of alterations (Crockett lingers longer in the entry to the gunpowder bunker) but on the whole remains unchanged.

The Theatrical Release does succeed in quickening the pace slightly, but the Director's Cut presents the fuller picture by filling in plot holes and fleshing out the dislike that Travis and Bowie have for each other. "You're a damn fool, Travis" and "you prissy jackass," are just two of the invectives used by Bowie to describe Travis in repeated verbal spats, the colonel counteracting with, "I'm better than that rebel" and "I've no respect for that knife-fighting adventurer," even labeling him "a traitor." But when Bowie and Crockett decide to stay on and fight with Travis, the three lining up in a sign of solidarity, Travis' mask slips, showing real feelings beneath that hard exterior and swagger. In modern vernacular, he gets choked up—and so will you.

Elsewhere, in the 39th minute (29th in the TR), Wayne gives us his profound thoughts on his political beliefs in his famous Republic eulogy: "Republic. I like the sound of the word. Means people can live free … Republic is one of those words that makes me tight in the throat," and demonstrates deft touches behind the camera, as in the poignant interlude with Linda Cristal beneath the towering tree, complemented by Dimitri Tiomkin's beautiful "The Green Leaves of Summer" refrains (Kenny Ball and his Jazzmen got to number seven in the British charts in 1962 with their rendition of this lovely tune). "I hope they remember. I hope Texas remembers," says a downcast Richard Boone as young Frankie Avalon charges off to join in the battle, but he's too late, the mission a smoking, corpse-littered ruin surrounded by the Mexican army as he views it from a ridge. And

Widmark and Wayne discuss a scene.

that battle is a corker: If you sit around for over two/three hours through all the preliminaries, you expect something pretty special for your buck and boy, do you get it; *The Alamo*'s dynamic final siege is one of cinema's, and the Western's, greatest of all set pieces, 13 minutes of pulverizing, no-holds-barred, smoke-filled action driven by Tiomkin's barnstorming score that will leave you exhausted after it finishes, a fantastic tragic finale that works on the emotional senses as you watch every one of those finely drawn characters you have lived with for all that cinematic length of time die to the last man (Wayne's death scene was influenced by Arthur Hunnicutt's demise in *The Last Command*.)

So to summarize: Forget about the in-fighting, the financial problems, the historical clangers and whether or not John Wayne was the right person behind the camera. Concentrate on Tiomkin's vibrant, richly textured, highly revered soundtrack, containing a multitude of leitmotifs to enhance the mood and nuances, William H. Clothier's superb photography, Wayne's conceptual vision, visual scope and craftsmanship, James Edward Grant's intelligent, sometimes humorous, at times moving, script and masterful acting from the entire cast. Wayne as Wayne in a coonskin cap (no bad thing), Widmark, sporting a giant knife and six-barrel volley gun, his usual highly charged self, smartly attired Harvey chewing the scenery with relish and solid, believable support from Chill Wills, Ken Curtis, Linda Cristal, Denver Pyle, Hank Worden, Joan O'Brien, Richard Boone and even 19-year-old, 5-foot-8 singer Frankie Avalon, among many others. Wayne's personal crusade weaves a darned fine story with colorful personalities to match, is heart-rending in all the right places, contains blistering, blood-pumping scenes of conflict and looks a treat (as it did in a theater over 50 years ago). Westerns come and go but *The Alamo* lives on in the hearts of Western fans, a timeless, multilayered American classic of the old-school, made with genuine passion that, like a good book, can be revisited and enjoyed time and time again by those who love and appreciate a motion picture that's either memorable or isn't—and Wayne's Western spectacular most certainly is.

CHAPTER 13

CAMERON: 1963-1966

After a six-year absence involving extensive television work (*State Trooper*; *Coronado 9*; *Laramie*), Rod found himself back wearing hat, gun and holster in Allied Artists' 1963 production *The Gun Hawk*, cast alongside Rory Calhoun. Ironically, it was a return to the genre for both actors after a lengthy spell away from it, perhaps the former cowboy stars thinking that they should give the Western, which had served them well in the past, one last throw of the loaded dice. As it's a Calhoun oater rather than a vehicle for Cameron, the film is reviewed in chapter 15. Rod played Sheriff Ben Corey, on the trail of old pal Calhoun, a notorious gunslinger hiding out in the remote mountain outlaw retreat of Sanctuary. It was a joy to see the old pros paired together (Cameron was 52, Calhoun 41) in a Western that gave early indications of how stale the horse opera would become in this decade; Rod looked brawnier than normal and his acting style was as terse as it had always been; he still had that heavyweight presence and, with Calhoun's swarthy charisma, kept the movie rolling by sheer machismo alone. But the truth is that if Rod and Rory hadn't had starred in director Edward Ludwig's final feature film, it would have sunk without a trace years ago.

During the second half of 1964, Rod Cameron traveled to Europe, like so many of his fellow Westerners, to star in the Italian/French/West German production *Bullets Don't Argue*, an early example of what would turn out to be a flourishing period for the continental Spaghetti Western. The Italian peplum era was coming to a close and those who

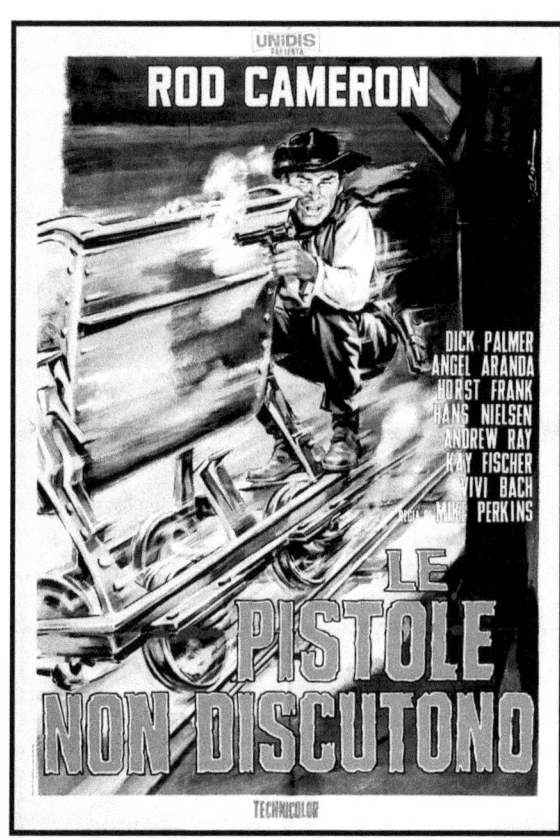

Original Italian poster for *Bullets Don't Argue*

had taken part in the sword and sandal bonanza were now lending their talents to the burgeoning Italian sagebrush revolution. *Bullets Don't Argue* was directed by Mario Caiano, the man behind seven classic peplums, while Mimmo Palmara and Andrea Aureli had been peplum stars for years, appearing in dozens of musclemen, torch and toga, swashbuckling, piratical, cavalier-type mini-epics; cinematographers Julio Ortas and Massimo Dallamano had also contributed greatly to the genre. Ennio Morricone's striking score was written around the same time he composed the groundbreaking soundtrack to Sergio Leone's *A Fistful of Dollars*, released in September 1964, one month earlier than Caiano's effort. *Bullets Don't Argue* has been left behind in the wake of Leone's masterful *Dollar* trilogy and others, but for those buffs not acquainted with the film, they're in for a pleasant surprise. Thankfully free of the overacting, buffoonery and comical absurdities that littered these movies from 1966 onward, Rod's initial foray into the world of Italian cinema is a real gem; streamlined, moderately violent (for the Italians) and put together with a genuine feel for traditional Western roots, with the big man in dominating form. DVD prints, although difficult to get hold of, are in pristine condition *and* in letterbox format, meaning a feast for the eye for those lovers of cowboy pictures not produced on American soil.

The story is simple, as most good Western plots should be: On Sheriff Pat Garrett's wedding day in River Town, two outlaws, Billy and George Clanton (Horst Frank and Ángel Aranda), rob the bank of $30,000, shooting the two officials on duty. Garrett (Rod, dressed in black) kisses his new bride (Giulia Rubini) goodbye and pursues the robbers across the Mexican border ("At $30 a month, I've got to get them men back.") where he has no jurisdiction, cornering them in a border town cantina after Frank has shot his horse from under him (the Bible-reading killer growls "Like the good book says, the bridegroom cometh," as he fires at the approaching beefy law officer). En route, Cameron has bumped into brother and sister Luis Durán and Vivi Bach who will figure in the action later on. Extricating the brothers from under the noses of the Mexican police force (Aranda is accidentally shot in the arm by Frank), the trio head for the forbidding Devil's Valley, a waterless tract of canyons, gulches and desert filmed around Almeria's Desierto de Tabernas region (this rugged, sun-blasted area features heavily in Sergio Leone's *For a Few Dollars More*), the brothers handcuffed on the end of a rope, all three feeling the intense heat. Buying three horses from a hacienda owner, bandido boss Mimmo Palmara enters the frame; having been informed by the hacienda chief that Cameron is carrying $30,000 on him, Palmara and his boys decide to follow Cameron and his captives and help themselves to those dollars. After several escape attempts instigated by Frank and shoot-outs with the bandidos, plus a brief sojourn in a ghost town, the threesome, almost dying from thirst, reach Bach's ranch, where Aranda's wound is tended to. Palmara launches the first of two assaults, boosted by a rival gang, Cameron handing over the cash to prevent a total massacre. But Aranda, who had ridden off in the night, returns with the cavalry; the bandidos are routed, and Palmara falls over a cliff with a knife in his chest after a fistfight with the sheriff. Cameron, aware that Frank had murdered the two bank officials, not his brother, lets Aranda off; the youngster has fallen for Bach and intend to stay with her to rebuild her burned-out ranch. Clutching the saddlebags containing the stolen loot, he returns to River Town and the arms of his loving wife with a cavalry escort.

From the opening scene of black-clad Frank riding over the parched Almeria hills to the final gun-blazing exchange of fire at Bach's homestead, *Bullets Don't Argue* is one of the better of the fledgling Euro-Westerns promoting an established American cowboy star in the lead role. It's as spartan-looking as Morricone's spare score, Caiano expertly framing his protagonists in longshot to take in that arid, sun-bleached scenery (Cameron appears very hot and bothered, later stating that, at nearly 54 years of age, he had difficulty in coping with the sweltering conditions), a lean Spaghetti horse opera made at a time when constant fooling around and mugging in front of the cameras *wasn't* de rigueur. Acting, direction, cinematography, script and music are all spot-on—Rod's entry into the continental Out West arena is a tightly edited winner that deserves an official release and further recognition.

The second of Rod's 1964 Euro-Westerns, the inferior Italian/Spanish/French-produced *Bullets and the Flesh*, had, like *Bullets Don't Argue* before it, several strong connections with the Italian peplum genre: Director Marino Girolami was the man behind the magnificent Troy-based epic *The Fury of Achilles* while Piero Lulli and Carla Calò starred in over 25 peplums each; leading man Bruno Piergentili (aka Dan Harrison), meanwhile, will forever be remembered in one of sword and sandal's all-time Italian schlock fantasy masterpieces, *Sinbad*

Against the Seven Saracens. Romeo and Juliet out in the Spanish West sums up Girolami's cowboys and Indians feature, filmed on the outskirts of Madrid at Hoyo De Manzanares, Piergentili playing a young Cherokee brave, Chata, passionately in love with Patricia Viterbo, daughter of logging magnate Rod Cameron (as Nathaniel Masters), autocratic head of the Masters clan. Once you get over the fact that what you are watching are unfamiliar Italian and Spanish actors in Western getup, a distinctly non-American background (far too green!), an Indian colony in leafy woods and even strange-looking holsters in light tan leather, then you have a fairly passable Chorizo oater made all the more palatable by Carlo Savina's melodic score (he composed the soundtracks to 22 peplum movies, from 1959-1966). Obviously, Big Rod objects to pretty-boy Piergentili slobbering all over Viterbo in the nearby lake, while the Indian's tribe, in return, objects to Cameron's men felling trees on what they regard as their land. It's all pretty basic fodder put across with pace, Lulli eating the scenery as a grizzled preacher on the side of the Cherokees, Ennio Girolami (the director's son) a loose-cannon killer and three thrilling five-minute showdowns to keep you interested: In the woods as the Cherokees attack Cameron's loggers; in town, between allies Lulli and Piergentili and the outraged citizens, Lulli shot through the heart; and in the climax, the Cherokee riding out into the hills where, following another lengthy gun battle, he's reconciled with Viterbo after wounding her by accident, Cameron letting them go, prevented by one of his own siblings from blasting Piergentili in the back.

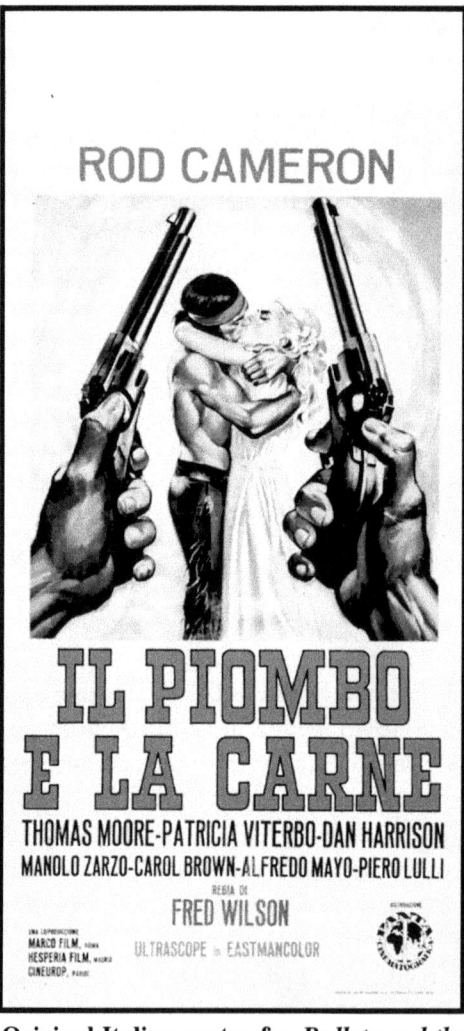

Original Italian poster for *Bullets and the Flesh*

Girolami pads out the narrative by focusing a lot on Piergentili's arrest, trial and release, but at least the picture doesn't resemble the standard Spaghetti Western emerging at this period (far less general silliness and exaggerated mugging at the cameras, for instance). Cameron doesn't do much other than scowl and reach for his gun (one disturbing scene has him beating Piergentili's dog to death with a club, a touch of Italian sadism creeping into the plot) while Piergentili himself, much like he was in his *Sinbad* outing, is totally miscast as the heroic, muscle-bound Indian lover, nice looking but vacant. A Cameron curio that, once seen, is immediately forgotten (on November 10, 1966, Viterbo was tragically killed at the age of 24 while filming a scene in a car; the vehicle reversed into a river and she was drowned).

In 1965, B-producer Alex Gordon (*Voodoo Woman*; *The She-Creature*) teamed up with B-director Spencer G. (Gordon) Bennet (*The Atomic Submarine*; *Killer Ape*) to knock out, back-to-back, a pair of Westerns that would embrace the traditional ideals set out in the genre's classic period, the 1950s. Embassy Pictures would distribute worldwide, each movie made on a budget of $194,000 and shot in Techniscope to attract the punters. Gordon decided to cram his homages with familiar names from the previous two decades: Rod Cameron, Stephen McNally, Dan Duryea, Audrey Dalton, Bob Steele, Johnny Mack Brown, Mike Mazurki, Fuzzy Knight, Boyd "Red" Morgan, Richard Arlen, Buster Crabbe, Frank Lackteen, Eddie Quillan, I. Stanford Jolley, Tim McCoy, Raymond Hatton, Zon Murray and Edmund Cobb, among others. These veterans knew full well how to promote and act in a low-budget oater and give the production the necessary expertise and bite. Roger Corman's favorite composer, Ronald Stein (*Attack of the Crab Monsters*; *Not of this Earth*), came up with two robust scores (as opposed to the by-now standard '60s wishy-washy efforts), Ruth Alexander scripted and Frederick E. West handled the photography. Compared to a lot of other cowboy films appearing in what many view as a declining period for the Western (Audie Murphy's pictures are the main exception), *Requiem for a Gunfighter* and *The Bounty Killer* cut it just fine, Bennet and Gordon basing their joint projects on crowd-pleasing foundations cemented in the past: a decent story, finely tuned pacing, fistfights, shoot-outs, no flannel and Cameron at his blunt best. One is great, the other a classic; for a couple of oaters made in the mid-1960s, they're pretty darned good as tributes go.

In *Requiem for a Gunfighter*, Rod plays a black-clad gunslinger (Dave McCloud) who meets circuit judge Tim McCoy out on the trail. The two get talking by the campfire, McCoy strictly opposed to Cameron's use of the gun as a weapon of law. "I'm a judge," he says. "Yeah? Of what?" is Cameron's sarcastic rejoinder, adding, "I'm the executioner. Only I use a bullet instead of a rope." "That's savagery," McCoy hits back, but the two start to form a bond of sorts,

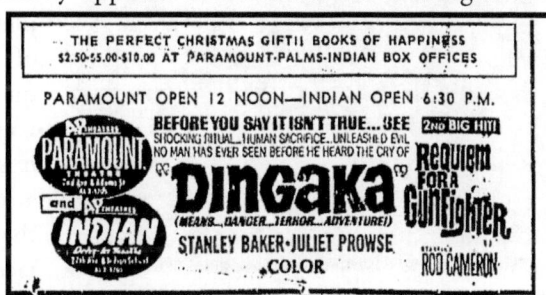

Cameron dismounts in *Requiem for a Gunfighter*.

brutally cut short when Bob Steele, one of Stephen McNally's henchmen, shoots McCoy from behind in an ambush to prevent him from arriving in Stopover Flats and testifying against another of McNally's boys, Lane Chandler, who has gunned down bartender Rand Brooks in a saloon prank—McNally has ambitions of being the town boss and won't let a judge stand in his way. Youngster Chris Hughes was a hidden spectator at the killing and rancher Chet Douglas, forever fussing over pregnant wife Olive Sturgess, is also at loggerheads with McNally; the slimeball wants to charge a tariff of $1 per head of cattle for Douglas to move his steers across land he claims is his, but which the cattleman states is stolen property. So the scene is set for Rod to stir up trouble with McNally and his rats when he canters into town; he's already killed Steele, so thug Mike Mazurki is itching to finish him off, as is trigger-happy Dickie Jones from a previous encounter. And when Rod accidentally drops McCoy's identity papers during a scuffle with Mazurki, McNally thinks that *he's* the judge, something which the gunman goes along with in order to bring this nest of vipers to trial for the murder of Brooks.

There are no romantic attachments in Rod's life in this picture, just himself in the guise of a judge, setting up court and quoting passages from McCoy's voluminous law book after confessing to Douglas and Sturgess at a dinner the previous evening that he isn't a magistrate at all, in fact just the opposite. "I'm not a judge. I'm a gunman. I just like being someone else," he tells them, becoming sick of his way of life without fully realizing it. At the trial, held in McNally's saloon, young Hughes is the star witness, anxious to testify ("He's a murderer," he shouts, pointing at smirking McNally), until preening Jones swaggers in, twirling his fancy six-shooters and blowing Cameron's cover ("That's Dave McCloud!"). Seizing the opportunity, McNally labels Rod an imposter and demands that he's hung, but it's too late in the day for the self-styled town tycoon; storekeeper Johnny Mack Brown, leading the town's upright citizens, carts him and his cohorts off to jail and in a street showdown, Rod blasts both pistols out of Jones' hands, then throws his own gun into the dust, departing from a cleaned-up Stopover Flats. On the edge of town, Hughes, an orphan, catches up with Cameron to convince him to return as the new law officer.

A 1965 Western in the semblance of a 1955 Western, *Requiem for a Gunfighter* comes as a pleasant surprise, especially Stein's stomping soundtrack that propels the action along nicely. Everyone gives it their best shot, a gritty, let's-get-down-to-basics exercise in traditional sagebrush saga themes that harks back to the good old glory days: This may have been on Cameron and the rest of the company's minds when they gathered together to make it; the cast of long-established old hands certainly take to their chosen roles like ducks to water.

Requiem for a Gunfighter's strong Western tropes continued apace in the second of Alex Gordon's oaters, the superb *The Bounty Killer*, which, if it had been released in the United Kingdom, might possibly have garnered an "X" certificate for its unrelenting, cold-blooded violence. Screen hardman Leo Gordon contributed to Ruth Alexander's intelligent script, a morality play centered on how a cycle of uncontrollable killing can poison one man's mind, in this case Dan Duryea's. He's a tenderfoot Easterner (Willie Duggan) coming out West from Vermont in smartly pressed black duds, waltzing into the Silver Lady saloon, chatting up unhappy bar singer Audrey Dalton and thus getting on the wrong side of her brutish boyfriend, Norman Willis. In the ensuing altercation, Cameron (as Johnny Liam), a notorious fast gun on the run from the law, comes to Duryea's assistance, plugging Willis without mercy ("You got 10 seconds to draw," he barks at the lout who's quaking in his boots). "Learn how to use this," Rod says to Duryea, handing him Willis' pistol. "Without this iron, you're nothing. A man carries the law on his hip." Intrigued, mild-mannered Duryea teams up with ex-sailor (and Rod's former '40s sparring partner) Fuzzy Knight, a grizzled old seadog nursing dreams of constructing a "wind wagon" that will carry him across the wide-open spaces minus the need of horses; they enroll as security guards, taking a payroll out to a distant mine. In an ambush, Duryea wipes out Boyd "Red" Morgan's gang almost single-handedly, collecting a $250 bounty. "Not bad!" he grins, and before you know it, the dude's attired in flashy clothes and sporting a gun, giving Dalton enough cash to enable the lass to quit her detested saloon existence and stay with her father, Richard Arlen, on his ranch. In their new roles as bounty hunters, Duryea and Knight focus their attentions on Buster Crabbe and his boys, worth $500 reward money. Mean as hell Crabbe is arrested and, handcuffed, rides off with the pair to jail, his cohorts following, Ronald Stein's doom-laden score, straight out of one of his 1950s horror productions, a menacing aural backdrop. In a shoot-out with Crabbe's men, Duryea and Knight are wounded; Knight is tied to a tree, Crabbe throwing knives at the trunk before shooting him dead, another bullet fired at his partner. Distraught at Knight's death, almost in mourning for the loss of his seafaring buddy, Duryea staggers onto the trail where he's picked up by none other than Arlen and taken to his ranch, tended over by Dalton who has fallen for him big time.

Duryea recovers—but he's not the same feller that Dalton fell for. "They're inhuman. They're gonna pay for what they did to us. I'll take 'em on. I'm going to take every last one of them, the dirty swine," the tortured soul rages to his sweetheart, burning with a desire to get even with Crabbe and asking Arlen to purchase a shotgun plus ammunition and belt. Armed with the sawn-off shotgun in its holster, he hits the vengeance trail as a bloodthirsty bounty killer, Arlen ordering him not to come back, having no desire to see his daughter get involved with a half-crazy gunman ("He's sick," he tells her). Thus begins Duryea's murder spree: In a series of bloody encounters, Crabbe and his bunch are blown to bits, all except one—Cameron! He's languishing in a cell, but when he learns of Crabbe's demise and the death of his brother who was a member of the gang, plus the identity of the man behind the slayings, he breaks jail and goes after Duryea, only to get both barrels in the stomach. Duryea, drinking heavily, has now become a shunned bounty hunter of fearsome repute, bent on a ruthless campaign of exterminating outlaws. Attending a church service held in the saloon, he regales the nervous congregation with his own murderous ungodlike creed, ranting "You miserable bunch of hypocrites. I do all your dirty work." In a fracas with Sheriff Johnny Mack Brown, who arrives to arrest Duryea, bartender Frank Lackteen receives a fatal shotgun wound. The bounty hunter himself has become a wanted man, fleeing to Arlen's ranch, a posse in pursuit. Against her father's wishes, Dalton decides to go with him, especially when he throws his weapon away and bitterly repents his self-destructive way of life, but it's not to be: Out on the trail, young gunslinger Peter Duryea (Dan's son), determined to make a name for himself, shoots Duryea, who dies in Dalton's arms, a vision of Knight's wind wagon forming in the sky as he expires.

Meaty stuff for 1965, 58-year-old Duryea giving a tremendous performance as the God-fearer turned bad, *The Bounty Killer* fully deserves a digital restoration job in widescreen to bring out its greatness; there's nothing sloppy, hokey or sentimental about *this* particular 1960s Western, only a cold, hard air of grim-faced revenge directed with the force of a sledgehammer by Spencer G. Bennet. Among a noteworthy cast of genre past masters, 85-year-old G.M. "Broncho" Billy Anderson makes a guest appearance (his last) as a barfly; the veteran of over 350 pictures made his movie debut in Edison's 1903 production of *The Great Train Robbery*; what a blistering Western to go out on.

Rod Cameron's final Western, *Winnetou and Old Firehand* (1966), took him back to Europe again, this time to Croatia, Yugoslavia and West Germany, one in a series of German/Yugoslavia produced films based on the novels of Karl May, written from 1875 to 1910. Pierre Brice starred as the heroic Apache in 11 *Winnetou* movies made between 1962 and 1968, Lex Barker partnering him as Old Shatterhand in seven, Stewart Granger as Old Surehand in three and Cameron as Old Firehand in one. Brice looked more like a neatly attired Comanche than a scruffy Apache chief, his warriors chased across the expansive Croatian grasslands (beautifully shot in Ultrascope by Karl Löb) by Harald Leipnitz and his cronies, the Silers, after rounding up wild mustangs. Meeting with Rod, mighty swell in a Davy Crockett coonskin cap and buckskins, the Indians plus Old Firehand's band of three (including Todd *Jason and the Argonauts* Armstrong) take to a high ridge where they open fire on the bandits who never seem to decrease in number despite heavy losses. The Silers retreat and director Alfred Vohrer adopts a narrative along *The Magnificent Seven* lines: The Mexican town of Miramonte is under siege by the Silers clan all because Billy-Bob Silers (Walter Wilz) is festering in jail, ex-peplum tough guy Rik Battaglia, the town's peace officer, having a hard time preventing the citizens from forming a lynch mob. Cameron and Brice draw up battle lines and the movie develops into a series of lengthy gun battles between the town's peasant population and Leipnitz's outlaws, a great deal of it exciting stuff, particularly when Wilz is shot in the back trying to escape, provoking more violence, and Mexican bandit captain Miha Baloh decides to join the outlaw gang but then turns against them when a priest holding a golden cross is sacrilegiously shot dead in the street. Sandwiched between the explosive skirmishes (wagons loaded with corpses and dynamite decimate parts of the town) and furtive sorties, Armstrong romances darkly attractive Marie Versini, Brice's sister, while Rod tries to rekindle *his* romance with ex-love Nadia Gray, busy being pursued by comical Englishman Victor de Kowa, acting as though he's just stepped from a farce direct off the London stage. There's bags of action in this last-but-one *Winnetou* outing, the rugged, sunny scenery a delight to behold—in a rousing climax, the bandits are forced down the slopes of a ravine, tumbling into a deep lake; likeable Armstrong expires from a bullet wound and detestable Leipnitz is pinned to a tree by an arrow fired by Rod, who finishes the thug off with another. Back in Miramonte, Cameron slugs his dopey English rival and resumes his affair with Gray, Brice and his braves continuing on their travels.

Cameron, Valdimir Medar, Todd Armstrong and Viktor de Kowa in *Winnetou and Old Firehand*

Although continental Karl May devotees were quick to criticize ("A poor and extremely brutal Western," "A bomb" and "The absolute nadir of the Karl May series" were some of the put-downs), *Winnetou and Old Firehand* is not without its merits, an invigorating Euro-Western to bow out on, burly Cameron smiling far more than he ever did in previous journeys out West and looking a sight happier—a nice performance in an enjoyable, fast-moving yarn. From 1966 to 1978, he concentrated mainly on television work, putting in an out-of-character appearance in Lexington's X-rated 1975 production *Psychic Killer*, an outrageous horror confection heavily cut by the British censor. Cameron's very last screen role was as Chief Gaffrey in an episode of *Project U.F.O.* in 1978. He then quit the business, living the quiet life near Lake Lanier in Northern Georgia, passing away at the age of 73 in Gainesville, Hall County, in December 1983. What did Rod Cameron leave behind him? What was his Western legacy? Well, any Hollywood player who between 1953 and 1955 figured in the movie capital's "Top 5" draws must have had something going for him, despite his basic performing skills. The fact of the matter is that he starred in a handful of classic Westerns (*Panhandle*; *Stampede*; *Brimstone*; *Short Grass*; *Southwest Passage*; *Santa Fe Passage*) a raft of respectable ones (his six Universal Fuzzy Knight outings; *Frontier Gal*; *Stage to Tucson*; *Ride the Man Down*), one truly bizarre oater in *Salome, Where She Danced*, a few that were not quite so classic (*Pirates of Monterey*; *Woman of the North Country*; *San Antone*; *Yaqui Drums*) plus a very decent Euro-Western (*Bullets Don't Argue*), all displaying, in one form or another, the Rod Cameron method of acting: Blunt delivery, grim expression, quick with fists and guns, and, as far as women were concerned, straight in for the kill, no messing around with formalities. In Rod Cameron, like so many others of his type during the movie heyday of the late 1940s and the whole of the 1950s, you had your standard no-frills B-Western movie star and as such, whatever he appeared in forms the traditional, much-loved Western that has long vanished from local cinema theaters the world over. Cameron gave the genre his best and that, after all, is what any fan can ask of their cowboy heroes. In his own unassuming, gruff way, he made an impact.

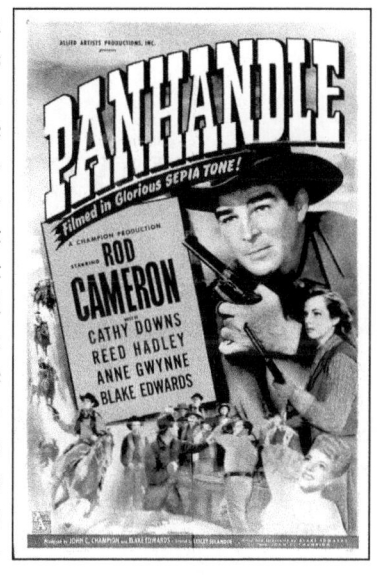

Essential Cameron
Panhandle
Stampede
Brimstone
Stage to Tucson
Short Grass
Ride the Man Down
Southwest Passage
Santa Fe Passage
Bullets Don't Argue
Requiem for a Gunfighter

CHAPTER 14

HAYDEN: 1957-1975

Stanley Kubrick's third movie *The Killing*, released in 1956, is briefly mentioned here for two reasons: Hayden, for once, actually fancied the part of Johnny Clay, and it's a paradox that the very best of the big man's talent can be found, not in a Western, but in this classic caper yarn (and, as mentioned, *The Asphalt Jungle*), unfolding in non-linear *noir* style. Hayden (he was paid $40,000 to take lead role) acts his socks off, spitting out his lines in rapid-fire delivery, commanding the attention, a tremendous hard-edged performance in a hard-edged movie; if only, one wonders, he could have put as much energy into his cowboy pictures as he did in Kubrick's seminal heist drama. And as proof of this, United Artists' 1957 offering *The Iron Sheriff* presented two sides of the Hayden coin; the lazy, uninterested look and the perked-up, now-I'm-interested look.

Where did that freshly minted silver dollar come from in the saloon takings? Whoever had been the owner could be responsible for the death of a stagecoach driver during a hijack—or are they? We're in Ellsworth, South Dakota, 1891 and Sheriff Sterling Hayden (Sam Galt) has his hands full. Son Darryl Hickman has been arrested for the driver's murder but claims he never did it, even though, on his deathbed, I. Stanford Jolley, also at the scene of the robbery and Hickman's future father-in-law, croaks to Hayden that he saw the boy commit the deed. With Hickman behind bars, Hayden sets about proving his son's innocence, opening up one can of worms after another en route, aided by whiskey-loving lawyer John Dehner, Range Detective Mort Mills and Marshal Walter Sande; Sande is there to make sure that if and when Hayden finds the real culprit, he won't fill him full of lead but bring him to trial in one piece, as all upright law enforcers should.

Sidney Salkow's *The Iron Sheriff* is a *noir*-type whodunit, cleverly written by Seeleg Lester, the narrative shifting backward and forward from courtroom drama to Hayden, appearing more morose than usual (if that was possible), ferreting out the truth behind the killing. The film could so easily have worked as a crime thriller, but United Artists opted for the Western format, popular with the public at that period. The labyrinthine plot is peppered with red herrings, one character after another in the frame for the murder, including Mills, Chinese laundryman Sammee Tong, newspaper chief Kent Taylor (Hayden's rival over the charms of Constance Ford), farm boy Peter Miller and owner of the Ace High saloon, William Phillips. Hayden, denounced by all for sheltering his son, is shunned by the citizens, who are crowing for a hanging ("Why don't you turn in your badge and get outta town."), making him ever more downcast (why, you might ask, doesn't he go ahead and knock the backbiting yellow bellies into shape?). At the trial, it transpires that Jolley objected to Hickman's physical relationship with his daughter, Kathleen Nolan, even though Hickman states that "I kissed Kathy once. I'd be ashamed to touch her before we got married." Telegraph operator King Donovan turns out to be the killer but messed things up; he ambushed the stage 1,000 yards down the trail *after* it had been robbed—by Jolley! Jolley took the $16,400 in gold and silver dollars, hiding it in a trunk, a gift to Hughes on her wedding day. A witness had seen Hickman open fire, but at Jolley who was galloping off; Donovan had shot the driver for nothing. Hayden, followed by Sande, who wants to prevent the sheriff from putting a bullet into Donovan, pursues the scared rabbit into the wooded hills (California's Simi Valley the location), shooting Sande's iron from his hand and sending him packing, tied to his horse. In a game of cat-and-mouse, he corners his quarry among rocks. Donovan begs to be spared; Hayden resists temptation, holsters his pistol and escorts his man into town, much to Ford's relief, who didn't want her future husband to be just one more cold-blooded gunman.

Emil Newman's melodramatic score (augmented by an uncredited Ernest Gold) blasts away in the background to a somber outing in which no one smiles, Salkow's pace leaden in parts except for the final 10 minutes where everything, including the leading man, comes to life. Hayden appears, in some instances, completely immobile, as though he's about to fall asleep, his mind elsewhere, drifting like one of his boats on the ocean currents, but, like it or not, that was his throwaway style, and it does add gravitas to a movie that overdoses itself on it. One great verbal exchange from scriptwriter Lester guaranteed to raise a laugh amid all the doom and gloom is when Tong bursts into Hayden's office, complaining that his cash has been stolen. "Money all gone," he moans. "No money left." "Well," drawls Hayden, seemingly disinterested, "that's what we got banks for." "What we got sheriff for?" says Tong, puzzled by Hayden's lack of response. *Variety* commented: "Interesting, offbeat oater."

Constance Ford and Hayden in a publicity photo from *The Iron Sheriff*

The Iron Sheriff was by no means your standard Western. Neither was Hayden's second trip out West in 1957, United Artists' bizarre *Valerie*, a curio among curios, based on Akira Kurosawa's 1950 groundbreaking, experimental Japanese drama *Rashomon,* in which a tale of multiple murder is related from several different angles. What led up to the killing of Anita Ekberg's parents (John Wengraf and Iphigenie Castiglioni) and the wounding of the vamp (or is she a vamp?) herself? Did she bring it all on her shoulders by treating her new husband, ex-Union major Sterling Hayden (John Garth) like dirt, dissatisfied with the luxurious Garth Manor and carrying out affairs with his brother, Peter Walker, and the local priest, Anthony Steel (Ekberg and Steel were married at the time)? The townsfolk reckon that the slut got all that she deserved, cattle rancher Hayden regarded with a certain amount of sympathy—he claims he opened fire in self-defense anyway. Hauled before a judge, Gage Clarke acting

208   Six-Gun Law

as his counsel, dour-faced Hayden, the caring, wronged husband, stands trial for murder and in three lengthy flashbacks, the same series of events leading up to the couple's wedding and its aftermath is told, from the viewpoint of Hayden, Steel and, lastly, Ekberg. We are first led to believe that Ekberg is a money-obsessed nymphomaniac, refusing to consummate her marriage to Hayden but bedding both Walker and Steel without a second thought. Then Steel appears to be the catalyst, a shotgun-toting reverend lusting after the blonde temptress. Finally, the court adjourns to Limerock's clinic where Ekberg, recovering on her bed, spills the beans on the whole business: Her immigrant parents coerced her into marrying Hayden to cement their position in Limerock, presenting the rancher with a $15,000 dowry which he used to clear debts. Walker was the man she loved, Hayden aware of this ("You seem frightened. You weren't frightened when you kissed my brother."), using his skills honed in prisoner interrogations during the Civil War to break her will, including stubbing his cigar on her lovely back, slapping her face hard, forcing liquor down her throat, ("Drink it!" he roars), forcing her to write incriminating letters to Steel so that he can sue her for divorce, raping her and, when he discovers that she's pregnant ("I don't want to have to support your brat."), subjecting his abused wife to a terrifying buggy ride in the hope that she'll miscarry. To prove that she's telling the truth, that Hayden is a monster in disguise, Ekberg's back is exposed to the jury, revealing livid cigar burns on her skin. Hayden, who has been lying all along, grabs two guns, his pal Jered Barclay another, and they seize Ekberg, dragging her into the street. Walker, who hates his domineering sibling, guns down the guilty pair and, hit in the arm, escorts Ekberg back into hospital.

In German director Gerd Oswald's overwrought Western courtroom non-actioner, Hayden goes from "I'm the innocent party" mode to psychotic manipulator with ease. Not so Ekberg, who struggles in her role of immoral demon to terrorized angel; her movie

Hayden and Anita Ekberg tie the knot in *Valerie*.

magazine sultry looks just about compensated for a halting, unconvincing performance. Oswald, who had made two United Artists' oaters prior to this oddity, *The Brass Legend* (1956) and *Fury at Showdown* (1957), was also let down by a twee violin-based score from Albert Glasser, sounding like music from a musty 1930s period drama. This was the composer who had galvanized horror-mad audiences with pounding soundtracks backing up memorable '50s guilty pleasures like *Indestructible Man*, *The Cyclops*, *Giant from the Unknown* and *The Amazing Colossal Man*. Here, he could have produced something more appropriate, although the static material may have been difficult to adapt to his usual bombastic style of notation. Oscar winner Ernest Laszlo (*Ship of Fools*, 1965) provided sharp monochrome photography, wasted on this occasion, and in one scene (included twice because of the repeated flashback format), the shadow of the camera crew can be seen quite clearly in the foreground when Hayden alights from a buggy to open the ranch gate.

Hayden, Ekberg and Peter Walker in *Valerie*

Valerie is a peculiar mix that hasn't worn well and is virtually unwatchable nowadays, a turgid 84 minutes that drags by, although admittedly the picture is not without interest. Judging by Hayden's pained expression, he didn't enjoy the experience, thankful to be on firmer ground in Allied Artists' *Gun Battle at Monterey* after putting in a guest appearance in TV's popular *Wagon Train*. On the face of it, Sterling's third 1957 Western didn't have a lot going for it: It was director Sidney Franklin, Jr.'s one and only film and co-director Carl K. Hittleman's third (he also produced). Moreover, composer Robert Wiley Miller had only scored four other features; this would be his final offering. Scriptwriters Jack Leonard and Lawrence Resner had 27 credits between them, mostly TV shows, although Leonard had been nominated for an Academy Award for his work

Mercedes McCambridge, Hayden and Robert Horton on the set of TV's *Wagon Train*

on RKO-Radio's *The Narrow Margin* in 1953. So, not a great deal of expertise behind the cameras, and no actual gun battle at Monterey either. What has it got to deserve the status of "underrated Sterling Hayden Western." An involving story spread over 67 minutes with fine interaction between the lead characters, a solid turn from Hayden and an unpredictable conclusion to round it all off.

Hayden (Jay Turner) and Ted de Corsia (a nice display of roguery from one of the screen's best-known "B" villains) have just robbed the Monterey Express Company, stashing the loot in a sea cave. De Corsia isn't too happy with the certainty that his world-weary partner wants to quit the life of crime after his $5,000 cut. "What's eatin' you?" barks de Corsia, throwing in a challenge: "How good are you with a gun?" As Hayden stands on a rock in the pounding surf, three bullets are pumped into him, one in the back, one in the arm and one in the chest. Found comatose on the beach by Pamela Duncan, he's patched up and nursed back to health, spending an idyllic four weeks with the lass, the couple falling in love. But Hayden is after de Corsia's blood, despite Duncan's solicitations for him not to hit the revenge trail. "Fish with us," she says, sitting by the sea. "I'd like to catch something now—and he isn't a fish," Hayden retorts. "I don't like shooting. Don't do it." begs Duncan. A dilemma has arisen—how not to upset his girl's feelings and wreck his romance by nabbing, and possibly killing, de Corsia. With this in mind, and the fact that the law thinks he's dead, he hatches a deviously cunning plan to bring the outlaw to justice without harming a hair on his head.

In Del Rey, de Corsia has taken over the Fortuna saloon by murdering proprietor Fred Sherman, blaming the act on self-defense; Sheriff Charles Cane is no help when it comes to an inquest, a dissipated sot, while snake-eyed Lee Van Cleef hovers by de Corsia's side, desperate to put a slug into anyone who upsets his corrupt boss. In strolls Hayden after 12 months of searching for his betrayer all over California, much to de Corsia's horror, claiming to be one John York from El Paso, just passing through. "Get a bead on him," de Corsia orders Van Cleef, sweating, Hayden denying all knowledge of their partnership ("It's him! I swear it!" cries de Corsia, getting jumpier by the minute), the casino boss instructing Mary Beth Hughes to seduce Hayden in his room in the hope that she'll spot any scars on his body. Hughes rips Hayden's shirt, licks her lips over that beefy torso, plants a smacker on his face and whispers "I aim to please" but still won't let on to Corsia what she did or didn't see. In the crowded saloon, Hayden grabs Van Cleef's cigar, lights his with it and hands the smoke back; yep, all this eight years before Van Cleef performed the same trick on Klaus Kinski in *For a Few Dollars More*! Sitting at a card table, Hayden deals the pack, de Corsia mumbling "He's no player. It's an act. He's faking it!" Hayden's scheme begins to work: Whipping Van Cleef in a brawl, he drags him off to jail and deputized for his efforts. Van Cleef then strangles the sheriff, is set free by Hughes but shot dead by Hayden, de Corsia tied up on a horse, ready to be taken to El Paso where, Hayden lies to the townsfolk, he's a wanted man. Hayden is now the town hero; they've been itching to get rid of all this lowlife for a year and the surly stranger has achieved it with no assistance from anybody.

Pamela Duncan, Ted de Corsia and Lee Van Cleef in a still from *Gun Battle at Monterey*

Out in the arid wilds (California's Red Rock Canyon), Miller's stirring soundtrack containing snatches of the old American folk song "Oh Shenandoah" comes into its own as de Corsia bitches to his old partner, "You're playing little games of revenge." "We're going to Monterey," says Hayden. "I'm taking you over to the sheriff for armed robbery and murder." "But you're alive!" yells de Corsia. "Three good reasons," is the terse reply, Hayden tossing three empty shell cases into the cooking pan, adding, "I'm gonna get you hung all nice and legal." In Monterey, de Corsia is handed over to an astonished Sheriff George Baxter; job done, Hayden gallops back to Duncan's loving arms.

"I found him."

"Killed him?"

"No. He's in Monterey, to be hung for murder."
"Whose?"
"Mine."

Duncan can't agree with this disreputable (in her eyes) turn of events; vengeance is wrong, she states, pricking Hayden's conscience. "Will you love me whatever happens?" he asks her. "Yes," is the answer. Mounting his horse, Hayden returns to Monterey and gives himself up, sharing a cell with de Corsia, both men roaring with laughter at the situation they now find themselves in.

Unusual in concept, continually twisting and turning and ultimately rewarding in an odd kind of fashion, *Gun Battle at Monterey* was to be the penultimate Western *proper* that Sterling Hayden would ever star in if you discount the comedy Italian oater *Cipolla Colt*, released in 1975/1976. His final Western, United Artists' *Terror in a Texas Town* (1958), was perhaps the one to hang up his spurs on; it's gained cult status over the years for various reasons. Writers Dalton Trumbo (a double-Oscar winner) and Ben L. Perry were blacklisted during the Joseph McCarthy commie-bashing era, as was actor/writer Nedrick (Ned) Young. Hayden himself had toyed with communism after the war (and held himself in contempt over his involvement with the Party) and this was to be hack-of-all-trades Joseph H. Lewis' last picture before entering the world of television. Another twice-Oscar winner, Ray Rennahan, was responsible for the deep, sharp-edged black-and-white photography, while Gerald Fried supplied an idiosyncratic, spare soundtrack made up principally of trumpet and strummed guitar, in complete contrast to his thumping horror scores (*I Bury the Living*, *The Vampire* and *Curse of the Faceless Man*, among others). Another interesting fact is that in England, the movie appeared on the billboards in some areas sporting an "X" rating. The British Board of Film Censors passed the picture as an "A" but the author

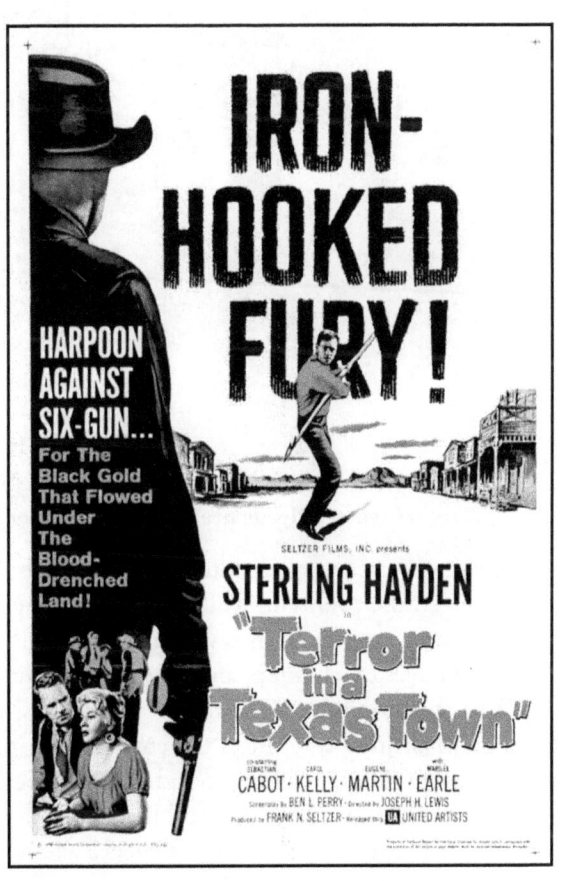

Hayden's deeds are torn up in *Terror in a Texas Town*.

recalls seeing it paired on a double "X" bill with *I Bury the Living* sometime in 1961; Surrey, the county in which it was showing, had, like other English counties, the power to impose its own classification if it deemed the material unsuitable for the eyes of children, and that may well have been the case here.

Why the prohibitive "X" and "A" certificates? Ned Young's black-clad, grim-faced gunman Johnny Crale is the embodiment of pure evil, a satanic entity in human form ("Death walking round in the shape of a man.") whose speciality is shooting his victims in the head, followed by five more into the still-twitching corpse. Girlfriend Carol Kelly is a slovenly whore, spending most of her time in

214 Six-Gun Law

bed, dreaming of a better life; and Young meets his Maker big-time, a whale harpoon plunged into his chest. It's these scenes, plus the adults-only air of *noir*-type violence, that makes *Terror in a Texas Town* unsuitable for the kids. Lewis frames his cast in close-up to add dynamism and imbues the production with a sweaty menace, a dazzling display of directorial nous that belies the man's penchant for dabbling in B-movies for most of his career.

The land bordering on Prairie City is rich in the black gold, oil, prompting ruthless land-grabbing magnate Sebastion Cabot to force pioneers off their land by offering them a pittance; those who decide to dig their heels in have their homes burned to the ground, their livestock run off or receive six bullets from Young's deadly left Colt .45 (his severed right hand, now a gloved metal claw, is useless; he wears a double holster for show). Swedish farmer Ted Stanhope is killed by Young for refusing to give up his land, challenging him with a harpoon: ex-seaman Hayden (as George Hansen) arrives in town, is told of his father's death and claims the homestead as his, even though oily, overweight Cabot claims it isn't; it was bought illegally by Stanhope, he says, and he now owns the deeds. The bull-headed Swede won't take "no" for an answer and comes up against Cabot's vicious henchmen and omnipresent Young, deciding to make a stand when young Mexican Victor Milan is pumped full of lead, leaving a grieving wife and three small children. But Milan's death prays on Young's conscience, has opened up a chink in his black armor; the Mexican wasn't afraid to die, and this troubles him. By now, Kelly has walked out on the psycho and Cabot sprawls on the plush carpeted floor, shot through arguing with Young. Hayden, meantime, has rallied the town's settlers and marches up the street to face the killer, armed with his father's harpoon (this sequence opens the picture). Young reaches for his gun and lets off a shot, collapsing in agony as the harpoon finds its target; Prairie City is at last free of tyranny.

An intense Western overflowing with ripe performances, Lewis' minimal near-classic showcases one of Western's vilest of all killers in Young's mesmerizing portrayal of a man in terminal decay, a cold-hearted, frozen-faced gunslinger to beat 'em all. Hayden, despite an erratic Swedish accent and wearing a suit two sizes too small for his build, also shines in a film that comes across as a thinly disguised pop at American attitudes toward racial harmony, loose morals in society and the lust for power over the masses, not surprising when you consider the names behind the making of it. Even the normally over-critical *New York Times* enthused: "Young a sardonically slithery villain ... trashy B-movie dialogue ... has required the reputation of a minor classic." "A sleeper," said *The Hollywood Reporter*, while *Variety* commented "A routine filler for the duals."

Peter Sellers and Hayden in *Dr. Strangelove*

Sterling Hayden then quit the Western genre, and on a high note, although he would have taken the role of the knife thrower Britt in John Sturges' *The Magnificent Seven* (United Artists, 1960); the part was given to James Coburn when Hayden became unavailable. Among other successes were parts in Stanley Kubrick's *Dr. Strangelove or: How I learned to Stop Worrying and Love the Bomb* (Columbia, 1964), the X-rated [in the UK] crime opus *Hard Contract* (Fox, 1964), a cameo in *The Godfather* (Paramount, 1972) and as Roger Wade in one of his own personal favorites, Robert Altman's *The Long Goodbye* (United Artists, 1973). In 1975, Universal was keen to have him take on the role of seadog Quint in Steve Spielberg's *Jaws*, something which would have suited nautical-mad Hayden right down to the ground but, at the time, he was heavily in debt to the IRS. Universal bosses thought they had hit upon a legal loophole to enable Hayden to join the crew: IRS officials got wind of the scheme and Hayden had to pull out, Robert Shaw making the part his own.

In order to pay off his IRS dues, Hayden went to Spain in 1975 to star alongside Franco Nero in Enzo G. Castellari's *Cipolla Colt*, also released as *Cry Onion*. After collecting his wages, it isn't too hard to figure out what the towering screen tough guy thought (or probably *didn't* think) of this frenetic, goofy, downright stupid farce/satire, if, of course, he ever got down to watching it, which, in his case, is doubtful. There's no middle ground on films such as these, where genre tropes are turned upside down just for the hell of it, 92 minutes of Nero (Onion Stark), munching the tear-inducing vegetables nonstop and drinking onion juice, dubbed in a James Stewart drawl, mugging furiously at the camera while all around embark on the kind of pranks witnessed among five-year-olds in the school playground—you either love them or loathe them. Backed by brothers Guido and Maurizio De Angelis' ludicrous music hall-cum-pop soundtrack, onion-loving Nero and wind-breaking horse Archibald trot into Paradise City to buy a plot of land from a recently murdered farmer. Martin Balsam (complete with mechanical right hand), boss of the Super Oil Company, wants the property as it lies in the middle of an oil field, so three gunslingers are sent to get rid of Nero, now residing on the homestead with two hard-drinking, hard-smoking kids named Al Capone and Dutch Schultz. Hayden (Henry "Jack" Pulitzer) owns the local rag, trying to expose town corruption, while his daughter, Emma Cohen, falls in love with Nero (red hearts are superimposed around their grinning faces), even though one puff of his breath can floor his opponents ("Onion or gun?" he calls out to those squaring up to him). When Balsam's metallic claw needs attention, a Hitler clone is on hand with a tool kit, as are two gender-bender pseudo-Nazis and a gang of motorcyclists (in 1910?); to cap it all, Sheriff Leo Anchóriz plays a lawman masquerading as an SS officer (the movie was partly financed in West Germany). Gray-whiskered Sterling looks totally bemused (as well he might) as Nero, ice-blue eyes staring maniacally, leaps, clowns and gags his way through one ridiculous situation after another, Balsam trying to steal Nero's land deeds, the whole shebang climaxing in a Keystone Cops-type chase through the muddy streets, ending with Nero drenched in oil as he and Balsam dig holes to plant (yes, that's right!) more onions.

Taking Terence Hill/Enzo Barboni's Spaghetti *Trinity* series as its template, *Cipolla Colt* is a colossal turnoff for most, except for continental Western aficionados who are tuned in to this kind of Spanish/Italian jokiness. Depressing fare for some, a laugh from beginning to end for others—the jury will be forever out on *Cipolla Colt*, a comedy/parody Western about as funny and appetizing as a bowl of cold Spaghetti—or onions!

Hayden faces the rope in *The Blue and the Gray*.

Sterling Hayden, after turning down a massive salary of $250,000 to star in *Charlie Chan and the Curse of the Dragon Queen* (he flew to Yugoslavia instead to cover the death of President Josip Broz Tito for *Rolling Stone* magazine and didn't make a dime, the article never completed), resigned from the movie business, a business he never professed to liking or enjoying, in 1981 (he was in the TV series *The Blue and the Gray* in 1982), pottering around with his boats until prostate cancer took him at the age of 70 on May 23, 1986 in Sausalito, California. Looking back, and bearing in mind his dismissive attitude, Hayden's forays into the Old West verged more on the psychological than the traditional, mirroring his preference for dark, *noir* thrillers. Hayden at his best (in a Western, that is), and even appearing to put just that bit more effort into his role playing, can be found in *Hellgate, Kansas Pacific, The Last Command, Shotgun, Top Gun, Gun Battle at Monterey* and *Terror in a Texas Town*. The big guy commendably (to some fans) bucked the Hollywood star factory trend, striding through the film capital with an air of disdain etched into his rugged features, a movie personality at odds with the whole filmmaking deal. One can picture him now, riding the ocean waves (NOT a horse!), the wind and spray blowing through his blond locks, glad to be away from it all, a one-off in an environment populated by fame-hungry wannabes. More master mariner than movie star, he led his life to the fullest, a king-sized character that brought something different to the silver screen through being mentally divorced from it. Bear that in mind the next time a Sterling Hayden Western appears on television and study him carefully: Behind that stern, unsmiling façade lies a man with one eye on the open sea, *not* on the camera lens!

Hayden aboard *Wanderer*, demonstrating his love of the sea.

Essential Hayden
Flaming Feather
Hellgate
Kansas Pacific
Johnny Guitar
Timberjack
Shotgun
The Last Command
Top Gun
Gun Battle at Monterey
Terror in a Texas Town

CHAPTER 15

CALHOUN: 1963-1990

From 1958 to 1960, Rory Calhoun completed work on his television series *The Texan*, deciding to concentrate his career on the motion picture industry rather than being tied down to a long-running TV show. Traveling to Italy, he donned a toga instead of a gun belt, taking on the lead role of Darios in Sergio Leone's epic $3,000,000 sword and sandal opus *The Colossus of Rhodes*, a huge hit with the public when released in 1961/1962 and earning the actor a tidy share of the profits. Staying in Italy, he followed it up with the British-produced swashbuckler *The Treasure of Monte Cristo* (*The Secret of Monte Cristo*) and starred as *Marco Polo* in the film of the same name, another sizeable earner. Calhoun then returned to the States in 1963 considerably better off than when he had left it, embarking on a number of B-Westerns made at a time when the once-popular oater was floundering in the water, not quite dead on its feet but getting there. Audiences didn't appear interested anymore, and this disinterest was reflected in lower '60s production values as opposed to higher '50s production values. All credit to stars like Calhoun and Audie Murphy (probably the one man during the 1960s to take on the mantle of the Western standard bearer), who refused to wave the white flag of surrender and carried on doing things in the traditional manner, despite public apathy and snipes from the critics, even though some of the product could be termed as bland, almost a facsimile of the genuine article. Rory's Westerns from here on in weren't a patch on those he had made prior to 1960, but some interesting, enjoyable and worthwhile features emerged that contained elements of what the genre used to be all about, and for that we must be truly thankful.

Allied Artists' *The Gun Hawk*, released in 1963, was the first of Rory's forays out West in the new decade, and the worrying difference between this, a typical

'60s Western, and Rory's last, *Apache Territory*, a typical '50s Western, was there for all the fans to see. The rot was beginning to set in—gone was the all-encompassing vibrancy and razzle-dazzle of the previous decade's hard-ridin', hard-shootin' dust-buster, replaced by muddy cinematography, insipid direction and one of the genre's most bizarre soundtracks courtesy of Jimmie Haskell: Rod Lauren warbling "A Searcher for Love" over the title credits (a bad omen) gives way to Haskell's irritating guitar-strumming tones containing echoes of what sounds like horses' hooves, as surreal in this setup as Hoyt Stoddard Curtin's score was in the legendary schlock howler *Mesa of Lost Women*. Rory himself looked tired in a production that exceeded its running time by at least 10 minutes; they should have kept it short like in the old days and cut out the fluff.

The Gun Hawk was director Edward Ludwig's final movie, his career dating right back to 1920 and taking in crime (*The Last Gangster*, 1937), adventure (*Swiss Family Robinson*, 1940), war (*The Fighting Seabees*, 1944) and even monster mayhem (*The Black Scorpion*, 1957). Calhoun played Blaine Madden, also known as El Gavilán Pistolero, a gunslinger dispensing his own brand of rough justice in the frontier town of Baxter, run by Sheriff Rod Cameron and his twitchy deputy, Morgan Woodward, the opening scenes regrettably enacted in a semi-jokey fashion. Rod Lauren is a cocky young gambling rebel anxious to make a name for himself, hitching his holster to Calhoun after the sharpshooter, against old pal

Calhoun looks for trouble in *The Gunhawk*.

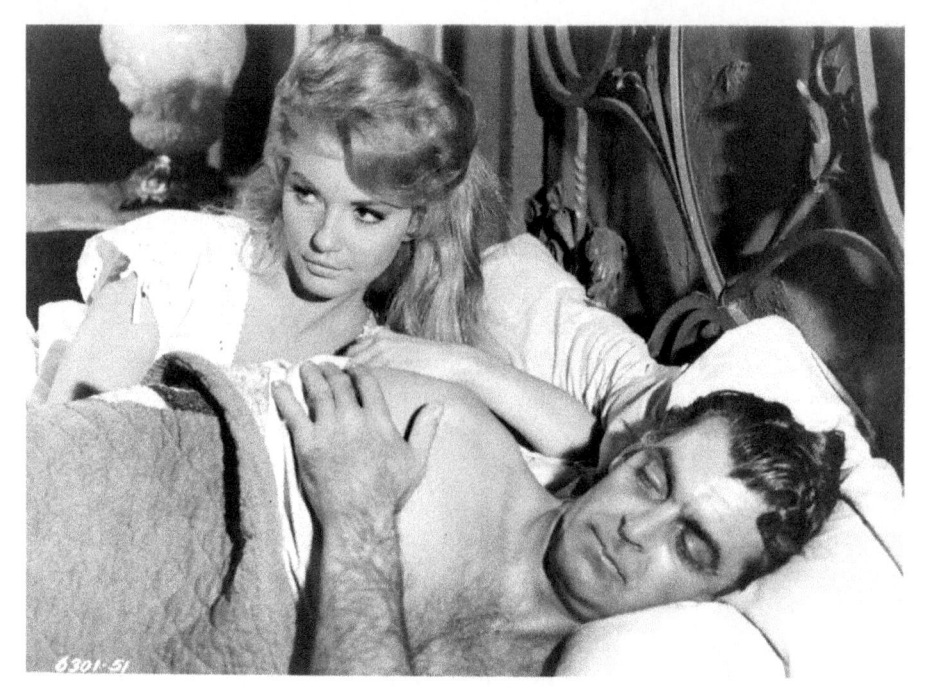

Ruta Lee comforts Rory in *The Gunhawk*.

Cameron's advice, drops the Sully brothers who have murdered his drunken father. Badly wounded in the right arm by Cameron, who refuses to shoot him in the back, Calhoun licks his wounds in the enclave of Sanctuary with Lauren, an odd little retreat surrounded by towering rock walls (filming took place in California's Bronson Canyon) where those wanted by the law seek refuge, Cameron and Woodward hot on his heels. Calhoun's the local hero in this remote backwater, the Gun Hawk of the title, and his word is law, even if the town, if you can call it that, boasts a population of around a dozen people. After a fistfight with sneering screen bad guy Robert J. Wilke, Calhoun's health deteriorates due to his infected bullet wound; it's then a case of whether he elects to die slowly in the arms of doting Ruta Lee, or go out in a blaze of glory by squaring up to Cameron.

The final 20 minutes of Ludwig's jaded Western drama drags: Calhoun lies sweating in bed from a fever, Lee, plastered in pink lipstick, wears a "startled rabbit" expression throughout, and Lauren tries his hand at impersonating Ricky Nelson in *Rio Bravo*, with variable results. Meanwhile, on a hill overlooking Sanctuary, grim-faced Cameron tries his best to prevent Woodward from taking out his spite on Calhoun. In the end, the so-called El Gavilán Pistolero opts for dying with dignity, provoking Lauren into a standoff. The professional gunslinger outdraws the young pretender to the throne but aims wide on purpose; Lauren doesn't, and Calhoun collapses in the street, Cameron looking on with a sense of sadness over the loss of his former friend. And wild kid Lauren has perhaps learned the error of his ways; it's the straight and narrow for him from now on.

Rory acts the part of the aging, taciturn gunman well and Cameron's burly presence fills the screen, but these two heavyweights of the B-Western genre were up against a dull script from the start (Joe Heims; who went on to write Clint Eastwood's psycho thriller *Play Misty for Me*) and one-dimensional stock situations; even the saloon sequences appear lifeless, matching the overall drabness of what's on offer, which in this case, wasn't much, the first poor Rory Calhoun Western in years.

Was the Western, once a dependable crowd-pleaser, fading into a cinematic twilight zone of sorts? Not if producer A.C. Lyles had anything to do with it. He approached Paramount Studios in 1963 with a view to making a series of low-budget oaters, shot in the space of 10-14 days, each on a budget of $300,000, much in the manner that Gordon Kay was doing over at Universal with Audie Murphy around the same time. Each movie (13 in all, 14 if you include 1975's *The Last Day* with Richard Widmark; 10 were scripted by Steve Fisher) would have a leading B-performer headlining the production as a promotional tool, with a host of familiar (and experienced) names making up the cast. Rory Calhoun was actually hired to star in the first of Lyles' oaters, *Law of the Lawless*, but pulled out because of health reasons, the role passed on to Dale Robertson at the last minute (he was woken without warning at 11:30 p.m., and told to be on set at six the next morning). After putting in guest appearances in TV's *Bonanza* and *The Virginian*, Rory took the role of Clint McCoy in the third of Lyles' cheapo Westerns, *Young Fury* (1964), playing, once again, the part of a close-mouthed gunslinger who's presence isn't welcomed by Sheriff Richard Arlen, particularly as four members of the Dawson bunch, led by John Agar, are hell-bent on riding into town to finish off Calhoun; he took a two-year stretch in prison for squealing on the gang, and they're looking for revenge, big time.

Unknown to Arlen, also heading his way is a group of young, boisterous gun-happy delinquents, The Hellions, Preston Pierce their leader and the

A scene from *Young Fury*

son of Calhoun ("The top dog in a wolf pack. That's the kind of animal we've raised," says Calhoun to Virginia Mayo). First seen roughing up a Mexican border town, this gang of punk wildcats charges into Arlen's domain, running the sheriff and his deputy out of town, causing a nuisance to every female who happens to catch their eye, getting roaring drunk in Mayo's saloon (horror legend Lon Chaney, Jr. is the bartender) and ransacking the hardware store. Only Calhoun can stop the rioting, but he's up against his own troubled son Pierce; the lad ("Blinkey" to his estranged parents) is unaware that Mayo is his long-lost mother and continually engages in fistfights with hothead Robert Biheller over who should or who shouldn't be boss. When news of Agar and his boys reaches the kids' ears, most turn tail and run for the less-dangerous delights of California; they may class themselves as tough, but those four hombres are a heap lot tougher! Calhoun, Pierce, Arlen and a couple of the braver Hellions are left to blast away at the Dawsons on the open street; Agar and company are wiped out in a blaze of gunfire and Mayo is killed, leaving Calhoun and Pierce to make their peace, the youngster deciding to set up house with petite blonde Linda Foster in the old abandoned family home.

Directed with energetic pace by Christian *The Thing from Another World* Nyby and containing a noisy Paul Dunlap score, *Young Fury* is a rowdy timepasser, more notable for its array of Hollywood faces (veteran William Bendix also pops up as a blacksmith) than anything else. Calhoun could have performed his by now customary gunslinger role in his sleep and is less livelier than usual (he had recently recovered from a bout of illness), but with Mayo, Chaney, Arlen, Bendix and Agar on set, it's not a case of who's doing what in this particular Western, more of catching sight of a fan's favorite from the 1950s. For a '60s oater made on a shoestring budget, it ain't all that bad. "Noisy cowboy fare," said *Variety*.

Like many American cowboy heroes in the mid-'60s, Rory Calhoun followed the well-trodden trail to Spain to take on the principal role in Sidney W. Pink's Paella oater *Finger on the Trigger*, distributed by Allied Artists in 1965. Spanish Westerns usually made little or no sense to devotees in other countries, and Pink's cockamamie end-of-Civil War confection was no exception to the rule. Shot in Almeria's sun-blasted hinterland of cliffs, gulches and gullies and cursed with a terrible score from José Solá, the story told of a ragbag bunch of hot, thirsty, war-battered Yankees, on their way to Santa Fe, encountering Indians and renegade Confederate Rebels, disguised as Bluecoats, hiding out in a fort masquerading as a Union P.O.W. camp; the Rebs are waiting for a wagon train to turn up, commandeered by Silvia Solar, seated daintily in a carriage. Calhoun (Larry Winton) ramrods the misfits, Major Aldo Sambrell tries to control treacherous Leo Anchóriz and his gold-hungry jackals (there's much talk of treasure, but where is it?), John Clarke does a laughable impersonation of a war chief with absurd dialogue to match his pantomime make-up ("Why there wagons and white woman? Me want know!" and "We go sleep at night. Fight in morning.") and for reasons best known to herself (but certainly not to the audience; it must have been lost in translation), Solar, having reached the fort, wants to turn on her pretty skirt hems and head straight back through the dusty wastes to Southernville and grab hundreds of gold horseshoes worth a million bucks, her aim being to return the fortune to the defeated Confederacy forces. One glaring blooper in these opening scenes—prismatic binoculars of the type the Graycoat major is handling in the ninth minute did *not* exist in the Wild West of 1865.

Antonio Macasoli's over-bright cinematography will have you reaching for your sunglasses as Calhoun and his motley outfit holes up in the deserted town of Southernville, hastily erected on the Almeria backlot by the looks of it; Rory has to deal with double-crossers Todd Martin and Brud (Bruce) Talbot, the rogues throwing their lot in with the whooping Indians, and eventually is forced to melt the precious horseshoes into cannonballs to drive back Clarke's braves in an admittedly exciting, slam-bang 10-minute climax. It's an exhausting experience to sit through, as exhausting in fact as the cast must have felt filming in those scorched, arid conditions, oddball characters nursing all kinds of hidden agendas that never come to light (why, for example, would Solar and her retinue go to all the trouble of journeying to Fort Grant, only to immediately turn back?) and plot holes by the dozen, almost a Spanish pastiche of a Hollywood B-Western but failing to hit the target. To his credit, Calhoun acts everyone else off the screen, but then, he was used to this sort of setup when others around him weren't; his fairly forceful turn, plus that smoke-filled finale, just about manages to prevent the mighty weird, deeply confusing, rarely seen *Finger on the Trigger* from being labeled a one-star Spanish clunker of the first order.

"Every Time He Comes To Town, Someone's Gonna Die!" So screamed the posters to 1965's *Black Spurs*, Calhoun's second Lyles/Paramount Western and reckoned to be one of the producer's best, which he starred in after turning up in the television series *Wagon Train* and *Gunsmoke*. Rory looked leaner and fitter, his mop of black hair now tinged with gray, while it was a treat for all lovers of vintage cinema to revel in the wily antics of Lon *The Wolf Man* Chaney, Jr., Bruce *King Kong* Cabot, Terry *Mighty Joe Young* Moore, DeForest *Star Trek* Kelley and the lovely Linda Darnell, who tragically died at the age of 41 in an accidental fire at her home in Glenview, Illinois not long after completing work on the picture. Writer Steve Fisher's script stuck closely to much-cherished Western ideals, complementing the acid delivery spat out by heavyweights Calhoun, Chaney and Cabot; composer Jimmie Haskell avoided the pitfalls that befell his soundtrack in *The Gun Hawk*, coming up with excellent guitar-strummed themes; and R.G. Springsteen, an old hand at directing TV Westerns (*Wanted: Dead or Alive*; *Wichita Town*; *Rawhide*; *The Tall Man*; *Tales of Wells Fargo*; *Wagon Train*), as well as working with the likes of Audie Murphy and George Montgomery, ensured a steady hand on the rudder. OK, there's not a great deal of depth on show, but do you need it within this kind of framework? No—this was a straightforward old-fashioned horse opera performed with gusto by the whole cast. It was almost like being back in the 1950s.

Calhoun played reformed gunman Santee, engaged to pretty but clinging Moore, the action set in Texas, 1885. Outdrawing bandit El Pescadore in a Mexi-

BLACK SPURS

AN A. C. LYLES PRODUCTION
TECHNICOLOR®
A PARAMOUNT RELEASE

STARRING RORY CALHOUN · LINDA DARNELL · SCOTT BRADY · LON CHANEY · RICHARD ARLEN · BRUCE CABOT and TERRY MOORE as ANNA
Directed by R. G. SPRINGSTEEN
Screenplay by STEVE FISHER

can backwater after tracking him for 10 months and collecting the reward of $3,000 needed for his wedding, he returns to find that his fiancée, fed up with waiting, has met and married James Best, the sheriff of Lark. Bitter over his loss, Rory dons the killer's black spurs (to match his black hat) and embarks on a lucrative career of bounty hunting over the next eight months, building himself a fearsome reputation in the process. Meanwhile, in the adjacent town of Kile, wealthy, greedy land baron Chaney is anxious that the government's new railroad franchise should include Lark, so hires Calhoun, now finished with bounty hunting, to open up the town. On a promise of $25,000 and 10,000 acres of land, he rides out to Lark to set up a gambling joint with Richard Arlen and bruiser Cabot, the plan to entice cattle drovers in and make the place more attractive as an investment to the rail bosses which in turn will line Chaney's ever-deepening pockets (Kile's corrupt law officer, Kelley, wanted the job, but he's gunned down after attempting to shoot Calhoun in the back). However, preacher Scott Brady doesn't want Calhoun, Cabot and their gambling den dirtying up Lark ("Get outta town," is his snarling welcome to Calhoun), and neither does Best, jealous of the ex-bounty hunter's past association with Moore. Saloon dame Darnell and her gals cast their womanly eyes over Calhoun, thinking him "cute," while Cabot throws his considerable bulk around, living up to his nickname of The Bouncer and determined to get rid of the law; Best orders Arlen to close the saloon down ("It's a hell town again.") but wisely backs away, a dozen gun barrels pointed at his chest. When Calhoun learns that Moore's young son Chad is his and not Best's, he has a fit of conscience, deciding to quit Chaney's underhand enterprise and leave town, giving his money back to the magnate who, infuriated, orders Cabot to sort things out—in other words, kill Calhoun, if he can.

Black Spurs is a bubbly, enjoyable mix containing rowdy saloon fights, drunken revelry, standoffs and spiky interaction between the three Cs, Calhoun, Cabot and Chaney, a worthy reminder of what true acting virtuosity combined with charisma was all about in those days. It ends with Best being tarred and feathered and Calhoun, a sheriff's badge pinned to his waistcoat, promising to clean Lark up, which he does, Cabot, Arlen and two sidewinders hitting the dirt after a furious gunfight—Cabot's body is dragged away by his horse, a foot caught in the stirrup. The badge is returned, those black spurs are left in the dust and the lone bounty hunter rides off to become, in Moore's words, "the sheriff of somewhere. I wonder?"

After putting in a guest appearance in TV's *Rawhide*, Calhoun rounded off 1965 with his third and final Western for A.C. Lyles, *Apache Uprising*, John Ford's *Stagecoach* among its many influences. Director R.G. Springsteen manufactured, with the help of Max Lamb and Harry Sanford's intelligent script, a frothy confection of baddies versus good guys versus Indians, all holed up in a way station and each at the mercy of the others' whims, for various reasons: Scar-faced John Russell, backed up by his two gun-happy partners, DeForest Kelley and Gene Evans, is in cahoots with Butterfield Stage Line's corrupt manager, Robert H. Harris, planning to steal a bag containing $80,000 in cash; strumpet Corinne Calvet, drummed out of town for being a bad influence on the womenfolk, eyes up good-looking drifter/gunman Calhoun; Kelley, forever on the prod, also eyes up Calhoun, out to beat him to the draw; grizzled mountain man Arthur Hunnicutt has captured a dying Tonto Apache chief to secure their safety; Russell and Calhoun go way back, old enemies who still mistrust one another; and coach driver Lon Chaney, Jr. hits the whiskey bottle with a vengeance, winding everybody up as the Apaches slowly move in for the kill.

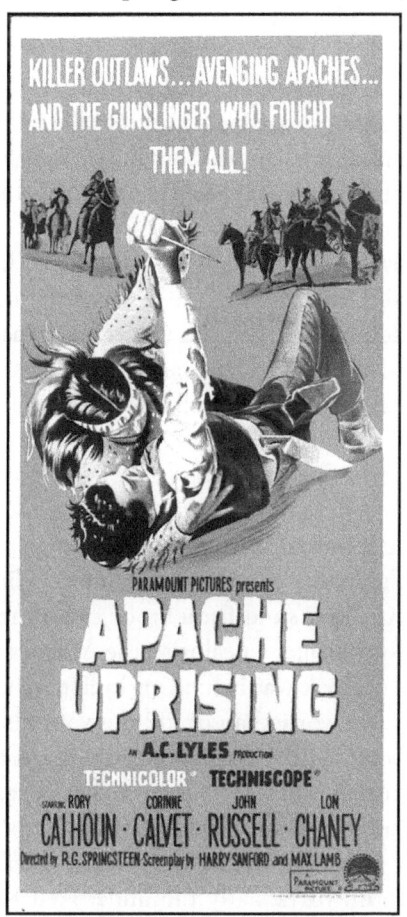

Apache Uprising commences with ex-Confederate Calhoun (as Jim Walker) and squaw man Hunnicutt riding across California's rugged Vasquez Rocks area, cinematographer W. Wallace Kelley's glossy colors highlighting the magnificent rocky scenery. Attacked by Indians, they join a cavalry detachment and ride into Apache Wells, where Springsteen introduces those main characters who will eventually end up together in the way station, Calhoun riding shotgun on the stage to Lordsberg. In his last appearance on celluloid, 61-year-old Johnny Mack Brown is a randy sheriff unsuccessfully trying it on with scarlet woman Calvet, clawed in the face for his efforts. The real pleasure to be had (and something of a revelation to "Bones" fans) in these opening scenes is in DeForest Kelley's juicy interpretation of psycho gunman Toby Jacks, similar to the outlaw role he played in *The Law and Jake Wade* (Kelley starred in nine Westerns and numerous television oaters, usually taking the part of a bad guy). One word spoken out of turn to the short-fused loony and he's reaching for his gun, eyes ablaze with fury. In the saloon, Calhoun gets on the wrong side of him. "Little man—big mouth," he sneers. Kelley explodes, almost foaming at the mouth, hand hovering over leather. "Big man—big gun!" he roars, but the expected standoff comes to nothing. Later, in the besieged station, Calhoun spits out a line worthy of a Randolph Scott Western (Scott was a master at delivering dry, withering dialogue) as he confronts loose cannon Kelley once again: "One of these days, you're gonna have to face a man all on your own. I just hope it's me," and when Kelley, grinning maliciously, puts two slugs in Harris' back, Calhoun growls, "Someday, somewhere, you're gonna get it." The Indians save him the trouble, firing two arrows into the unhinged killer. "The mark of a two-legged polecat," is Hunnicutt's description of scarred Russell who gets jumpy when the Indians approach. "What's the matter sonny? Your spine crawling?" Following a roll in the hay with Calvet (Calhoun's old flame from 1947; they must have enjoyed *that* tender moment!), Rory strikes a deal with the Apaches: Their sick chief is handed over plus Russell; the crook was behind an Indian massacre some six years back and is now due for a fate worse than death; everyone else is free to leave in 24 hours, which they do, boarding the stage to Lordsberg after giving Hunnicutt, shot by Russell, a decent burial. And Calvet seems to have bagged a man unconcerned about her lurid past, judging by the signals she's flashing in Calhoun's direction.

A smart little trail buster, then, with Calhoun and company in blistering form, particularly the underrated Kelley. But it's badly let down in one major department, the soundtrack. Jimmie Haskell's bland music sounds like something out of an American sitcom, harmlessly burbling along without having the slightest effect on the action. What *Apache Uprising* needed for greater impact was the type of bulldozing score conjured up by David Buttolph, Paul Sawtell and Hans J. Salter in the halcyon days of the 1950s; even one of Joseph Gershenson's stitched-together Universal stock musical arrangements would have made one hell of a difference. Many Westerns produced in this decade suffered from ineffectual incidental scoring and *Apache Uprising* was prey to a similar fate, a B-Western of some merit lumbered with a grade Z score, a real shame as this was to be the last traditional American Western that Rory Calhoun would ever make, his next, *Mission to Glory: The Father Kino Story*, released in 1977, a time when the genre was submerged under the weight of bank-busting space operas, hugely expensive disaster flicks and X-certified essays into the Devil and all his works—not a Western in sight on the cinematic horizon.

The last three Westerns that Rory Calhoun starred in are dispiriting affairs to admirers of his previous work; quite honestly, what he gave to the genre ended with *Apache Uprising*. Moreover, he was devoting more and more of his time to television anyway, a jobbing actor going where the work beckoned in order to pay the bills. But we will nevertheless give them a brief hearing; they hardly merit anything else. *Mission to Glory* was the tale of Padre Eusebio Francisco Kino, a roving priest who created 24 missions in his 50 journeys across Old California in the

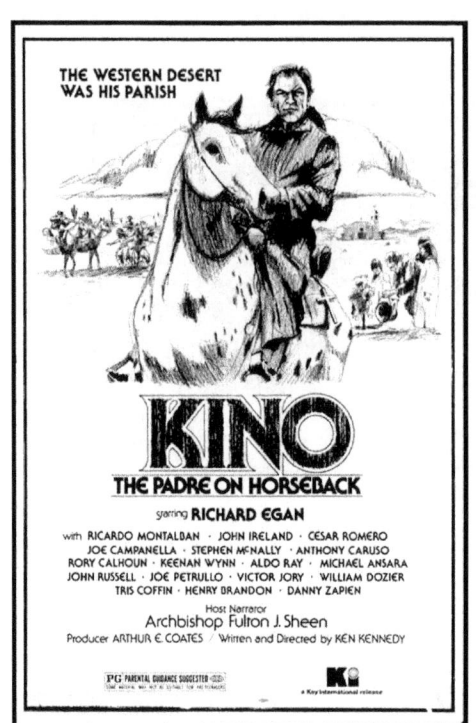

1680s, involving himself in the day-to-day lives of the persecuted native Pima Indians. Richard Egan played the part with commendable straight-faced nobility, a gaggle of aging regulars in cameo roles boosting the cast list: John Ireland, Ricardo Montalban, Keenan Wyn, Victor Jory, Aldo Ray, Cesar Romero and John Russell. Rory trotted on screen in the film's latter part, playing Spanish captain Juan Monje. Dressed to the nines, he doesn't say or do a lot in a rambling, unstructured exercise in religious piousness that will test the patience of even those who attend church on a regular basis; the film is overlong, dull and, from an entertainment point of view, artistically bankrupt.

Even worse was Rory's second outing of 1977, the dire comedy Western *Mule Feathers* in which our former charismatic gunslinging hero found himself teamed up with a talking mule (voiced by Don Knotts, who also narrated). Rory starred as Bonaparte Shelby, a preacher not on the side of God ("A dealer in death," states Knotts, or the mule), first seen dressed as a cavalry officer and relieving a train of its payroll. He then rides over to Natchez and gets caught up in a crazy hunt for a lost gold mine carried out by even crazier townsfolk, all one step away from being committed to the nearest lunatic asylum. Can this really be the same man who was so captivating in *Red Sundown*, *Utah Blaine* and *The Saga of Hemp Brown*? Rolling his eyes in the manner of Jack Elam, Calhoun (and it hurts to say it) is an embarrassment to watch, as are the rest of the cast as they clown, mug and overact their silly way through this patently unfunny farce. Available as part of a family 4-pack DVD set, even today's kids would find little to smile about in *Mule Feathers*, the only faintly amusing line on offer when Rory

Six-Gun Law

Cast and director from *Bad Jim*

complains to his four-legged buddy, "I risk my life while you sit around eating leaves all day." *Not* recommended!

From 1978 to 1990, Rory Calhoun contented himself with appearing in TV shows (*Hawaii Five-O, The Blue and the Gray, Alfred Hitchcock Presents, Capitol*—he turned down a role in *Dallas*), making a bit of a comeback for a newer generation of cinemagoers with parts in horror/crime spoofs *Motel Hell* (1980), *Angel* (1984), *Avenging Angel* (1985) and *Hell Comes to Frogtown* (1988). *Bad Jim*, released in 1990, related the story of three cowpokes (James Brolin, Richard Roundtree and John Clark Gable) who take to a life of crime after Gable has bought Billy the Kid's horse (the Bad Jim of the title) from an outlaw on the run. Sixty-one minutes in, Rory enters the frame for around a minute, as ranch boss Sam Harper, and it comes as something of a shock to see the 67-year-old actor looking so thin, gaunt and gray-haired, although the sparkle in those striking blue eyes of his is still in evidence. The picture, shot in Tucson, Arizona, doesn't amount to much, only the sunny scenery of any real interest, plus the fact that it was our hero's last stint, however short, in a Western.

Aged 70, Rory Calhoun made one final movie, *Pure Country* (1992), a country and western musical, before

Rory Calhoun—Glamour Cowboy

quitting the business to devote his time to his favorite hobby, painting. He died in Burbank, California in April 1999, aged 76, after health complications arising from years of smoking. Had he left his mark in Hollywood's Western Hall of Fame? In 2016, I asked seven of my friends, all over 65 and all frequent moviegoers over the years, if they had ever heard of Rory Calhoun. One said yes, six said no. Therefore, you can argue that, from a mainstream audience perspective, maybe he didn't make his mark. But from a Western perspective he unquestionably did, albeit in an unassuming way. The 13 oaters he made between 1954 and 1958, from *The Yellow Tomahawk* to *Apache Territory* (including *The Spoilers*), plus *Massacre River*, *Way of a Gaucho*, *The Silver Whip*, *Powder River* and a couple of the A.C. Lyles trail busters, are highly respectable contributions to the genre's rich tapestry, as good as the Western gets. And has there ever been a better-looking gunslinger on film than Rory Calhoun, those blue eyes twinkling under a mop of dark, unruly hair, that easy grin lighting up those attractive, swarthy features? Perhaps not.

French poster for *Powder River*

Essential Calhoun
Way of a Goucho
Powder River
Dawn at Socorro
Four Guns to the Border
Red Sundown
The Hired Gun
Domino Kid
The Saga of Hemp Brown
Black Spurs
Apache Uprising

CHAPTER 16

WIDMARK: 1961-1988

After the trials and tribulations of working on John Wayne's *The Alamo*, not an easy shoot for the affable, intelligent Widmark, matters settled down a bit, his second Western of the 1960s, John Ford's *Two Rode Together* (Columbia, 1961), placing him in cavalry uniform for the first time, as First Lieutenant Jim Gary. Following that unbroken run of eight superlative oaters from 1948 to 1960, *Two Rode Together* was Widmark's poorest film per se in years, as it was director Ford's and leading star James Stewart's. Commencing around 1960/1961, the hard-hitting, all-guns blazing, slam-bang, gritty bravado that hallmarked the traditional Hollywood '50s Western, the genre's undisputed heyday, began to go into meltdown, owing to studio and audience apathy; still-popular cowboy star Audie Murphy was about the only person on the Hollywood backlot attempting to keep the spirit of that productive decade alive. A general malaise had set in, and Ford's unofficial "sequel" to his magnificent *The Searchers*, regarded by many as the best Western ever made, lacked sparkle, showing all the worrying (to fans) attributes of the horse opera in the first stages of its declining period: Muddy photography (Charles Lawton, Jr.), awful folksy music (George Duning), a large cast of secondary characters with nothing to say, a semi-comic screenplay (Frank S. Nugent), much too leisured in execution and a listless turn from Stewart. Ford hated the script and denounced the movie as "crap," claiming to his critics that he only made it as a favor to Columbia boss Harry Cohn, a close friend of his who had died in 1958. The money also came in handy—a salary of $225,000 plus 25% of net profits. However, profits in this case were hard to come by and the public stayed away; *Two Rode To-*

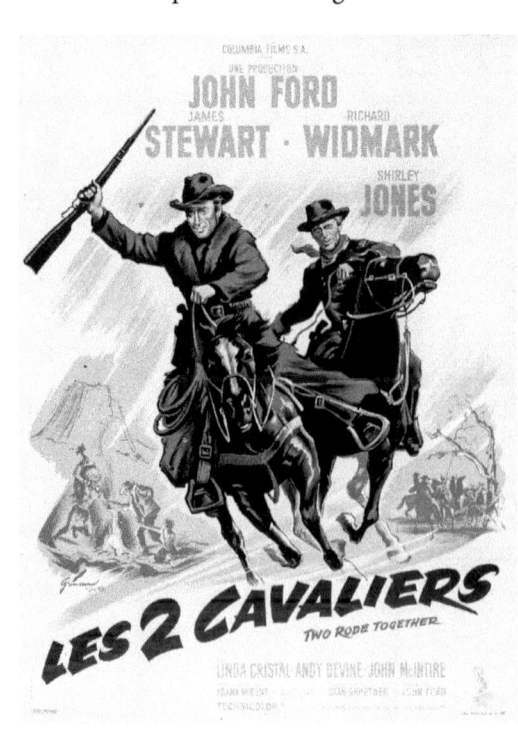

French poster for *Two Rode Together*

Jimmy Stewart gets tough in *Two Rode Together*

gether turned out to be a box-office flop despite warm critical reaction in some quarters, the *New York Times* stating it had "a clean economical style ... compelling." The author remembers seeing it in October 1961 at Leatherhead's Crescent Cinema (A-rated in England) and being bored to tears.

Has it got *anything* going for it? Well, Stewart and Widmark made a watchable pair as one would expect, Widmark's Jim Gary the straight man to Stewart's amoral, boozy money-grabbing Marshal Guthrie McCabe, *not* the usual Stewart honest good guy by any stretch of the imagination. The warring pair go to Fort Grant (John Wayne's Alamo village was used for location work) where they are given the task by Major John McIntire to infiltrate Comanche Chief Henry Brandon's camp (he memorably played Chief Scar in *The Searchers*) to trade guns and ammunition for white folk abducted years back, at the risk of breaking the current peace treaty. Any found will be returned to their families, a bunch of argumentative, highly wrought settlers milling around the fort compound in covered wagons. Trouble comes in the shape of Woody Strode (Stone Calf) who goes into a war-dancing frenzy when his white woman squaw (Linda Cristal) is taken away by Stewart and Widmark, young David Kent the only male brought back—and he's in an uncontrollably savage state.

Can white persons who have lived among Indians ever be rehabilitated into their own society, and at what cost? That's the message in Nugent's jokey script, flatly and disjointedly put across by Ford. Cristal, viewed as tainted goods, even-

Widmark and Stewart in *Two Rode Together*

tually looks to Stewart for salvation after being shunned at a dance while Kent murders his own mother and is hanged (this scene was cut in Britain by the censor). To magnify the feeling that what you are experiencing is a third-rate rehash of Ford's 1956 masterpiece, as well as Brandon, the director's stock company of John Qualen, Harry Carey, Jr., and Ken Curtis crops up, the last two indulging in a slapstick fistfight with Widmark; rotund, grinning Andy Devine provides jocular amusement in a scenario that refuses to take itself all that seriously. Ford allows Stewart and Widmark to bond in one five-minute unbroken sequence on a riverbank, the two rambling on about life, love and women, a nice moment showing the star chemistry that existed between the pair, even though the comedic elements appear forced, while Annelle Hayes plays Belle, the saloon tart with a heart of gold who has had an on/off history with Stewart. Shirley Jones puts in a touching performance as the girl looking for her brother, missing for nine years, playing a tune on her music box to remind her of happier times past (the 27-year-old actress fell in love with Widmark during filming). A more-or-less upbeat ending sees Widmark proposing to Jones (that must have pleased her) and Stewart, riding stage, heading off to California to play house with Cristal, all over in a flash, the damp climax to an uninteresting John Ford picture riddled with inconsistencies, bereft of any barnstorming action and no real answers to its many questions, and saddled with a drab, dreary aspect to boot. Perhaps, on this showing, the two *shouldn't* have ridden together, this being about the only Western Widmark starred in that isn't worth a second look.

Following another key role as prosecutor Colonel Tad Lawson in Stanley Kramer's 186-minute courtroom drama *Judgement at Nuremberg* (United Artists, 1961), Widmark was part of a huge star-studded cast in MGM's grand-scale $14,500,000 Western *How the West Was Won* (1962), playing hard-as-nails railroad boss Mike King, upsetting the Arapaho Indians by introducing the dreaded Iron Horse to their sacred territories. Widmark appeared after 108 minutes had ticked by, but *How the West Was Won* wasn't really about individuals as such (Widmark's screen time amounted to around eight minutes, five more than co-star John Wayne); it was all about scenic grandeur, one of only two major dramatic motion pictures to be shot using the three-strip Cinerama format (the first was MGM's *The Wonderful World of the Brothers Grimm*). Thereafter, because of the numerous technical difficulties encountered in the three-strip process (plus those infuriating vertical lines), the spate of Cinerama productions that appeared during the mid- to-late 1960s were shot in Ultra Panavision 70 and stretched out onto massive curved screens in those major theaters built to handle the job of exhibiting a giant viewing experience to transfixed audiences, giving the same all-embracing optical panoramic effect (the author can testify to the power of Cinerama, having seen *How the West Was Won* in all its glory in London, January 1963).

George Peppard and Richard Widmark disagree on how to deal with hostile Indians.

METRO-GOLDWYN-MAYER and CINERAMA present "HOW THE WEST WAS WON" in Metrocolor

A distinguished cast including James Stewart, Carroll Baker, John Wayne, Gregory Peck, Henry Fonda, Karl Malden, Lee J. Cobb, Robert Preston, Walter Brennan, Carolyn Jones, Debbie Reynolds and Eli Wallach; narration by Spencer Tracy; 41 location sites ranging from Tucson, Arizona to Utah's Monument Valley; 12,000 extras; a concise script from James R. Webb; over a year in the making; and three noted Western directors at the helm in Henry Hathaway, John Ford and George Marshall: *How the West Was Won*'s impressive credentials said it all, probably the last of the old-fashioned Hollywood Western epics, but perhaps lacking in one essential cinematic ingredient—intimacy between the leading players. The bulk of MGM's spectacular Super Western was filmed in longshot to principally take in those wide-open spaces, ruling out a recognizable degree of rapport in the various relationships, Hathaway commenting that he "hated that damned Cinerama. You couldn't get close up to the actors." Ford also moaned that lining up shots to avoid visible "joins" in the finished print was a headache, while those participating were unable to make proper eye contact in several scenes due to awkward positioning of the Cinerama cameras to ensure correct frame synchronization. The episodic scenario, presented as a series of vignettes, charted the fortunes of the Prescott family from 1839 to 1889, mainly through the eyes of Debbie Reynolds' Lilith, the crucial character linking all five segments seamlessly together: The Rivers, The Plains, The Outlaws, directed by Hathaway; The Civil War, directed by Ford; and The Railroad, directed by Marshall. Highlights embraced a hair-raising trip down rapids, a Cheyenne Indian attack on a wagon train, a Civil War battle, the famous thundering buffalo stampede and a pulsating shoot-out climax aboard a train stacked with dangerously shifting logs. The film won three Oscars (it was nominated for eight); the pristine, pin-sharp cinematography was absolutely out of this world, as one would expect from William H. Daniels, Milton R. Krasner, Charles Lang, Jr. and Joseph LaShelle, all four being previous Oscar winners; and composer Alfred Newman provided a rousing, instantly recognizable opening credits score, one of the greatest Western title themes of all time.

It wasn't a particularly happy shoot in some areas. James Stewart, at 54, probably turned in the finest performance as mountain man Linus Rawlings (although Reynolds wasn't that far behind), a part originally earmarked for Gary Cooper until the actor's untimely death in May 1961. But Karl Malden, his prospective father-in-law, was four years *younger*, leading to much banter between the two concerning the need for toupees. Buffalo hunter Henry Fonda felt "uneasy and detached" in such a sprawling enterprise, a feeling voiced by many other cast members, and there was no love lost between Gregory Peck and Henry Hathaway; Peck found the temperamental director a "cigar-chewing tyrant," while Hathaway called Peck a "cold, indifferent son-of-a-bitch." Although most applauded *How the West Was Won*'s sheer over-the-top magnitude and brash style, many critics were far from kind, Pauline Kael stating the movie "should be retitled 'How the West Was Lost.'" The *New York Times* savaged the picture: "A mammoth patchwork of Western fiction clichés ... no pictorial style ... random episodes ... little or no imagination," and finishing with "How the West was Done—to Death." They even poured vitriol on Webb's script, claiming it was "horribly written," even though it earned Webb an Oscar! Unusually, the movie was premiered in London, on November 1, 1962 and those critical put-downs were ignored by the public, the film going on to become the year's top-grosser, eventually bringing in a hefty $50,000,000 profit for MGM. Current DVD issues show restored prints in breathtaking clarity, a testament to MGM in bringing their "all-star fairground attraction" to the larger-than-normal screen, a one-off in Western terms that has never been, and will never be, repeated. Despite negligible faults here and there, it entertains and tells a story, and those splendid American wilderness landscapes are gob-smacking, worthy of inclusion in the pages of *National Geographic Magazine*, a visual treat for the eyes. Surely, isn't that what *How the West Was Won* is all about?

Outside of the Western sphere, Widmark continued to make a success of everything he appeared in: Both Jack Cardiff's *The Long Ships* (Columbia, 1964) and Michael Anderson's *Flight from Ashiya* (United Artists, 1964) were box-office hits, his blond reprobate, Rolfe the Viking in *The Long Ships*, counting as one of his most engaging roles. Western number 11 was another expensive, large-in-scope undertaking, Warner Bros.' $4,200,000 *Cheyenne Autumn*, notable for being John Ford's final horse opera, a lengthy homage to two things of paramount importance in the eyes of the director: Utah's majestic Monument Valley and the injustices forced upon the Native American Indian by Hollywood moviemakers since the 1920s. Widmark played Captain Thomas Archer, in love with schoolteacher Carroll Baker, a Quaker. It's September 1878: When a party of over 300 Cheyenne, sick of the white man's broken promises, quit their reservation in Oklahoma, deciding to trek 1,500 miles north to the ancient Cheyenne stamping grounds in Wyoming, Indian sympathizer Widmark has his work cut out in trying to ensure that they make it in one piece, despite government interference, divisions within his ranks *and* divisions within the Indian ranks; old chief Victor Jory dies, leaving feuding chiefs Ricardo Montalban and Gilbert Roland to eventually part company, hothead Sal Mineo stirring up trouble en route. Baker, helped by English-speaking "Spanish lady" Dolores del Rio, goes along with the Indians on their desperate struggle to survive, mainly to keep an eye on the children, while in Washington, Secretary of the Interior Edward G. Robinson has to fend off demands to put an end to the perceived Indian threat, even if it means exterminating the lot of them.

Never has Utah's mighty rock formations in Monument Valley looked so stunningly gorgeous as in *Cheyenne Autumn*, dressed in William H. Clothier's glowing colors (he was nominated for an Oscar and should have won it). Western movie buffs will recognize many of the locations used by Ford to such iconic effect in *The Searchers* and which have supplied the genre with so many classic images over the years—the buttes, the towering sandstone crags, the wide rivers, the deep-shaded canyons, the lofty mesas red in the sun's rays, a pictorial feast that plays an equally important, almost symbolic role, as that of the marching, starving Indians on their long, perilous passage back to home territory. One can't help feeling that the director was saying a personal fond farewell to his beloved locale in his use of numerous panoramic longshots; the first 80 minutes are splendidly visual, even though the pace is leisurely, livened up by one large-scale cavalry versus Indian shoot-out in a canyon ambush (Ford employed Navajo Indians in cameos, many of whom had worked with him on previous pictures). In the type of picture where the grandeur of scenery can swallow an actor whole, Widmark, to his credit, is assertive in his major part as the short-tempered cavalry officer, holding the scenario together when it threatens to drift in the hot breeze; he doesn't look happy, what with fretting over Baker, dealing with Patrick Wayne's insubordination and coping with the stress of command, but he grabs the attention, a forceful piece of role playing from one of Tinseltown's most reliable leading men. Widmark also found Ford to be likeable but a "nutball" and erratic on set, due to the director's frequent bouts of heavy drinking, resulting in long spells spent in bed instead of getting on with the job of completing the picture.

Then it all goes horribly wrong for 20 minutes, a semi-comic interlude featuring James Stewart as a dim-witted, half-drunk Wyatt Earp in Dodge City, more concerned with the state of his poker game than marauding savages. After shooting Indian killer Ken Curtis in the foot with a derringer pistol, Stewart rounds up a motley posse consisting of John Carradine, Arthur Kennedy (as Doc Holliday), most of the townsfolk and a bevy of saloon gals decked out in red, and heads out into the wilds to face the Cheyenne. There's a lame attack, and then it's time for the intermission. Why did Ford include this slice of farcical nonsense which undermines all that has gone before? Some say that, because of the film's length (originally, it ran to 170 minutes, then was re-edited to 158 minutes), Ford joked to Stewart that patrons would take a much-needed bathroom break when it came on, an intermission of sorts before the *real* intermission. Others reckon it was Ford doffing his cap to the era of the Silent Western. Against Ford's wishes, Warner Bros. cut the segment completely on the picture's release date because of unfavorable audience reaction, but it features on modern DVD releases. This is one occasion where the "skip" button on your remote will come in very handy.

Part two of *Cheyenne Autumn* fails to measure up to the meandering magnificence of part one, Alex North's discordant, somber soundtrack disappearing off the radar for extended interludes, the action bogged down and muddled. The Indians are faced with an unknown terror in the shape of the Iron Horse and, 700 miles from Nebraska, split up, the smaller party going to Fort Robinson commanded by Karl Malden, a wild-eyed alcoholic German; Malden overacts like crazy, a jarring, unlikeable turn from the veteran. The Cheyenne are locked in a room and left to starve; Widmark and Malden come to blows over what should be done with them; the Indians break out with smuggled rifles, Malden, raving and full of liquor, confined to quarters. The storyline then becomes fragmental at times, what with Baker coming and going, Wayne reinventing himself as an honest soldier, the Cheyenne reuniting and Robinson traveling West to broker another peace deal. The wandering Cheyenne home at last in the closing reel, Mineo is shot dead for stealing Roland's younger wife and Widmark, Baker and a young Indian girl canter off in a buggy to play house. Ford ends his final Western as he should have done, a sunset shot over the wilderness, his heartfelt salute to the region that served him so well in so many classics.

Cheyenne Autumn, though, falls short of the classic mark. Although the *New York Times* called it "Beautiful and powerful," *Variety* was less than enthusiastic, labeling the film "a rambling episodic account." Film critic Stanley Kauffmann was scathing: "The acting is bad, the dialogue trite … the pace funereal … the climaxes puny." "Ponderous and disjointed," wrote Moira Walsh. The punters stayed away—1964 was on the cusp of the ultra-violent X-certified Spaghetti Western and Ford's worthy, elegiac essay into the plight of the Redskin seemed like a throwback to another age. Granted, it *is* old-fashioned and slow-moving, but Widmark is in top form, plus those fantastic Monument Valley vistas and the fact that this was legendary director John Ford's very last journey out West, make *Cheyenne Autumn* just that little bit special, despite its numerous shortcomings and that terrible, jarring Wyatt Earp 20-minute segment.

Following yet another critical and commercial success in Columbia's 1965 Cold War thriller *The Bedford Incident* (Widmark was in outstanding form as Soviet sub-chasing Captain Eric Finlander, blind to the fact that his obsessive actions in hunting down a Russian submarine could trigger a nuclear war), Widmark starred as Confederate Colonel Tom Rossiter in Edward Dmytryk's oddball, lackluster *Alvarez Kelly* (Columbia, 1966), second-billed to William Holden. If it wasn't for the magnetic pairing of Widmark and Holden, this dull tale of Confederates stealing 2,500 herd of prime Mexican steer from under Union noses

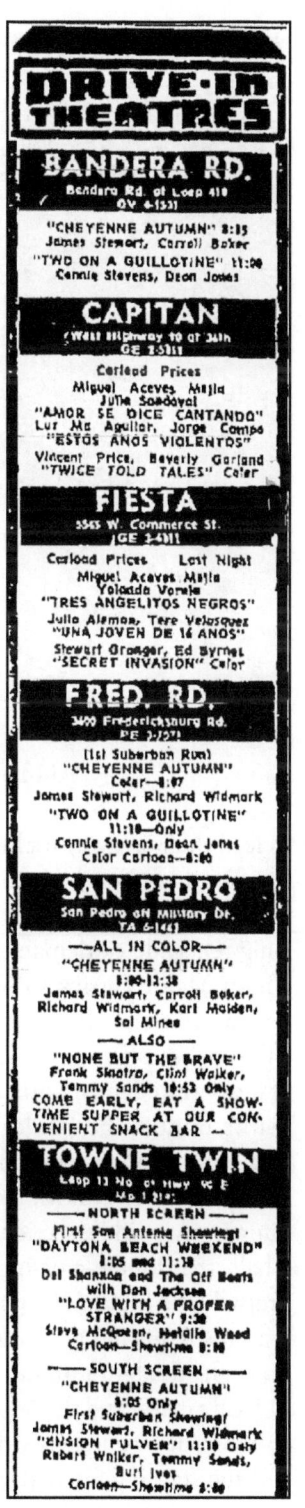

Widmark the Confederate in *Alvarez Kelly*

to feed their army in Richmond wouldn't be worth a dime. Taking place in 1864, The Brothers Four's rendition of the title theme, folksy and twee, didn't bode well for what was to come: Holden, the eponymous lead character, is a womanizing renegade cattleman, not loyal to the North or South, who sells his herd to Union Major Patrick O'Neal for $50,000; he's then led up the garden path by sexy plantation owner/Southern belle Victoria Shaw, abducted by Widmark, has a finger shot off and is forced to rustle the cattle for the Confederacy under threat of death. Holden's mantra in life is "Money, whiskey and women," pinching Widmark's bride-to-be (Janice Rule) and rubbing up the battle-weary Confederate leader the wrong way. Widmark, wearing an eye patch and speaking in a peculiar slurred Southern drawl, looks strained throughout a picture which lapses into tedium in the middle section, focusing on bouts of flirting in Rule's mansion during a ball, the double-crossing Holden/Rule relationship and a prolonged visit to a brothel (the House of Joy) that stretches to the limit the patience of those Western fans requiring a bit more action to enliven the pace. Things eventually perk up in the final 40 minutes, Widmark and Holden organizing a successful raid on O'Neal's cattle and driving the steers through woods and swamps, culminating in a shoot-out by a rickety bridge; the bridge is destroyed, O'Neal's troops withdraw and the starving Confederate army gets to feast on the beef. The rivalry, enmity

Widmark fires a shot in *Alvarez Kelly*.

and finally the grudging mutual respect is finely played to the hilt by the two leads (that famous Widmark chuckle can be heard in the 50th minute), holding the rambling scenario together where John Green's tepid score patently fails to do so, *Variety* calling the script and film "underdeveloped and uneven."

Alvarez Kelly is a typical mid-'60s uninspired Western depicting the horse opera floundering under a barrage of adult-rated crime/detective/sex dramas prevalent in cinemas at the time, Dick Widmark himself entering that particular arena after his next cowboy film, Andrew V. McLaglen's $2,500,000 *The Way West* (United Artists, 1967). The critics sharpened their knives for this one in the form of a Western backlash: "Washed out in scripting, direction and pacing," said *Variety*, while the *New York Times* wrote, "hackneyed hash," stating that old Western fans "will get up and walk out." The *New Yorker*'s notorious film critic, Pauline Kael, was even more viperish than usual: "A jerk's idea of an epic; big stars ... bad jokes, folksy-heroic music to plug up the holes and messy hang-ups." In a year where audiences were flocking to see Arthur Penn's ultra-violent *Bonnie and Clyde*, it's a wonder that *The Way West* stood even the slightest chance of making any money at the box-office, what with its old-fashioned Western values amalgamated with new-age sex (nymphet Sally Field, 21, in her screen debut), a graphic hanging to keep in with current cinematic fads and three old pros (Widmark, Kirk Douglas and Robert Mitchum) simply going through the motions, as some believed. But this rambling tale of the Liberty wagon train heading out to Oregon from Independence, Missouri in 1843 for a new life had a lot going for it, apart from seeing Widmark, Douglas and Mitchum starring together in a movie. McLaglen, much like John Ford was wont to do, framed his wagon train in a series of beautifully composed landscape shots among Oregon's striking rock formations, bathed in William H. Clothier's sumptuous colors (the scene of the wagons crossing a prairie at night during a thunderstorm is absolutely breathtaking); Bronislau Kaper's rowdy score *did* contain those irritating folksy elements detested by Kael (a blight in many '60s Western soundtracks) but kept the momentum going; Mitch Lindemann and Ben Maddow's fairly complex script was far from washed-out; and the three leads were eminently watchable: Widmark (Lije Evans) tough, hard-working and honest; ex-senator and wagon train leader Douglas a hard taskmaster, and a masochist to boot; and sleepy-eyed, master of the slow drawl Mitchum, the trail guide suffering from fading eyesight, a wise, somewhat cynical, buckskin-clad loner at one with his beloved wilderness.

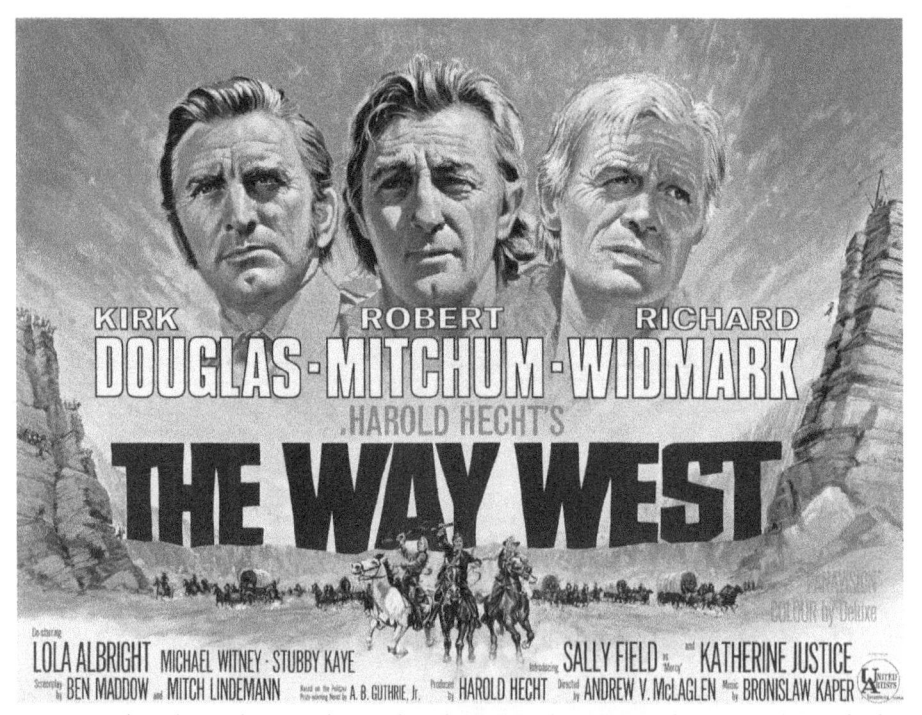

The covered wagons leave Missouri for Oregon ("I gotta go where I not bin," says Widmark to wife Lola Albright, who's unhappy at the idea of moving to pastures new) and right from the off, the blond one and the laid-back one are questioning the dimpled-chin one's ruthless leadership tactics, leading to much friction. A perilous river crossing is followed by Douglas making a play for Albright, while Michael Witney takes full advantage of Field's youthful lust, his frigid wife

Wagons roll over the Oregon trail in *The Way West*.

(Katherine Justice) unable to consummate the marriage. During a drunken revelry involving a party of whiskey-loving Sioux, Witney shoots dead, by mistake, the chief's young son, disguised as a wolf; to prevent a wholesale massacre, Douglas orders the hanging of Witney in front of the Indians to prove justice has been carried out according to white man's law. Fort Hall is reached, Widmark's son Michael McGreevey marries pregnant Field, there's talk of a defection to California because of a rumored gold strike and after several more escapades and incidents (Douglas' son is killed in an accident and he's deposed as wagon master; and there's a hazardous trek across a desert), the settlers reach Crooked River Gorge, having to lower wagons, oxen, horses and each other down into the depths on a rope winch. Raving Justice, out of her mind, cuts Douglas' rope and he plummets to his death. After his burial, Widmark, Mitchum and company carry on down the ravine to their eventual goal, the movie closing to the homespun refrains of The Serendipity Singers chorusing the title theme.

Viewed nearly 50 years later, McLaglen's semi-epic *The Way West* hugely entertains, even more so when one considers the real fact that in 1967, the traditional American Western wasn't in vogue with a pronounced adult-oriented shift in moviemaking ideals, appeasing a newer clientele. All in all, it's a pretty eventful trip spread over two hours, the all-conquering '50s-style horse opera *almost* re-

They don't make them like this anymore. Three screen legends: Douglas, Mitchum and Widmark

visited (maybe that's what McLaglen and his team were striving for, to recapture those former Western glories), bolstered by sweeping location work and expert role playing by everyone concerned (how could you *ever* elicit a poor performance out of macho men Widmark, Douglas and Mitchum in this kind of setup?). An anachronism, perhaps, in a year overloaded with X-rated gangster flicks, rogue cop dramas, spy thrillers and banned sex pictures, but a charming, in some ways invigorating, anachronism all the same, very much underrated on first release, a "Get out the Coke and popcorn and put up your feet" kinda movie, great fare for a Saturday night in.

Dick Widmark was a noted activist for the enforcement of gun control laws in America; he also denounced violence of any kind, feeling a sense of guilt over many of the tough, edgy roles he had played, even once remarking that he felt remorse at netting a trout while fishing with friends. So it comes as something of a surprise that he took on the role of hard-boiled New York detective Dan Madigan in Don Siegel's *Madigan* (Universal, 1968), the one picture he made in the 1960s that was a crystallization of all of Widmark's character traits as an actor: Determined, uncompromising, stalwart, charming, cultivated, volatile, snappy and able to handle himself in any situation, spitting out lines of dialogue through that disarming, easy grin, everything totally believable in his portrayal. We won't review the movie as such, but *Madigan*, one of two films he made that received an "X" certificate in the United Kingdom and a return to his early '50s *noir* roots, was one of his biggest success stories to date, the public turning up in droves to catch yet another in a long line of X-rated urban cop thrillers featuring a rebellious law enforcement officer refusing to play things by the book—Frank Sinatra's trio of *Tony Rome* (Fox, 1967), *Lady in Cement* (Fox, 1968) and *The Detective* (Fox, 1968); Steve McQueen in *Bullitt* (Warner Bros., 1968), among others; and later, Donald Sutherland in *Klute* (Warner Bros., 1971), culminating in the most savage cop show of them all, Clint Eastwood as *Dirty Harry* (Warner Bros., 1971), again directed by Siegel who Widmark rated highly. *Madigan* was so popular (and made Universal a lot of money) that Widmark went against his personal grain and entered the world of television, revising Dan Madigan (now a sergeant) in a six-episode series made in 1972/1973, even though in the original screenplay, he had been shot to death outside Steve Ihnat's apartment in one of copdom's most ferocious climactic gunfights. It's a vital, key essential Widmark performance on riveting display in *Madigan*, no doubt about it, Siegel tackling police corruption at the highest level, on-the-street violence and adult sexual shenanigans in equal doses; perhaps, in hindsight, his latter-day forays into the West could have benefited from some of this particular director's pace, grit and bite to push them more into the classic category instead of being, on occasions, just that little bit ordinary.

Don Siegel was also behind *Death of a Gunfighter* (Universal, 1969), but only when Widmark had drafted him in to complete the picture after television director Robert Totten had been replaced following a major artistic dispute and falling-out. To avoid contractual hassles, a compromise was reached, the pseudonym "Alan Smithee" used on the film's title credits after consultation with The Directors Guild of America (Widmark refused to have Totten's name shown on the list of credits and dug his boot heels in over the issue). Considering *Death of a Gunfighter* was produced during a period when the much-loved American Western

Widmark protects bride Lena Horne in *Death of a Gunfighter*.

itself was dying out, Siegel, Totten and Widmark somehow managed to manufacture a first-rate if downbeat "passing of the Old West" fable, violent and gutsy, the star himself, looking tired and world-weary, turning in a sublime performance as Frank Patch, a professional gunman-turned-town marshal who has outstayed his welcome in Cottonwood Springs, Texas; the mealy mouthed council, shocked at the gunning down of quivering, sexually inadequate (catch the opening scene in a whore's bedroom: "You ain't no plumber!") James Lydon in the first few minutes, demands that Widmark quit, even though Lydon ambushed the lawman in a livery stable for personal reasons and fired the first shot ("We don't want a man that good anymore," states Mayor Larry Gates. "This is a new town. He's all used up."). Widmark has to go; he's old-style, a square peg in a round hole, at odds with a new century where rickety motor vehicles are slowly replacing horses on the streets. In fact, every male in the film apart from Widmark and young sidekick Michael McGreevey (the two reprised their relationship from *The Way West*) is a spineless coward, afraid of Widmark's authority and deadly gun power; even County Sheriff John Saxon, who arrives to arrest Widmark, departs with his tail between his legs and a cut on his cheek, slugged by a marshal that won't stand for any nonsense from anybody.

Like Gary Cooper's Will Kane in *High Noon*, Widmark is the only person around with backbone and guts in a town packed to the sidewalks with lily-livered milksops: Councilor Kent Smith puts a rifle to his head after he's unable to kill Widmark, the result being that the marshal puts a bullet in Smith's son, Mercer Harris, after he comes gunning for him. On the day of Widmark's wedding to Lena Horne, town bully/saloon owner Carroll O'Connor decides to finish him off with the aid of a couple of cohorts; two bite the dust, O'Connor wounded, lassoed, dragged unceremoniously through the streets and hauled behind bars. Badly wounded himself, Widmark visits Lydon's widow in church (did he have an affair with her?) and walks down the church steps into the main street to his doom, riddled with rifle bullets in a brutal *Bonnie and Clyde*-type climax artfully orchestrated from a high crane shot, those cowards at the town council doing the dirty deed. The movie closes where it began, newly widowed Horne catching a train out of Cottonwood Springs, her husband's body in its coffin placed on board with her.

"Marshal. Do you know anything about sex?" asks McGreevey to Widmark, the two relaxing by a river, fishing, *not* a line you would expect to hear in a pre-1960s Western! But Joseph

Horne and Widmark tie the knot.

Widmark's Western low-point? *A Talent for Loving*

Calvelli's script steers well clear of that dreaded pseudo-comical whimsy which affectively ruined many Westerns at the tail end of the decade, as does Oliver Nelson's serious score—thankfully, not the sound of a jangling banjo or harmonica to be heard. And Andrew Jackson's period photography is as sharp as a knife. Above all else, in a feature the *New York Times* described as "sharply directed," *Death of a Gunfighter* is Richard Widmark's show from start to finish, the camera quite often closing in on those blond, finely etched features and blue eyes, a persuasive, acutely observed character study by the actor of a man whose usefulness to society no longer figures in gradually changing climates. Just for a moment, even as late as 1969, the '50s Western flame flickered into life, mainly due to Widmark's undeniable screen presence and effortless role playing, an underrated drama set within the confines of a small town, with all its inbred paranoia, tensions, hidden secrets and back-stabbing rising to the surface, one that Western purists should enjoy watching over and over again, which is more than can be said for his next offering, Paramount's downright bizarre *A Talent for Loving*, released in 1969.

In December 1965, producer Walter Shenson offered The Beatles' manager, Brian Epstein, Richard Condon's script of *A Talent for Loving*, earmarked as a possible follow-up to United Artists' *Help!* Although cowboy-mad Ringo was marginally interested, the Fab Four rejected the project as being "not us." After viewing the film, it's difficult to work out which Beatle would have fitted into what part, but one thing's for certain: Lennon and McCartney would have come up with a far more tuneful title theme and soundtrack than Ken Thorne's limp, quasi-Mexican tonalities. Columbia's 1965 *Cat Ballou* has a great deal to answer for: Elliott Silverstein's just plain silly horse opera began a (thankfully) short-lived trend in comedy spoof Westerns, where everyone acted the goat, where absurd characters were greatly exaggerated and where there was too much stupid horseplay, all backed by a banjo-plucking, harmonica-based corny score, the whole cast caught up in some huge private joke at the expense of audience involvement. The critics hated it, the public seemed to like it. If you're one of those fans who detests spoof movies of *any* kind, then *A Talent for Loving* will cause severe indigestion after a few minutes in; if you're willing and brave enough to persevere, then Richard Quine's much-maligned Western farce *might* tickle the funny bone now and again; it's not as ghastly as you may think, but it ain't all that great, either.

The ramshackle farrago of a plot goes something like this: Widmark (Major Patten—but he's not a major, that's just his name, cue for joke number one!) wins 1,500 acres from his old rival, roisterous Mexican bandit Topol, in a poker game. Widmark takes up residency in Cesar Romero's opulent mansion (the film was shot in Spain), crammed full of suggestive nude statues, scantily dressed servants (Romero's concubines) and sexually rampant Fran Jeffries; she's been afflicted by an Aztec curse brought on by a stunted priest (his body resides in a suit of armor) who ravaged 634 Aztec virgins in 11 months. Widmark marries Jeffries, the slut quickly wearing him out; Topol, meanwhile, is dying to lay his hands on a stash of rifles hidden away in the mansion (hence the film's alternative title, *Gun Crazy*); Milo Quesada's daughter is abducted by Indians; and Jeffries runs off with four

Fran Jeffries wears Widmark out in *A Talent for Loving*.

Hungarian acrobats from a circus—they will no doubt satisfy her wanton needs more than worn out Widmark is able to do. Six years later, we have a bullfight and Topol is still staggering around half-drunk, trying to rape Geneviève Page in a bathtub (she's now a widow, hubbie Romero dead from a heart attack); Widmark finds himself the object of Page's lustful desires. Another 12 years go by, one ridiculously convoluted situation after another piled on to dull, rather than heighten, the senses; we are now firmly in sex-farce territory. Widmark's daughter, busty Caroline Munro, is under the Aztec curse, looking to bed Mircha Carven and Judd Hamilton in one hit ("She's twitchin' all over," shouts Widmark, Munro licking her lips, yelling "I want them both!"), even though Carven's promised to Topol's daughter, 17-year-old virgin Janet Storti, and Hamilton to Marie Rogers, a man-eating beef buyer. Libby Morris, Quesada's kidnapped daughter (she's Carven's sister; pay attention at the back!), plays Jacaranda, now a plump, not very attractive, loud-mouthed squaw, the Indians led by London-born actor Joe Melia, mumbling in a Cockney accent. A Beatles connection pops up in the shape of dithering Derek Nimmo (he was in *A Hard Day's Night*), the traveling salesman setting his cap at hot chick Munro, and numerous drink-related brawls, street standoffs and misunderstandings later, the climax has Topol (in pink Napoleon uniform) and his gunslingers converging on a train carrying the entire cast (and those pesky carbines) at the same instance that Melia's Indians are on the warpath, all after rifles which, it turns out, are rusty with age and refuse to fire. The final overhead crane shot sees every main character (plus minor ones)—Widmark, Page, Munro, Nimmo, Carven, Storti, Hamilton, Rogers, Topol's Mexicans—in one almighty hugging/kissing session, the Indian horses encircling them in a gigantic heart, a cue for the audience to breathe "Ah!" or reach for the sick bucket, whatever takes your fancy!

How does our leading man fare in this headache-inducing hokey nonsense put out under the guise of a Western? There is one sequence near the beginning where Jeffries is whistling Handel's "Water Music" and pouting like mad; Widmark parodies her whistle in a series of sweaty pants brought on by lust and it's excruciatingly embarrassing to observe. Otherwise, he does okay, perhaps content to simply go along with the ride, or the money. *A Talent for Loving* was never afforded a cinema release in America or Britain, appearing on American television's ABC network in 1974, and it's not all that difficult to understand the reasons why—today, or even in 1969, it would empty an auditorium in 10 minutes flat. In fact, you'll need as much tequila that Topol tips down his slobbering gullet to have the stamina to sit through it to the bitter end. Widmark's worst-ever Western? Probably yes, even though, to his credit, he appears comfortable and keeps his head (apart from that aforementioned scene) when all around him are losing theirs, overacting like there is no tomorrow. As I write, the picture is only obtainable on gray market discs, Paramount obviously not seeing the viability in issuing a commercial copy. And on this showing, why should they?

The 1970s saw a spate of rodeo movies hitting theaters; *J. W. Coop* (Columbia, 1971), *Junior Bonner* (ABC, 1972), *Black Rodeo* (Utopia, 1972) and *The Electric Horsemen* (Columbia, 1979), among others. Stuart Millar's *When the Legends Die* (20th Century Fox, 1972) was probably one of the best of the bunch, Widmark once more giving a marvelous performance as Red Dillon, a whiskey-loving huckster who takes shameless advantage of Ute Indian Frederic Forrest's natural skill as a bronco-buster, promoting him on the rodeo circuit to earn a fast buck, by fair means or foul ("I own you. You're mine!"). Wily Widmark, after showing Forrest the ropes to toughen him up, places bets, instructs his protégé to take a tumble in the first round, increases the odds and rakes in the cash after Forrest wins the tournament. Eventually, the two have a bitter parting of the ways, conscience-stricken Forrest defying Widmark's underhand tactics, sheer exploitation of his talents and shouted orders to "take my boots off," striking out on his own and becoming a major success on the big city circuits. Following Forrest's brief fling with nurse Luana Anders, a reunion eventually takes place, but Forrest's former mentor is now a spent force, years of hard drinking having taken its toll; he's contracted cirrhosis of the liver and dies in a hotel room. Forrest burns Widmark's dilapidated shack to the ground, Indian-style, and returns to looking after horses, his favored profession. At last, after enduring a stormy life-changing rite of passage, he's discovered how to live in harmony with the wilderness *and* civilization.

The opening spell of *When the Legends Die* would have you believe that

we're out in the Old West: Young Tillman Box (Tom Black Bull) lives an idyllic existence in the mountains with his pet bear cub, Richard H. Kline's gleaming photography highlighting the golden-leafed woods, rugged snow-capped peaks, waterfalls and blue skies (filming took place in Colorado), the boy's parents both dead. When he's dragged off to town by John War Eagle to learn "the new ways," it comes as a shock to see cars on the highway—we're actually out in the New West! Disobedient and absconding from school, he's tracked down in the wilds and recaptured, forced to say farewell to his big cuddly friend, a moving, heartfelt moment underlined by Glen Paxton's lilting, unobtrusive score. Flash forward several years and Box (his one and only feature; he was just 44 when he died) is now Forrest (this was trumpeted as his debut, even though two films preceded it), showing an uncanny prowess in breaking untamed horses, and that's where Widmark enters the fray. He sees Forrest in action and dollar signs light up; soon, the two are making waves on the rodeo circuit, a friendly association which gradually deteriorates when Widmark's greed takes over. Forrest is regarded as a meal ticket, pure and simple, whether the Ute likes it or not, the old cowhand introducing the naïve lad to liquor and loose women and cheating customers by the dozen until their profit-making scam comes to light. The frequent rodeo sequences are orchestrated with a ferocious, in-your-face intensity, making you feel every lurch, bump, kicking hoof and mouthful of dirt Forrest is experiencing, while out on the road in Widmark's battered pickup truck, Kline and Millar take full visual advantage of New Mexico's splendid limitless horizons in a series of colorful panoramic longshots.

"Tough and funny," said the *New York Times* of Widmark's star turn and they weren't wrong; in the Western's twilight years, his expertise gave the genre all he had got, which is considerable, an older, more grizzled Widmark that could still conjure up a twinkle in those blue eyes, plus that look of withering disdain capable of stopping a man dead in his tracks. He plays off Forrest's innocence beautifully, realizing that, near the end, what they once had, whether or not it was worth a dime, is no more. "You need me," he almost pleads with Forrest, who brusquely replies, "Last year I won $17,000," implying that he did so without his help. The Widmark/Forrest on/off relationship is a magical winner, thanks to Robert Dozier's intelligent script, Millar's fast-paced direction and a gentleness that lies beneath all the frenetic rodeo machismo on display. It may not have set the box-office alight and remains one of Widmark's least-seen pictures, but *When the Legends Die*, a modern-day Western *par excellence*, exudes charm, is good to look at and undoubtedly is worth seeking out.

On October 5, 1892 at 9:30 a.m., the Dalton gang, comprising Bob Dalton, Grat Dalton, Emmett Dalton, Bill Power and Dick Broadwell, rode into Coffeyville, Kansas, with the intention of holding up two banks: The First National Bank and C.M. Condon and Company's Bank. Bob Dalton was hell-bent on becoming more notorious than the Jesse James gang, but in the ensuing gun battle he was shot to death along with brother Grat, Power and Broadwell. Emmett Dalton received 23 gunshot wounds but survived, serving a 14-year prison sentence in Lansing penitentiary. Producer A.C. Lyles specialized in knocking out low-budget Westerns during the 1960s, 13 made between 1964-1968, including *Law of the Lawless*, *Town Tamer*, *Red Tomahawk*, *Hostile Guns*, *Black Spurs* and *Buckskin*. The Coffeyville raid had previously been covered in two classic vintage Randolph Scott oaters, *When the Daltons Rode* (Universal, 1940) and *The Doolins of Oklahoma* (Columbia, 1949), also figuring in Audie Murphy's *The Cimarron Kid* (Universal, 1951). In *The Last Day*, Lyles hired the experience and bankable name of Richard Widmark to take on the role of ex-gunfighter Will Spence whose credentials have never been fully established; Spence, a blacksmith living in Coffeyville at the time of the incident, was (apparently) a hated enemy of Bob Dalton through the killing of his outlaw friend Jake (Jim) Younger. Unfortunately, unlike Lyles' 1960s Western potboilers, each featuring stars that were (not to sound unkind) past their prime and all released through Paramount, *The Last Day* was never afforded a theatrical release, the company, quite correctly, of the opinion that in 1975, the Western film genre as such was dead in the water, lacking in both audience appeal and possible box-office receipts. Therefore, Vincent McEveety's barebones Western went straight onto the television networks where, over the years, it has garnered quite a healthy reputation among diehard fans for being an honest, semi-documentary account of those violent times, enacted over a four-

German poster for *The Last Day*

day period, narrator Harry Morgan describing who is who and relating a time frame of events leading up to the twin robberies.

McEveety, a highly experienced television director/producer of the 1960s through to the 1990s, starts the ball rolling by showing sepia-tinted prints behind the credits, seguing into color, to set the right period mood. Robert Conrad (Bob), Richard Jaeckel (Grat), Tim Matheson (Emmett), Christopher Connelly (Dick) and Tom Skerritt (Bill) converge on the Dalton homestead run by Conrad's wife, Daisy (Loretta Swit) to discuss plans of the proposed bank robbery hit ("Be like licking a candy store."). In Coffeyville, reformed gunman Widmark lives with wife Barbara Rush and their young boy, having not used his six-gun for three long years. When information leaks out that the Daltons are planning a raid and Conrad has an old score to settle with Widmark, the townsfolk turn into cowards; Widmark, because of his feared reputation, is somehow blamed for what's about to occur, while stern-faced Marshal Morgan Woodward, in another town, decides to get in on the action. McEveety's low-key Western is a joy to behold, everyone looking suitably grimy as befits a cowboy flick from the '70s, the dialogue (Jim Byrnes, Steve Fisher) pithy, the whole cast acting their parts to perfection. The only minus point is Robert Bain and Carmine Coppola's modernistic musical score which jars, completely at odds with the carefully wrought 1890s period feel. Matheson, the youngest of the bunch, wants to quit, then changes his mind and, on the fateful day, Widmark straps on his gun belt against the wishes of his distraught wife. The climax is a belter, a suspenseful, seven-minute blazing shoot-out which leaves four of the lawbreakers plus five of Coffeyville's citizens dead, a thrilling Sam Peckinpah *Wild Bunch*–type sequence that can hold its own against bigger-budgeted, more better-known movies of this type. The outlaws' bodies are put on display and photographed, Widmark packs away his six-shooter for good, deciding to stay in Coffeyville despite the spineless attitude exhibited by the town council, and Woodward belatedly arrives on the scene, having missed out on all the gunplay. A punchy, gritty little actioner with Widmark in fine fettle and looking a lot younger than his 61 years, *The Last Day*, even for a movie consigned to the relative obscurity of the small screen, proved conclusively that a handful of filmmakers in the industry were still determined to preserve the Western myth and all that it stood for in a cinematic climate where, sadly, the once-revered genre counted for little or nothing.

No one could ever accuse Richard Widmark of not keeping busy after completion on *The Last Day* to his next Western, *Mr. Horn* (Lorimer Productions, 1979): In Peter Sykes' X-rated *To the Devil a Daughter* (Hammer, 1976) he went to England and played an occult novelist alongside Christopher Lee, later denouncing the role as his least rewarding in 45 years of moviemaking; in Peter Collinson's *The Sell Out* (Warner Bros., 1976), he was a CIA operative; in Robert Aldrich's *Twilight's Last Gleaming* (Allied Artists, 1977) a General; Stanley Kramer's *The Domino Killings* (Associated General Films, 1977) had him cast as a criminal boss; James Goldstone's *Rollercoaster* (Universal, 1977) saw him playing an agent; in Michael Crichton's *Coma* (MGM, 1978) he was a doctor; and in Irwin Allen's *The Swarm* (Warner Bros., 1978), he was a General, another movie he had no fond recollections of, as did the entire cast (*The Swarm* has regularly been listed as one of the 100 worst films ever made). Whatever artistic merit these movies may or may not have possessed, they at least demonstrated that Widmark was quite willing and able to turn his hand to any number of roles if need be, content *not* to hog the top billing slot on the billboards, an egotistical bone of contention among many of his more fame-hungry contemporaries.

The Last Day

In 1978, writer William Goldman presented a script outlining the life of Tom Horn—hired gunman, frontier scout, range detective, Indian tracker and Pinkerton agent—to Steve McQueen, Don Siegel to direct a possible picture. McQueen and Siegel fell out with Goldman over the handling of the material, McQueen going on to star in his own version of events, *Tom Horn*, budgeted by Warner Bros. at $3,000,000, TV director William Wiard at the helm. Goldman's rejected screenplay was revamped and turned into a three-hour television production in 1979 entitled *Mr. Horn*, Jack Starrett directing, David Carradine hired for the lead role and Richard Widmark his mentor, Al Sieber. Aged 64 when filming commenced, Widmark looked wearier and slightly grizzled around the edges, taking on greenhorn Carradine to join him in the hunt for renegade Apache chief Geronimo (Enrique Lucero), and what a lengthy hunt it turned out to be: The first two hours, set in 1885, mostly consists of a cavalry detail plus Indian scouts trekking across bleak and barren wilderness (location shooting took place in Mexico), a few humorous incidents thrown into the mix, sandwiched between repeated ferocious Apache attacks and ambushes in gullies which admittedly are well staged. Karen Black is introduced as Carradine's love interest, Stafford Morgan's General Miles is a belligerent martinet, bent on covering himself in personal glory, while Widmark, suffering from the effects of 28 old wounds, teaches Carradine a few tricks and rants against the army's ill-treatment of Indians ("All soldiers are jackasses!"), a kind of Rooster Cogburn-type character played to the hilt by the veteran actor.

The final cavalry slog across the arid wastes is interminable and lacking in dramatics, hindered by Jerry Fielding's damp score; Geronimo, after talking at length with Carradine, surrenders, eventually packed off to Florida, Widmark more or less disappearing from the scenario as we are now in Cheyenne, Wyoming in 1901. The next lethargic hour concentrates on Carradine's attempts to prevent cattle rustling and put a stop to town corruption. He also rekindles his sexual liaison with widow Black, much to Sheriff Richard Masur's dismay; the uptight lawman is romancing Black and views the lofty gunfighter as a possible threat to their on/off relationship.

Tom Horn was hanged on November 20, 1903, the day before his 43rd birthday, for the killing of 14-year-old farm boy William Nickell; it was never actually proved that Horn was responsible and, in 1993, he was posthumously acquitted of the crime. Legend states that the corrupt townsfolk wanted the former gun hand (17 notches on his belt) out of the way because he began poking his nose into their unscrupulous affairs, framing him for the murder. In the film, Carradine seems to realize this but resigns himself to his unjust fate—even Masur believes him to be innocent. His hanging is watched by Widmark (on crutches) who has previously bemoaned to town officials, "Why do we have to bring him down? There ain't no reason."

If shorn by an hour and tidied up, the modest *Mr. Horn* would have been deserving of a limited cinema showing on the peripheral circuits but perhaps a decade earlier; by 1979, cinemagoers had forgotten all about the once-mighty American Western and, as a reflection of this increase in audience apathy, it would be another nine long years before Widmark starred in his very last horse opera, Burt Kennedy's *Once Upon a Texas Train* (Brigade, 1988), which, like *Mr. Horn*, failed to get a theatrical release.

Willie Nelson (55); Richard Widmark (74); Angie Dickinson (57); Chuck Connors (67); Ken Curtis (72); Royal Dano (66); Jack Elam (68); Gene Evans (66); Kevin McCarthy (74); Dub Taylor (81); Stuart Whitman (60); Harry Carey, Jr. (67); and Hank Worden (87): Yes, like Jean Yarbrough's *The Over-the-Hill Gang* (Thomas/Spelling, 1969) before it, a vintage cast of thespians, all in their prime, was rolled out into the Arizona cactus-strewn terrain and given another crack at the ailing Western genre courtesy of writer/producer/director Burt Kennedy, an old boys' reunion if ever there was one. What we had here was a nostalgic trip down memory lane, nothing more, nothing less; there *was* a story, but the real joy was in seeing this bunch of seasoned professionals acting their boots off without a care in the world—they must have had a real ball making it! Nelson (John Henry Lee) emerges from the Texas territorial prison after serving a 20-year sentence for train robbery. Straight away, the notorious outlaw hitches up with his former gang, blasts the Bank of Texas in Del Rio to matchwood and makes off with $20,000. Hot on his trail comes Widmark (Captain Owen Hayes), an ex-Texas

Widmark as Tom Horn

Ranger and Nelson's love rival for the hand of Angie Dickinson, still a picture of loveliness at 57. He's got his own bunch of old-timers with him, determined to grab the stolen cash from Nelson and put him back behind bars. But when young gun Shaun Cassidy (a mere 30!) and his three confederates butt in on the action, hankering after that $20,000 and reckoning it's about time those old fellows cashed in their chips, Widmark and Nelson join forces to teach these upstarts a lesson in the harsh realities of frontier life. It all ends in the vein of a Spaghetti Western, a street shoot-out in which no one gets killed (it's not that sort of film): Cassidy and his boys are winged, sprawled in the dirt, Widmark hitches up with Dickinson, the stolen loot is returned to Del Rio and Nelson is let loose to lead an honest life ("Git goin' you old buzzard."); judging by the look on his grizzled features when he hears a locomotive's whistle in the distance, that honest life will last all of five minutes!

Widmark and Angie Dickinson in *Once Upon a Texas Train*

"Thank you kindly," chortles 87-year-old Hank Worden (in an old folk's home), a line straight from *The Searchers* in which Worden memorably played rocking chair-loving Mose Harper; then we have short-sighted Jack Elam riding a battered bike instead of a horse, while Dub Taylor overturns his rig at every given opportunity, Royal Dano (Nitro) keeps dropping explosives all over the place and Nelson's past-their-best outlaws shoot wide off the mark during a practice session. "Aren't you a little old to go runnin' round chasin' after an outlaw?" Kevin McCarthy asks Widmark. "Well, ain't he a little old to go runnin' round robbin' banks?" he replies, referring to Nelson. Yes, the accent is firmly on old age and the encroaching years, but poked fun of in a gentle way; Ken Lamkin's photography of the Old Tucson wilderness is crystal-clear and Arthur B. Rubinstein's jaunty soundtrack complements Kennedy's snappy direction, which blends new-age machismo with old-style machismo between interludes of reminiscing about times gone by. An entertaining, sweet-natured TV Western which, like *Mr. Horn*, would have done okay in smaller independent cinemas at the time.

For many of the cast, *Once Upon a Texas Train* was near-enough their movie swansong. It was Richard Widmark's final journey out West; low-key, perhaps, but enjoyable in a cozy kinda way. He made three other insignificant pictures before retiring from the industry in 2001: In 2008, aged 93, he died at his home in Roxbury, Connecticut after a long illness. How to extol the virtues of one Richard Weedt Widmark in a single short sentence? Well, in the words of the British, he was "a bloody good actor and a nice bloke." I challenge anyone to name a poor Widmark performance, because none exist on celluloid. Whatever type of film he appeared in, he gave the part his all, at the same time coming over to an audience as a natural, as though he wasn't really acting, only being Richard Widmark, up there on the big screen, blond and unpredictable. As mentioned before, he wasn't a Western leading star like Wayne or Stewart, but those he did star in were worth the price of admission *because* of his unorthodox presence. Numerous images spring to mind: His taut-as-a-whip gambler in *Yellow Sky*; his quiet tête-à-tête with Gary Cooper in a Mexican saloon during the opening scene of *Garden of Evil*; his standoff with Henry Silva in *The Law and Jake Wade*; his angst-ridden cowpoke in *Backlash*; controlling his trigger-happy pals when Henry Fonda makes his entrance in *Warlock*; coming on to Felicia Farr while chained to a wagon wheel in *The Last Wagon*; his upright Jim Bowie in *The Alamo*; his doomed marshal in *Death of a Gunfighter*; and, outside the Western sphere, his tough cop in *Madigan*. "I'll always be remembered as that guy with the giggle," he once said in an interview, talking of his Tommy Udo in *Kiss of Death*. Let it be said that one of Hollywood's key, and more atypical, iconic players would be remembered

Felicia Farr and Widmark in *The Last Wagon*

for a great deal more than that, as the eight classic Westerns he made from 1948 to 1960 testify. This author's personal favorite? *The Law and Jake Wade*, in which you'll find the spirit of Widmark burning brightly, a peak showing from the unassuming star that holds the attention throughout 86 minutes without ever letting go. In this author's mind, his undisciplined, murderous, cunning but highly charismatic outlaw, Clint Hollister, elevates Richard Widmark into the Western Hall of Fame, and deservedly so.

Essential Widmark
Yellow Sky
Garden of Evil
Backlash
The Last Wagon
The Law and Jake Wade
Warlock
The Alamo
Death of a Gunfighter
When the Legends Die
The Last Day

CHAPTER 17

FILMOGRAPHY

Film Ratings

Dead Shot *****
Hits the target ****
Finger on the trigger ***
Half-cocked **
Firing blanks *

RICHARD WIDMARK

Yellow Sky
20th Century Fox 1948; 98 minutes; Producer: Lamar Trotti; Director: William A. Wellman
Gregory Peck; Anne Baxter; Richard Widmark; James Barton; John Russell; Harry Morgan; Charles Kemper; Robert Arthur *****

Garden of Evil
20th Century Fox 1954; CinemaScope/Technicolor; 100 minutes; Producer: Charles Brackett; Director: Henry Hathaway
Gary Cooper; Susan Hayward; Richard Widmark; Cameron Mitchell; Hugh Marlowe; Victor Manuel Mendoza; Rita Moreno; Antonio Bribiesca *****

Broken Lance
20th Century Fox 1954; CinemaScope/Technicolor; 96 minutes; Producer: Sol C. Siegel; Director: Edward Dmytryk
Spencer Tracy; Robert Wagner; Jean Peters; Richard Widmark; Katy Jurado; Hugh O'Brian; Earl Holliman; E.G. Marshall *****

Backlash
Universal 1956; Technicolor; 84 minutes; Producer: Aaron Rosenberg; Director: John Sturges
Richard Widmark; Donna Reed; John McIntire; William Campbell; Roy Roberts; Harry Morgan; Robert J. Wilke; Jack Lambert *****

The Last Wagon
20th Century Fox 1956; CinemaScope/DeLuxecolor; 98 minutes; Producer: William B. Hawks; Director: Delmer Daves
Richard Widmark; Felicia Farr; Tommy Rettig; Susan Kohner; Nick Adams; Ray Stricklyn; Stephanie Griffin; Douglas Kennedy *****

The Law and Jake Wade
MGM 1958; CinemaScope/Metrocolor; 86 minutes; Producer: William B. Hawks; Director: John Sturges
Robert Taylor; Richard Widmark; Patricia Owens; Henry Silva; DeForest Kelley; Robert Middleton; Eddie Firestone; Burt Douglas *****

Warlock
20th Century Fox 1959; CinemaScope/DeLuxecolor; 122 minutes; Produced and Directed by Edward Dmytryk
Richard Widmark; Henry Fonda; Anthony Quinn; Dorothy Malone; Dolores Michaels; DeForest Kelley; Tom Drake; Wallace Ford *****

The Alamo
United Artists 1960; Todd-AO/Technicolor; 202 (167) minutes; Produced and Directed by John Wayne
John Wayne; Richard Widmark; Laurence Harvey; Linda Cristal; Richard Boone; Frankie Avalon; Chill Wills; Patrick Wayne *****

Two Rode Together
Columbia 1961; Eastmancolor; 109 minutes; Producers: Stanley Shpetner and John Ford; Director: John Ford
James Stewart; Richard Widmark; Linda Cristal; Shirley Jones; John McIntire; Henry Brandon; Andy Devine; Paul Birch **

How the West Was Won
MGM 1962; Cinerama/Metrocolor; 164 minutes; Producer: Bernard Smith; Directors: Henry Hathaway, John Ford and George Marshall
Carroll Baker; James Stewart; Karl Malden; Henry Fonda; Gregory Peck; Debbie Reynolds; Richard Widmark; George Peppard *****

Cheyenne Autumn
Warner Bros. 1964; Super Panavision 70/Technicolor; 158 minutes; Producers: John Ford and Bernard Smith; Director: John Ford
Richard Widmark; Carroll Baker; Karl Maiden; Edward G. Robinson; Dolores del Rio; Ricardo Montalban; Gilbert Roland; Sal Mineo ****

Alvarez Kelly
Columbia 1966; Panavision/Pathecolor; 116 minutes; Producer: Sol C. Siegel; Director: Edward Dmytryk
William Holden; Richard Widmark; Patrick O'Neal; Victoria Shaw; Janice Rule; Arthur Franz; Harry Carey, Jr.; Richard Rust **

The Way West
United Artists 1967; Panavision/DeLuxecolor; 122 minutes; Producer: Harold Hecht; Director: Andrew V. McLaglen
Kirk Douglas; Robert Mitchum; Richard Widmark; Sally Field; Lola Albright; Michael McGreevey; Michael Witney; Katherine Justice ****

Death of a Gunfighter
Universal 1969; Technicolor; 99 minutes; Producer: Richard E. Lyons; Directors: Don Siegel and Robert Totten (credited to Alan Smithee)
Richard Widmark; Lena Horne; Michael McGreevey; Carroll O'Connor; Larry Gates; Kent Smith; John Saxon; Dub Taylor ****

A Talent for Loving
aka *Gun Crazy*
Paramount 1969; Technicolor; 110 (95) minutes; Producer: Walter Shenson; Director: Richard Quine
Richard Widmark; Topol; Cesar Romero; Fran Jeffries; Geneviève Page; Derek Nimmo; Caroline Munro; Mircha Carven **

When the Legends Die
20th Century Fox 1972; CinemaScope/DeLuxecolor; 107 minutes; Produced and Directed by Stuart Millar
Richard Widmark; Frederic Forrest; Luana Anders; Vito Scotti; John War Eagle; Herbert Nelson; Roy Engel; Tillman Box ****

The Last Day
A.C. Lyles Prods./Paramount Television 1975; Color; 100 minutes; Producer: A.C. Lyles; Director: Vincent McEveety
Richard Widmark; Barbara Rush; Robert Conrad; Richard Jaeckel; Tim Matheson; Christopher Connelly; Tom Skerritt; Loretta Swit ****

Mr. Horn
Lorimer Productions 1979; Color; 183 minutes; Producers: Robert L. Jacks and Elliott Kastner; Director: Jack Starrett
David Carradine; Richard Widmark; Karen Black; Jack Starrett; Jeremy Slate; Enrique Lucero; Richard Masur; Stafford Morgan **

Once Upon a Texas Train
aka *Texas Guns*
Brigade Prods./Rastar Films 1988; Color; 87 minutes; Produced and Directed by Burt Kennedy
Willie Nelson; Richard Widmark; Angie Dickinson; Shaun Cassidy; Chuck Connors; Jack Elam; Dub Taylor; Royal Dano ***

RORY CALHOUN

Massacre River
Windsor Pictures/Allied Artists 1949; Sepiatone/Black-and-White; 78 minutes; Producers: Julian Lesser and Frank Melford; Director: John Rawlins
Guy Madison; Rory Calhoun; Carole Mathews; Cathy Downs; Johnny Sands; Steve Brodie; Iron Eyes Cody; Art Baker ****

Sand
20th Century Fox 1949; Technicolor; 78 minutes; Producer: Robert Bassler; Director: Louis King
Mark Stevens; Coleen Gray; Rory Calhoun; Charles Grapewin; Robert Patten; Robert Adler; Paul E. Burns; Harry Cheshire ***

A Ticket to Tomahawk
20th Century Fox 1950; Technicolor; 90 minutes; Producer: Robert Bassler; Director: Richard Sale
Dan Dailey; Anne Baxter; Rory Calhoun; Will Wright; Walter Brennan; Chief Yowlachie; Mauritz Hugo; Charles Kemper ****

Return of the Frontiersman
Warner Bros. 1950; Technicolor; 74 minutes; Producer: Saul Elkins; Director: Richard L. Bare
Gordon MacRae; Julie London; Rory Calhoun; Jack Holt; Fred Clark; Edwin Rand; Raymond Bond; Matt McHugh **

Way of a Gaucho
20th Century Fox 1952; Technicolor; 91minutes; Producer: Philip Dunne; Director: Jacques Tourneur
Rory Calhoun; Gene Tierney; Richard Boone; Hugh Marlowe; Everett Sloane; Enrique Chaico; Jorge Villoldo; Ronald Dumas *****

The Silver Whip
20th Century Fox 1953; 73 minutes; Producers: Michael Abel and Robert Brassler; Director: Harmon Jones

Dale Robertson; Rory Calhoun; Robert Wagner; Kathleen Crowley; James Millican; Lola Albright; John Kellogg; J.M. Kerrigan ****

Powder River
20th Century Fox 1953; Technicolor; 78 minutes; Producer: André Hakim; Director: Louis King
Rory Calhoun; Corinne Calvet; Cameron Mitchell; Penny Edwards; Carl Betz; John Dehner; Robert J. Wilke; Frank Ferguson *****

River of No Return
20th Century Fox 1954; CinemaScope/Technicolor; 91 minutes; Producer: Stanley Rubin; Directors: Otto Preminger and Jean Negulesco (uncredited)
Robert Mitchum; Marilyn Monroe; Rory Calhoun; Tommy Rettig; Murvyn Vye; Douglas Spencer; Fred Aldrich; Don Beddoe **

The Yellow Tomahawk
Bel-Air/United Artists 1954; Color/B&W; 82 minutes; Producer: Howard W. Koch; Director: Lesley Selander
Rory Calhoun; Peggie Castle; Noah Beery, Jr.; Warner Anderson; Peter Graves; Lee Van Cleef; Rita Moreno; Dan Riss ****

Dawn at Socorro
Universal 1954; Technicolor; 81 minutes; Producer: William Alland; Director: George Sherman
Rory Calhoun; Piper Laurie; David Brian; Kathleen Hughes; Edgar Buchanan; Mara Corday; Alex Nicol; Skip Homeier *****

Four Guns to the Border
Universal 1954; Technicolor; 83 minutes; Producer: William Alland; Director: Richard Carlson
Rory Calhoun; Colleen Miller; Walter Brennan; Charles Drake; John McIntire; George Nader; Jay Silverheels; Nestor Paiva *****

The Treasure of Pancho Villa
RKO-Radio 1955; SuperScope/Technicolor; 92 minutes; Producer: Edmund Grainger; Director: George Sherman
Rory Calhoun; Gilbert Roland; Shelley Winters; Joseph Calleia; Fanny Schiller; Carlos Múzquiz; Pasquel Pena; Tony Carbajal ****

The Spoilers
Universal 1955; Technicolor; 84 minutes; Producer: Ross Hunter; Director: Jesse Hibbs

Anne Baxter; Jeff Chandler; Rory Calhoun; Ray Danton; Barbara Britton; John McIntire; Wallace Ford; Carl Benton Reid **

Red Sundown
Universal 1956; Technicolor; 82 minutes; Producer: Albert Zugsmith; Director: Jack Arnold
Rory Calhoun; Martha Hyer; Dean Jagger; Robert Middleton; James Millican; Grant Williams; Lita Baron; Trevor Bardette *****

Raw Edge
Universal 1956; Technicolor; 76 minutes; Producer: Albert Zugsmith; Director: John Sherwood
Rory Calhoun; Yvonne De Carlo; Mara Corday; Neville Brand; Emile Meyer; Rex Reason; Herbert Rudley; Robert J. Wilke ****

Utah Blaine
Clover/Columbia 1957; 75 minutes; Producer: Sam Katzman; Director: Fred F. Sears
Rory Calhoun; Susan Cummings; Angela Stevens; Paul Langton; Max Baer; George Keymas; Ray Teal; Ken Christy ****

The Hired Gun
MGM 1957; CinemaScope; 64 minutes; Producers: Rory Calhoun and Victor M. Orsatti; Director: Ray Nazarro
Rory Calhoun; Anne Francis; Chuck Connors; Vince Edwards; John Litel; Salvador Baguez; Guinn "Big Boy" Williams; Robert Burton *****

Domino Kid
Columbia 1957; 74 minutes; Producers: Rory Calhoun and Victor M. Orsatti; Director: Ray Nazarro
Rory Calhoun; Kristine Miller; Andrew Duggan; Eugene Iglesias; Robert Burton; Yvette Duguay; Peter Whitney; Roy Barcroft *****

Ride Out for Revenge
United Artists 1957; 78 minutes; Producer: Norman Retchin; Director: Bernard Girard
Rory Calhoun; Lloyd Bridges; Gloria Grahame; Vince Edwards; Joanne Gilbert; Michael Winkelman; Richard Shannon; Frank DeKova ****

The Saga of Hemp Brown
Universal 1958; CinemaScope/Technicolor; 80 minutes; Producer: Gordon Kay; Director: Richard Carlson

Rory Calhoun; John Larch; Beverly Garland; Fortunio Bonanova; Russell Johnson; Morris Ankrum; Trevor Bardette; Allan Lane ****

Apache Territory
Columbia 1958; Eastmancolor; 77 minutes; Producers: Rory Calhoun and Victor M. Orsatti; Director: Ray Nazarro
Rory Calhoun; Barbara Bates; John Dehner; Tom Pittman; Carolyn Craig; Leo Gordon; Myron Healey; Frank DeKova ****

The Gun Hawk
Allied Artists 1963; DeLuxecolor; 92 minutes; Producer: Richard Bernstein; Director: Edward Ludwig
Rory Calhoun; Rod Cameron; Rod Lauren; Ruta Lee; Morgan Woodward; Robert J. Wilke; John Litel; Lane Bradford **

Young Fury
Paramount 1964; Techniscope/Technicolor; 80 minutes; Producer: A.C. Lyles; Director: Christian Nyby
Rory Calhoun; Virginia Mayo; Preston Pierce; Lon Chaney, Jr.; John Agar; Linda Foster; William Bendix; Richard Arlen ***

Finger on the Trigger
aka *Blue Lightning*
FISA/Allied Artists 1965; Techniscope/Technicolor; 91 minutes; Produced and Directed by Sidney W. Pink
Rory Calhoun; Aldo Sambrell; Silvia Solor; Leo Anchóriz; James Philbrook; Todd Martin; Brud Talbot; John Clarke **

Black Spurs
Paramount 1965; Techniscope/Technicolor; 81 minutes; Producer: A.C. Lyles; Director: R.G. Springsteen
Rory Calhoun; Scott Brady; Lon Chaney, Jr.; Terry Moore; Bruce Cabot; Linda Darnell; James Best; DeForest Kelley ****

Apache Uprising
Paramount 1965; Techniscope/Technicolor; 90 minutes; Producer: A.C. Lyles; Director: R.G. Springsteen
Rory Calhoun; Corinne Calvet; John Russell; Lon Chaney, Jr.; DeForest Kelley; Arthur Hunnicutt; Gene Evans; Robert H. Harris ****

Mission to Glory: The Father Kino Story
21st Century Fox 1977; Technicolor; 116 minutes; Producer: Arthur E. Coates;

Director: Ken Kennedy
Richard Egan; Cesar Romero; Ricardo Montalban; John Ireland; Keenan Wyn; John Russell; Michael Ansara; Rory Calhoun **

Mule Feathers
BAM Productions/Monarch 1977; Technicolor; 79 minutes; Produced and Directed by Donald R. von Mizener
Rory Calhoun; Don Knotts (narrator); Arthur Roberts; Angela Richardson; Ken Smedberg; Ken Johnson; Theodore Lehmann; Cathy Caribu *

Bad Jim
Delaware Pictures/MGM 1990; Technicolor; 90 minutes; Producers: Clyde Ware, Stephane Mermet and Joseph Wouk; Director: Clyde Ware
James Brolin; John Clark Gable; Richard Roundtree; Harry Care y, Jr.; Rory Calhoun; Ty Hardin; Pepe Serna; Suzanne Wouk **

ROD CAMERON

Boss of Boomtown
Universal 1944; 58 minutes; Associate Producer: Oliver Drake; Director: Ray Taylor
Rod Cameron; Tom Tyler; Fuzzy Knight; Vivian Austin; Jack Ingram; Marie Austin; Robert Barron; Sam Flint ***

Trigger Trail
Universal 1944; 59 minutes; Associate Producer: Oliver Drake; Director: Lewis D. Collins
Rod Cameron; Eddie Dew; Fuzzy Knight; Vivian Austin; George Eldredge; Lane Chandler; Michael Vallon; Ray Whitley ***

Riders of the Santa Fe
aka *Mile a Minute*
Universal 1944; 60 minutes; Associate Producer: Oliver Drake; Director: Wallace W. Fox
Rod Cameron; Fuzzy Knight; George Douglas; Eddie Dew; Ray Whitley; Jennifer Holt; Lane Chandler; Earle Hodgins **

The Old Texas Trail
aka *Stagecoach Line*
Universal 1944; 60 minutes; Associate Producer: Oliver Drake; Director: Lewis D. Collins

Sterling Hayden; Fuzzy Knight; Marjorie Clements; Eddie Dew; George Eldredge; Edmund Cobb; Virginia Christine; Joseph J. Greene ***

Beyond the Pecos
aka *Beyond the Seven Seas*
Universal 1945; 58 minutes; Associate Producer: Oliver Drake; Director: Lambert Hillyer
Rod Cameron; Fuzzy Knight; Eddie Dew; Jennifer Holt; Gene Roth; Frank Jaquet; Robert Homans; Jack Ingram ***

Renegades of the Rio Grande
aka *Bank Robbery*
Universal 1945; 57 minutes; Associate Producer: Oliver Drake; Director: Howard Bretherton
Rod Cameron; Fuzzy Knight; Eddie Dew; Jennifer Holt; Ray Whitley; Glenn Strange; John James; Edmund Cobb **

Salome, Where She Danced
Universal 1945; Technicolor; 90 minutes; Producer: Walter Wanger; Director: Charles Lamont
Yvonne De Carlo; Rod Cameron; David Bruce; Walter Slezak; Albert Dekker; Marjorie Rambeau; J. Edward Bromberg; Abner Biberman * or *****

Frontier Gal
aka *The Bride Wasn't Willing*
Universal 1945; Technicolor; 92 minutes; Producers: Michael Fessier and Ernest Pagano; Director: Charles Lamont
Yvonne De Carlo; Rod Cameron; Sheldon Leonard; Andy Devine; Fuzzy Knight; Beverly Simmons; Frank Lackteen; Jan Wiley ****

Pirates of Monterey
Universal 1947; Technicolor; 77 minutes; Producer: Paul Malvern; Director: Alfred L. Werker
Maria Montez; Rod Cameron; Gilbert Roland; Phillip Reed; Mikhail Rasumny; Tamara Shayne; Gale Sondergaard; Robert Warwick *

Panhandle
Allied Artists 1948; Sepiatone; 85 minutes; Producers: John C. Champion and Blake Edwards; Director: Lesley Selander
Rod Cameron; Reed Hadley; Anne Gwynne; Cathy Downs; Blake Edwards; Jeff York; Dick Crockett; Rory Mallinson *****

River Lady
Universal 1948; Technicolor; 78 minutes; Producer: Leonard Goldstein; Director: George Sherman
Yvonne De Carlo; Dan Duryea; Rod Cameron; Helena Carter; Lloyd Gough; John McIntire; Florence Bates; Jack Lambert **

The Plunderers
Republic 1948; Trucolor; 87 minutes; Associate Producer and Director: Joseph Kane
Rod Cameron; Forrest Tucker; Ilona Massey; Adrian Booth (Lorna Gray); Paul Fix; George Cleveland; Grant Withers; Taylor Holmes ***

Belle Starr's Daughter
20th Century Fox 1948; 86 minutes; Producer: Edward L. Alperson; Director: Lesley Selander
George Montgomery; Ruth Roman; Rod Cameron; Wallace Ford; Charles Kemper; William Phipps; Isabel Jewell; J. Farrell MacDonald ***

Stampede
Allied Artists 1949; Sepiatone; 76 minutes; Producers: John C. Champion and Blake Edwards; Director: Lesley Selander
Rod Cameron; Gale Storm; Johnny Mack Brown; Don Castle; Donald Curtis; John Miljan; Jonathan Hale; John Eldredge *****

Brimstone
Republic 1949; Trucolor; 90 minutes; Associate Producer and Director: Joseph Kane
Rod Cameron; Walter Brennan; Jim Davis; Jack Lambert; James Brown; Forrest Tucker; Adrian Booth (Lorna Gray); Guinn "Big Boy" Williams *****

Dakota Lil
20th Century Fox 1950; Cinecolor; 88 minutes; Producers: Jack Jungmeyer and Edward L. Alperson; Director: Lesley Selander
George Montgomery; Marie Windsor; Rod Cameron; John Emery; Wallace Ford; Jack Lambert; Walter Sande; Larry Johns ****

Stage to Tucson
aka *Lost Stage Valley*
Columbia 1950; Technicolor; 81 minutes; Producer: Harry Joe Brown; Director: Ralph Murphy
Rod Cameron; Wayne Morris; Kay Buckley; Roy Roberts; Sally Eilers; Harry Bellaver; Carl Benton Reid; Douglas Fowley ****

Short Grass
Allied Artists 1950; 84 minutes; Producer: Scott R. Dunlap; Director: Lesley Selander
Rod Cameron; Cathy Downs; Morris Ankrum; Johnny Mack Brown; Alan Hale, Jr.; Jonathan Hale; Raymond Walburn; Riley Hill *****

Oh! Susanna
Republic 1951; Trucolor; 84 minutes; Associate Producer and Director: Joseph Kane
Rod Cameron; Adrian Booth (Lorna Gray); Forrest Tucker; Chill Wills; Jim Davis; William Ching; Douglas Kennedy; John Compton **

Cavalry Scout
Monogram 1951; Cinecolor; 78 minutes; Producer: Walter Mirisch; Director: Lesley Selander
Rod Cameron; Audrey Long; Jim Davis; James Millican; James Arness; Stephen Chase; John Doucette; Rory Mallinson ***

Fort Osage
Monogram 1952; Cinecolor; 73 minutes; Producer: Walter Mirisch; Director: Lesley Selander
Rod Cameron; Morris Ankrum; Jane Nigh; Douglas Kennedy; John Ridgely; William Phipps; Francis McDonald; Myron Healey ***

Wagons West
Monogram 1952; Cinecolor; 70 minutes; Producer: Vincent M. Fennelly; Director: Ford Beebe
Rod Cameron; Peggie Castle; Michael Chapin; Frank Ferguson; Henry Brandon; Riley Hill; Noah Beery, Jr.; Anne Kimball ***

Woman of the North Country
Republic 1952; Trucolor; 90 minutes; Associate Producer and Director: Joseph Kane
Rod Cameron; Ruth Hussey; Gale Storm; J. Carrol Naish; John Agar; Jim Davis; Jay C. Flippen; Barry Kelley **

Ride the Man Down
Republic 1952; Trucolor; 90 minutes; Associate Producer and Director: Joseph Kane
Brian Donlevy; Rod Cameron; Forrest Tucker; Ella Raines; Barbara Britton; Chill Wills; J. Carrol Naish; Jim Davis ****

San Antone
Republic 1953; 90 minutes; Associate Producer and Director: Joseph Kane
Rod Cameron; Arleen Whelan; Forrest Tucker; Katy Jurado; Rodolfa Acosta; Bob Steele; Harry Carrey, Jr.; James Lilburn *

Southwest Passage
aka *Camels West*
United Artists 1954; Pathecolor; Orig. in 3-D; 75 minutes; Producer: Edward Small; Director: Ray Nazarro
Rod Cameron; John Ireland; Joanne Dru; Guinn "Big Boy" Williams; John Dehner; Stuart Randall; Douglas Fowley; Morris Ankrum *****

Santa Fe Passage
Republic 1955; Trucolor; 91 minutes; Producer: Sidney Picker; Director: William Witney
John Payne; Faith Domergue; Rod Cameron; Slim Pickens; George Keymas; Irene Tedrow; Leo Gordon; Anthony Caruso *****

Yaqui Drums
Allied Artists 1956; 71 minutes; Producer: William F. Broidy; Director: Jean Yarbrough
Rod Cameron; J. Carrol Naish; Roy Roberts; Mary Castle; Robert Hutton; Denver Pyle; Ray Walker; Keith Richards *

Spoilers of the Forest
Republic 1957; Naturama/Trucolor; 68 minutes; Produced and Directed by Joseph Kane
Rod Cameron; Vera Ralston; Ray Collins; Edgar Buchanan; Carl Benton Reid; Sheila Bromley; Hillary Brooke; John Compton ***

The Gun Hawk
Allied Artists 1963; DeLuxecolor; 92 minutes; Producer: Richard Bernstein; Director: Edward Ludwig
Rory Calhoun; Rod Cameron; Rod Lauren; Ruta Lee; Morgan Woodward; Robert J. Wilke; John Litel; Lane Bradford **

Bullets Don't Argue
Jolly Film/Trio Films/Constantin Film Produktion 1964; Ultrascope/Eastmancolor; 92 minutes; Producer: Fernando Rossi; Director: Mario Caiano
Rod Cameron; Ángel Aranda; Horst Frank; Mimmo Palmara; Vivi Bach; Giulia Rubin; Luis Durán; Andrea Aureli ****

Bullets and the Flesh
Bercol Films/Cines Europa 1964; Ultrascope/Eastmancolor; 93 minutes; Producer: Jacques-Paul Bertrand; Director: Marino Girolami
Rod Cameron; Patricia Viterbo; Bruno Piergentili; Piero Lulli; Ennio Girolami; Manuel Zarzo; Alfredo Mayo; Carla Caò **

Requiem for a Gunfighter
Embassy Pictures 1965; Techniscope/Technicolor; 91 minutes; Producer: Alex Gordon; Director: Spencer G. Bennet
Rod Cameron; Stephen McNally; Tim McCoy; Chet Douglas; Olive Sturgess; Johnny Mack Brown; Mike Mazurki; Lane Chandler ****

The Bounty Killer
Embassy Pictures 1965; Techniscope/Technicolor; 92 minutes; Producer: Alex Gordon; Director: Spencer G. Bennet
Dan Duryea; Rod Cameron; Audrey Dalton; Fuzzy Knight; Buster Crabbe; Johnny Mack Brown; Richard Arlen; Boyd "Red" Morgan *****

Winnetou and Old Firehand
aka *Thunder at the Border*
Columbia/Jadran Film/Rialto Film 1966; Ultrascope/Eastmancolor; 98 minutes; Producer: Hortst Wendlandt; Director: Alfred Vohrer
Pierre Brice; Rod Cameron; Marie Versini; Todd Armstrong; Harald Leipnitz; Rik Battaglia; Miha Baloh; Nadia Gray ***

STERLING HAYDEN

El Paso
Paramount 1949; Cinecolor; 103 minutes; Producers: William H. Pine and William C. Thomas; Director: Lewis R. Foster
John Payne; Gail Russell; Sterling Hayden; Dick Foran; George "Gabby" Hayes; Henry Hull; Robert Ellis; Eduardo Noriega **

Flaming Feather
Paramount 1952; Technicolor; 77 minutes; Producer: Nat Holt; Director: Ray Enright
Sterling Hayden; Forrest Tucker; Barbara Rush; Arleen Whelan; Victor Jory; Edgar Buchanan; Richard Arlen; Carol Thurston ***

Denver and Rio Grande
Paramount 1952; Technicolor; 89 minutes; Producer: Nat Holt; Director: Byron Haskin

Edmond O'Brien; Sterling Hayden; Dean Jagger; Lyle Bettger; Laura Elliot (Kasey Rogers); J. Carrol Naish; Zasu Pitts; Paul Fix ***

Hellgate
Commander Films/Lippert Pictures 1952; 87 minutes; Producer: John C. Champion; Director: Charles Marquis Warren
Sterling Hayden; Joan Leslie; Ward Bond; James Arness; Robert J. Wilke; Peter Coe; John Pickard; James Anderson *****

Kansas Pacific
Allied Artists 1953; Cinecolor; 73 minutes; Producer: Walter Wanger; Director: Ray Nazarro
Sterling Hayden; Eve Miller; Barton MacLane; Reed Hadley; Harry Shannon; James Griffith; Tom Fadden; Myron Healey ****

Take Me to Town
Universal 1953; Technicolor; 81 minutes; Producers: Leonard Goldstein and Ross Hunter; Director: Douglas Sirk
Ann Sheridan; Sterling Hayden; Phillip Reed; Lee Aaker; Harvey Grant; Dusty Henley; Lee Patrick; Larry Gates **

Arrow in the Dust
Allied Artists 1954; Technicolor; 79 minutes; Producer: Hayes Goetz; Director: Lesley Selander
Sterling Hayden; Coleen Gray; Keith Larsen; Tom Tully; Tudor Owen; Jimmy Wakely; Lee Van Cleef; John Pickard ***

Johnny Guitar
Republic 1954; Trucolor; 110 (105) minutes; Producer: Herbert J. Yates; Director: Nicholas Ray
Joan Crawford; Sterling Hayden; Mercedes McCambridge; Scott Brady; Ward Bond; Ernest Borgnine; Ben Cooper; Royal Dano *****

Timberjack
Republic 1955; Trucolor; 94 minutes; Producers: Herbert J. Yates and Joseph Kane; Director: Joseph Kane
Sterling Hayden; Vera Ralston; David Brian; Adolphe Menjou; Chill Wills; Hoagy Carmichael; Howard Petrie; Jim Davis ****

Shotgun
Allied Artists 1955; Technicolor; 80 minutes; Producer: John C. Champion; Director: Lesley Selander

Sterling Hayden; Yvonne De Carlo; Zachary Scott; Guy Prescott; Robert J. Wilke; Paul Marion; John Pickard; Ralph Sandford *****

The Last Command
Republic 1955; Trucolor; 110 minutes; Producers: Herbert J. Yates and Frank Lloyd; Director: Frank Lloyd
Sterling Hayden; Richard Carlson; Arthur Hunnicutt; Ernest Borgnine; J. Carrol Naish; Anna Maria Alberghetti; Ben Cooper; John Russell *****

Top Gun
United Artists 1955; 73 minutes; Producer: Edward Small; Director: Ray Nazarro
Sterling Hayden; Karin Booth; John Dehner; James Millican; William Bishop; Rod Taylor; Regis Toomey; Hugh Sanders ****

The Iron Sheriff
United Artists 1957; 73 minutes; Producer: Jerome C. Robinson; Director: Sidney Salkow
Sterling Hayden; Constance Ford; John Dehner; Darryl Hickman; Walter Sande; Mort Mills; Kathleen Nolan; Kent Taylor ***

Valerie
United Artists 1957; 84 minutes; Producer: Hal R. Makelim; Director: Gerd Oswald
Sterling Hayden; Anita Ekberg; Anthony Steel; Peter Walker; Jered Barclay; Gage Clarke; John Wengraf; Iphigenie Castiglioni **

Gun Battle at Monterey
Allied Artists 1957; 67 minutes; Producer: Carl K. Hittleman; Directors: Sidney Franklin, Jr. and Carl K. Hittleman
Sterling Hayden; Pamela Duncan; Ted de Corsia; Lee Van Cleef; Mary Beth Hughes; I. Stanford Jolley; Charles Cane; Fred Sherman ****

Terror in a Texas Town
United Artists 1958; 80 minutes; Producer: Frank N. Seltzer; Director: Joseph H. Lewis
Sterling Hayden; Ned Young; Sebastion Cabot; Carol Kelly; Victor Milan; Frank Ferguson; Tyler McVey; Marilee Earle *****

Cipolla Colt
aka *Cry Onion*
CIPI Cinematografica S.A. 1975; Eastmancolor; 92 minutes; Producers: Carlo Ponti and Zev Braun; Director: Enzo G. Castellari

Franco Nero; Sterling Hayden; Martin Balsam; Emma Cohen; Leo Anchóriz; Helmut Brasch; Massimo Vanni; Romano Puppo * or ***

BIBLIOGRAPHY AND ACKNOWLEDGMENTS

There's very little in-depth literature on the market relating to the four stars featured in this book apart from the following volumes:

Richard Widmark: A Bio-Bibliography by Kim R. Holston (Greenwood Press, 1990). A straightforward account detailing Widmark's movie career, including television work and a few anecdotes.

Rory Calhoun: 159 Success Facts by Cynthia Bryan (Emereo Publishing, 2014). Virtually comprising a list of basic facts regarding Calhoun's film repertoire. Rod Cameron is also included in this e-book series under the title **Rod Cameron: 82 Success Facts**, by Nicholas Salinas.

Wanderer by Sterling Hayden (Knopf, 1963. Reprinted in 1998 by Sheridan House). Hayden's autobiography of his time spent on the ocean waves rather than treading the Hollywood sound stages gives an insight into the big man's inner wanderings and his personal outlook on life. What made the highly complex actor that was Sterling Hayden tick can be found within the pages of this book.

More thorough background particulars regarding the stars' early lives/careers has been gleaned from online sites **Wikipedia** and **IMDb**; the covers and inserts to DVDs sometimes provide useful facts not found elsewhere, and occasionally, rooting around for an obscure site compiled by a fan or film society will throw up the odd interview, story, quote or unusual snippet of information. Popular cowboy fan-based online site **https://fiftieswesterns.wordpress.com** has reviews of most Westerns made by Rod Cameron and Sterling Hayden, written by Boyd Magers, plus articles on Rory Calhoun and Richard Widmark.

Thanks to Larry Springer for providing several photographs.

If you enjoyed this book,
write for a free catalog of
Midnight Marquee Press titles
or visit our website at
http://www.midmar.com

Midnight Marquee Press, Inc.
9721 Britinay Lane
Baltimore, MD 21234
410-665-1198
mmarquee@aol.com